SCHAUM'S OUTLINE OF

THEORY AND PROBLEMS

OF

COST ACCOUNTING

Third Edition

•

RALPH S. POLIMENI, Ph.D., CPA, CCA

Professor and Chairman
Department of Accounting
Hofstra University

SHEILA A. HANDY, M.B.A, CPA

Instructor of Accounting
Hofstra University

JAMES A. CASHIN, M.B.A, CPA

Emeritus Professor of Accounting
Hofstra University

SCHAUM'S OUTLINE SERIES

McGRAW-HILL, INC.

New York St. Louis San Franscisco Auckland Bogotá Caracas
Lisbon London Madrid Mexico City Milan Montreal
New Delhi San Juan Singapore Sydney
Tokyo Toronto

RALPH S. POLIMENI is Chairman of the Department of Accounting and Business Law, and Chaykain Distinguished Professor of Accounting, at Hofstra University. He is also Director of the Chaykain CPA Review Program at Hofstra.

Dr. Polimeni is a recipient of the Hofstra University Distinguished Teaching Award. He has authored seven textbooks and written extensively in both domestic and international accounting journals including *The International Journal of Accounting Education and Research*, *Cost and Management*, and *The CPA Journal*. His article in *The Internal Auditor* won the outstanding contribution award for that year.

Dr. Polimeni received his Ph.D. degree in accounting from the University of Arkansas and is a CPA in New York State and a Certified Cost Analyst (CCA). He was employed as an auditor for Deloitte and Touche and has served as a consultant to Coopers and Lybrand, the City of New York, the New York State Special Prosecutor's Office, and several law firms.

SHEILA A. HANDY is an Instructor of Accounting at Hofstra University, where she is also an instructor in the Chaykain CPA Review Program. Prior to teaching at Hofstra, she was employed in the Tax Department of Arthur Andersen and Co.

Mrs. Handy received her B.B.A. in accounting and her M.B.A. in taxation from Hofstra University and is a CPA in New York State. She is a consultant to a law firm and is a member of the AICPA and the New York Society of CPAs.

JAMES A. CASHIN, deceased, Emeritus Professor of Accounting, was formerly Chairman of the Accounting Department of Hofstra University. He also taught in the Graduate School of City University of New York and at New York University. Professor Cashin earned a B.S. degree in Accounting from the University of Georgia and an M.B.A. degree from New York University; he was a CPA and Certified Internal Auditor and had wide experience in business and government agencies.

Schaum's Outline of Theory and Problems of
COST ACCOUNTING
International Editions 1994

This edition combines and updates material from Schaum's Outline of Cost Accounting I, 2nd ed., © 1984 and Schaum's Outline of Cost Accounting II, 1st ed., © 1983.

2 3 4 5 6 7 8 9 0 SLP PMP 9 8 7 6

Sponsoring Editor: Jeanne Flagg
Production Supervisor: Leroy A. Young
Editing Supervisor: Patty Andrews
Front Matter Editor: Maureen Walker
Cover design by Amy E. Becker

Library of Congress Cataloging-in-Publication Data

Polimeni, Ralph S.
Schaum's outline of theory and problems of cost accounting / by Ralph S. Polimeni, Shelia A. Handy and James A. Cashin. - 3rd ed.
p. cm. - (Schaum's outline series)
"This book, the third edition, combines the previous editions of Cost accounting I and Cost accounting II" - Pref.
Includes index.
ISBN 0-07-011026-3
1. Cost accounting - Problems, exercises, etc. I. Handy, Shelia A. II. Cashin, James A. III. Title.
HF5686.C8P5955 1993
657'.42'076-dc20 93-23908
CIP

When ordering this title, use ISBN 0-07-113592-8

Printed in Singapore

Preface

This book, the third edition, combines previous editions of *Cost Accounting I* and *Cost Accounting II* and reflects the latest issues, concepts, and procedures in the field of cost accounting. As in prior editions, the solved problems approach is used, with emphasis on the practical application of fundamental cost accounting concepts and techniques. The student is provided with:

1. Concise definitions and explanations in easily understood terms
2. Examples which illustrate the concepts and techniques developed in each chapter
3. Fully worked-out solutions to a large range of representative problems (against which students can check their own solutions)

This volume parallels the full-year cost accounting course offered in most schools. The subject matter has been carefully coordinated with leading textbooks, so that any topic can easily be found in the table of contents or the index.

The modern use of cost accounting in all phases of business activity reflects its usefulness as a management tool for planning, control, and decision making. Indeed, the diversity of its uses has stimulated its own growth, so that today cost accounting embraces such sophisticated advances as those in quantitative techniques and decision models, productivity and performance standards, behavioral science concepts, human resources accounting, learning curve theory, and advanced marketing concepts. In addition, important changes have been made in the field. These include the establishment of the Cost Accounting Standards Board (CASB) and the examination program for the Certificate in Management Accounting (CMA) given by the National Association of Accountants (NAA). Thus, cost accounting, once concerned primarily with manufacturing operations, is now recognized as appropriate for nonmanufacturing activities of all kinds.

The topics treated in this book comprise perhaps the most difficult area of study in the accounting curriculum. Cost accounting is a highly specialized field, requiring an in-depth understanding and mastery of complex concepts and techniques that are unparalleled in other accounting courses. The theory-and-solved-problems approach of this book is designed to clarify the detailed subject matter and provide students with the practical applications they need to be completely familiar with the methodology.

In addition to its usefulness in formal course work, this book will provide excellent preparation and review for the Uniform CPA Examination and for the CMA Examination. It will also serve the needs of those interested in acquiring cost accounting knowledge through independent study, such as students majoring in business and economics areas outside accounting, and business owners, managers, and executives.

We wish to thank Jeanne Flagg, a sponsoring editor for the Schaum's Outline Series, and Jeffrey Hecht for their assistance on this project.

Ralph S. Polimeni
Sheila A. Handy

Contents

Chapter 1

The Role, Concepts, and Classifications of Cost Accounting

1.1 PLACE IN THE COMPANY

Cost accounting provides management with costs for products, inventories, operations or functions and compares actual to predetermined data. It also provides a variety of data for many day-to-day decisions as well as essential information for long-range decisions.

1.2 MANAGERIAL FUNCTIONS

The managerial functions are carried out by the *top management group,* the president, vice-presidents and other executives; the *middle management group,* the division managers, branch managers and department heads; and the *lower management group,* the supervisors. These groups require comprehensive analytic cost data provided on a timely and systematic basis. Essentially the various managerial groups assist in establishing company objectives and determining that the objectives are realized. There are four basic managerial functions that are common to all activities, no matter how large or small the enterprise: (1) planning, (2) organizing, (3) directing, and (4) controlling.

Planning. The process of establishing organizational goals (i.e., setting objectives) and a strategy for their accomplishment is known as planning. It is concerned with the future—immediate and/or long range. Middle and lower management planning stems from the goals (i.e., the plan) set by top management. Examples of primary objectives are improvements in market standing, productivity, profitability, managerial performance, and public responsibility.

Organizing. Once objectives are set and a basic plan is established, the process of organizing involves developing a framework for the activity and making specific work assignments. *Authority* originates with top management and is delegated to the various management levels. A closely related factor is *responsibility*—the obligation to account for a particular function. The supervisor has the authority to delegate the particular work, the employee has the responsibility for performance. *Accountability*—a facet of responsibility—is the obligation to report results to higher authority. This is an important feature of budgetary control and standard costing, since it aids in the comparison of actual performance with predetermined standards and an analysis of causes of difference.

Directing. This is the process by which management achieves its objectives. It requires the ability to supervise and motivate employees in order to obtain optimal levels of productivity conforming to established plans (e.g., budgets or standards for sales, production, costs, etc.)

The modern concept of motivation involves creating a work environment that stimulates superior levels of productivity. On the manager's part, it means providing subordinates with a clear picture of what is expected, necessary guidance, and the feeling that their work represents an important contribution to the achievement of the enterprise's ultimate goals. By effectively communicating with employees and encouraging feedback from them, managers are able to satisfy employee needs.

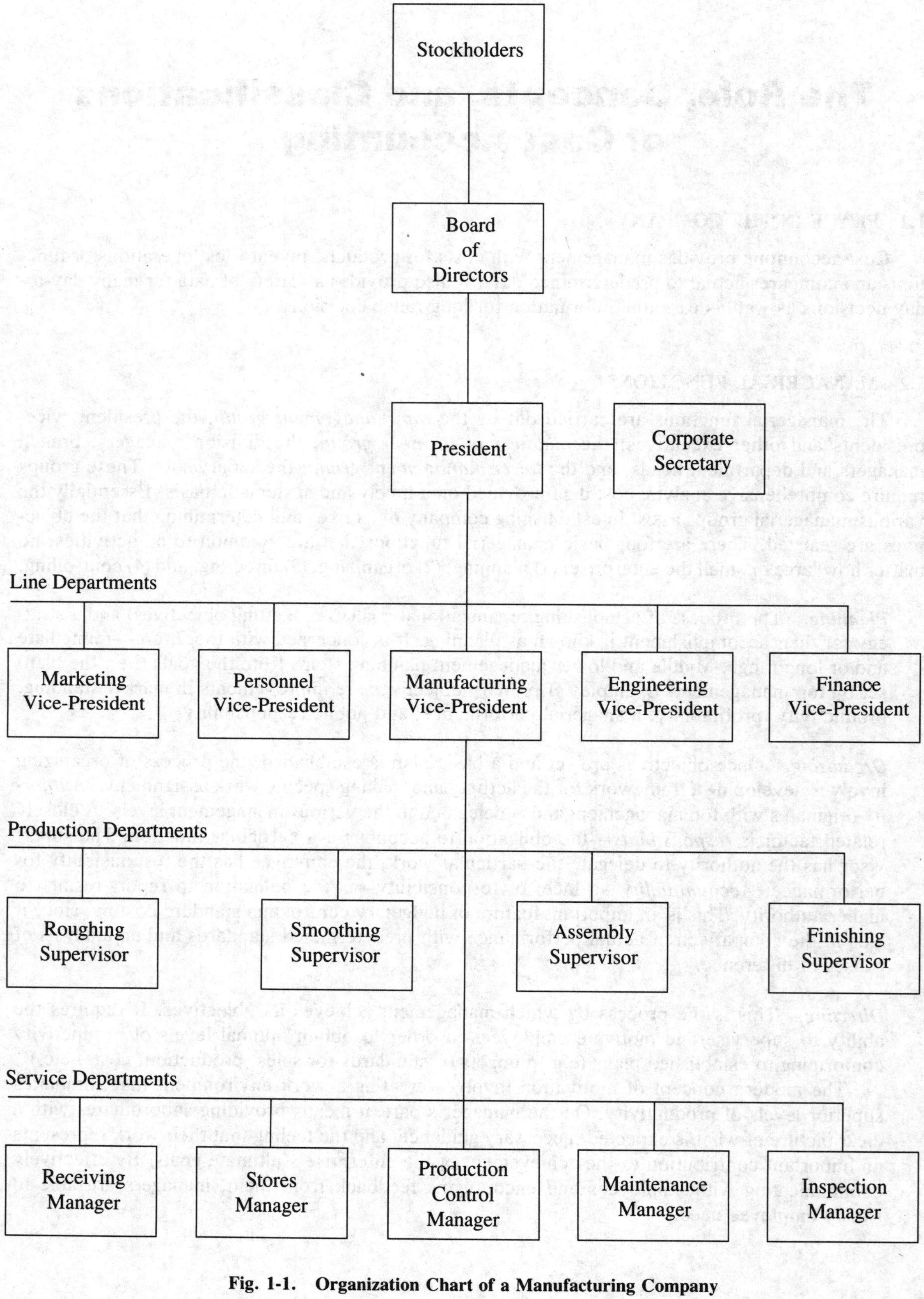

Fig. 1-1. Organization Chart of a Manufacturing Company

Controlling. The process of review, evaluation and reporting monitors the achievement of goals. It involves comparing actual results with those projected in planning as well as against actual performance in past periods. There are two facets to reviewing the enterprise's activities: (1) the comparison of actual to projected results and (2) individual traits. This is done because discrepancies on paper can often be traced to employee achievements and/or failures (e.g., good and bad decisions, exceptional or insufficient supervision and motivation, etc.)

Another kind of appraisal is the *internal audit*. This is a systematic review and evaluation made by a staff of internal auditors to assure management that established controls are operating as planned. Internal auditing today covers accounting, financial and other business operations, such as evaluations of policies, managerial performance, methods, etc. An important part of any review is the reporting of deficiencies and effective recommendations for their prompt correction.

1.3 ORGANIZATION CHARTS

An organization chart establishes the flow of authority and responsibility by defining the relationships among the major management positions of the enterprise. As such, it identifies those persons to whom the various kinds of cost accounting information (see Section 1.5) should go.

For purposes of cost accounting there are two organization charts that we should consider:

(1) ***Company Chart.*** This chart depicts the flow of authority and responsibility downward from the stockholders, through the Board of Directors, the President, the respective Vice-Presidents and other executives to the operating levels. See Fig. 1-1.

(2) ***Controller's Division Chart.*** The controller is the top accounting officer in the company. As a member of the top management team, his or her attention should be directed to providing services to all levels of management and to all functions of the company. The technical and detailed activities for which the controller is responsible are prepared by a staff of specialized accountants. See Fig. 1-2.

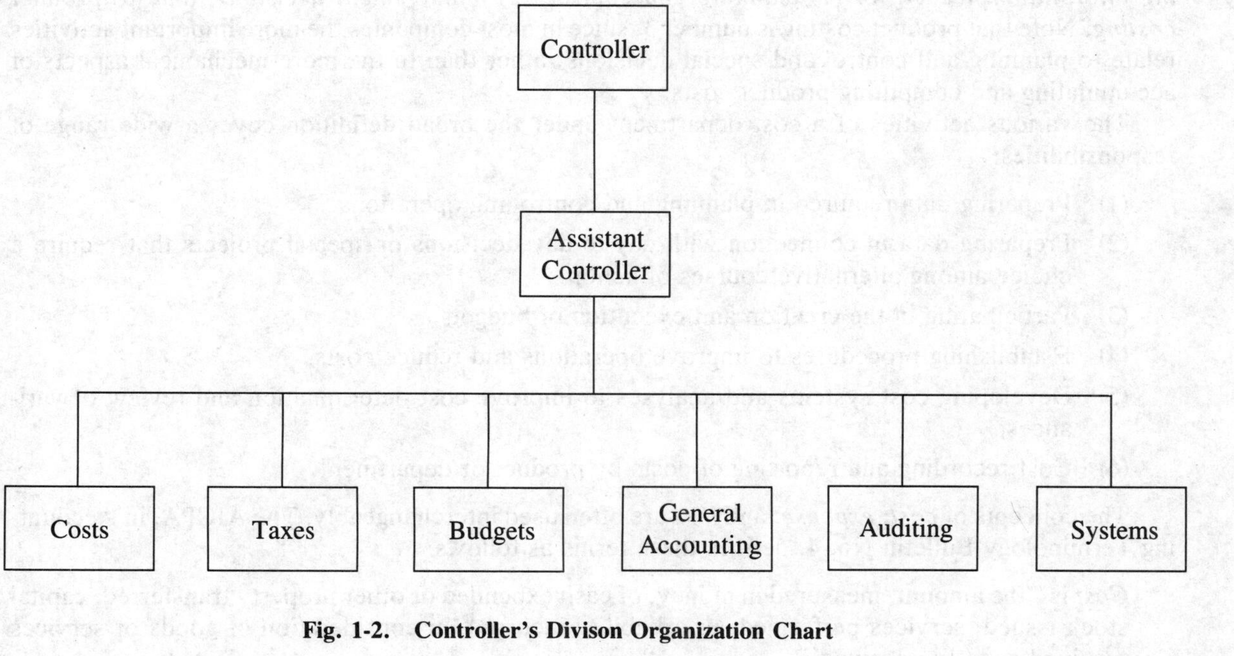

Fig. 1-2. Controller's Divison Organization Chart

1.4 LINE AND STAFF RESPONSIBILITY

Most responsibilities in a company can be divided into line and staff functions. The *line function* has the responsibility for decision making, guidance and supervision. The *staff function* provides advice and service to the line function, but cannot require implementation of its findings. Thus, the controller has line responsibilities (i.e., those that affect his or her own department) as well as staff responsibility with respect to other departments.

1.5 THE COST DEPARTMENT

The cost department is usually supervised by a controller or chief cost accountant. It is responsible for developing and reporting cost data with respect to materials, labor and overhead, and maintaining the necessary underlying records.

The extent to which the cost department participates in management decisions is prescribed by the definition of cost accounting used by the company. In some cases, the cost department is responsible only for compiling product costs, and has no part in analysis for decision making. In others, the wide variety of cost data needed in making day-to-day operating decisions is provided by a staff of cost accountants who have the ability to provide all types of cost information. See Section 1.6.

EXAMPLE 1

Suppose that a manufacturing firm must decide whether to produce a part necessary for one of its products or purchase it from a supplier. Under the limited definition of cost accounting, the cost computations needed for the decision would not be made by the cost department. In the broader sense, the cost department would be responsible for such computations as well as any related analyses.

1.6 NATURE OF COST ACCOUNTING

The broad definition of cost accounting is *the process of identifying, summarizing and interpreting information needed for (1) planning and control, (2) management decisions, and (3) product costing*. Note that product costing is number 3, since in most companies the more important activities relate to planning and control and special decisions rather than to the more mechanical aspects of accumulating and computing product costs.

The various activities of a cost department under the broad definition cover a wide range of responsibilities:

(1) Preparing data required in planning and controlling operations.
(2) Preparing data in connection with day-to-day decisions or special projects that require a choice among alternative courses of action.
(3) Participating in the creation and execution of budgets.
(4) Establishing procedures to improve operations and reduce costs.
(5) Developing cost systems and analyses to improve cost determination and review of variances.
(6) Cost recording and reporting of costs by product or department.

The concepts of *cost, expense,* and *loss* are often used interchangeably. The AICPA, in Accounting Terminology Bulletin No. 4, defines these terms as follows:

Cost is "the amount, measured in money, of cash expended or other property transferred, capital stock issued, services performed, or a liability incurred, in consideration of goods or services received or to be received."

Expense is "all expired costs which are deductible from revenues." Revenue is defined as the price of goods sold and services rendered. In a narrower sense "the term 'expense' refers to operating, selling, or administrative expenses, interest, and taxes." Items included in cost of manufacturing, such as materials, labor, and overhead, should be described as costs, not expenses.

Loss is "(1) the excess of all expenses, in the broad sense of that word, over revenues for a period, or (2) the excess of all or the appropriate portion of the cost of assets over related proceeds, if any, when the items are sold, abandoned, or either wholly or partially destroyed by casualty or otherwise written off. When losses such as those described in (2) are deducted from revenues, they are expenses in the broad sense of that term."

1.7 COSTS AND THEIR CLASSIFICATION

Classification of costs is necessary in order to determine the most suitable method of accumulating and allocating cost data. The principal methods of accumulating costs are described below.

(1) ***Function***

Manufacturing. Costs applied to producing a product.

Marketing. Costs incurred in selling a product or service.

Administrative. Costs incurred in policy-making activities.

Financial. Costs related to financial activities.

(2) ***Elements***

Direct material. Material which is an integral part of the finished product.

Direct labor. Labor applied directly to components of the finished product.

Factory overhead. Indirect materials, indirect labor, and the manufacturing expenses that cannot easily be allocated directly to specific units, jobs or products.

(3) ***Product***

Direct. Costs which are charged directly to the product.

Indirect. Costs which must be allocated.

(4) ***Department***

Production. A unit in which operations are performed on the part or product.

Service. A unit not directly engaged in production and whose costs are ultimately allocated to a production unit.

(5) ***When Charged to Income***

Product. Costs included when product costs, as defined above, are computed. Product costs are included in inventory when the product is produced and in cost of sales when the product is sold.

Period. Costs associated with the passage of time rather than with the product. These costs are not inventoried and are closed to income summary each period since no future benefits are expected.

(6) ***Relation to Volume***

Variable. Costs which change in total in direct proportion to changes in related activity. The unit cost remains the same over a wide range of volume (referred to as the relevant range).

Fixed. Costs which do not change in total over wide ranges of volume. The unit costs decrease as volume increases.

(7) ***Period Covered***

Capital. Costs which are expected to benefit future periods and are classified as assets.

Revenue. Costs which benefit only the current period and are thus expensed as incurred.

(8) ***Degree of Averaging***

Total. The cumulative cost for the established category.

Unit. The total cost divided by the number of units of activity or volume.

1.8 COST SYSTEMS

The cost system must be closely tailored to the organizational structure of the company, the manufacturing process, and the type of information desired and required by executives. Numerous cost systems exist, each with its own advantages and disadvantages. The principal types of cost systems, classified according to their particular attribute, are described below.

(1) ***Periodic Cost Accumulation Systems.*** These provide only limited cost information during a period and require quarterly or year-end adjustments to arrive at the cost of goods manufactured. Periodic physical inventories must be taken to adjust inventory accounts and arrive at the cost of goods manufactured. A periodic cost accumulation system is *not* considered a complete cost accumulation system since the costs of work in process and finished goods can only be determined after physical inventories are taken. Because of this limitation, periodic cost accumulation systems are generally used by small manufacturing companies.

(2) ***Perpetual Cost Accumulation Systems.*** These provide continuous information about work in process, finished goods, and cost of goods manufactured. Cost data are accumulated through a work-in-process account. These systems are used by most medium and large manufacturing companies. Perpetual cost accumulation systems are usually organized under either of two cost formats:

Job Order Cost. The cost unit is the job, and costs are accumulated by job. This format is most suitable where each job or order is different, such as in a printing shop.

Process Cost. The cost unit is the average cost for the units produced in a specified period of time. This format is most suitable where a high volume of similar products are produced, such as in a paper mill.

1.9 UNIT COSTS

The total cost figure is usually unsatisfactory from a control standpoint since the quantity of production varies greatly from period to period. Therefore, some common denominator, such as unit costs, must be available for comparison of varying volumes and amounts. The unit cost figure can be readily computed by dividing total costs by the number of units produced. Unit costs may be stated in terms of tons, gallons, pounds, feet, individual units, etc.

EXAMPLE 2

Unit costs facilitate the computation of amounts for closing inventory and for cost of goods sold. For example, assume that 3,000 units are produced at a total cost of $4,500, or $1.50 per unit. If 2,500 units are sold and 500 remain in inventory, the computation is as follows:

Description	Units	Cost	Unit Cost
Production cost	3,000	$4,500	$1.50
Cost of goods sold			
(2,500 units @ $1.50)	2,500	3,750	1.50
Closing inventory			
(500 units @ $1.50)	500	$ 750	$1.50

1.10 FIXED AND VARIABLE COSTS

For proper budgeting and cost control it is necessary to make a distinction between *fixed* and *variable* total costs. Most costs fit easily into one category or the other; however, various items of factory overhead can be classified as *semivariable* costs and must be carefully examined to determine their relationship to changes in the volume of production.

Fixed Costs. Those which continue unchanged in total within a relevant range despite wide fluctuations in volume or activity. There is a fluctuation in fixed cost *per unit* with volume change. Examples of fixed costs are property taxes and production executives' salaries.

Variable Costs. Those which change in total in direct proportion to changes in volume or activity. There is a uniform cost *per unit* with changes in volume or activity within the relevant range of production. Direct materials and direct labor are generally considered variable costs. Included in this category are such items as factory supplies and payroll taxes.

Semivariable Costs. Those which vary but not in direct proportion to volume or activity. For example, the payroll department costs may remain unchanged up to a certain number of production employees. Additional volume usually requires additional production employees and causes an increase in the payroll department costs. Other examples of semivariable costs are salaries of production department supervisors and machinery repairs.

1.11 INCOME STATEMENTS

The income statements of a manufacturing company and a merchandising company reflect the basic difference in operations of these two types of enterprises. The manufacturing company transforms raw material into finished goods through the use of labor and factory facilities (for example, a company producing finished furniture from lumber). A merchandising company, such as a retail furniture store which buys finished furniture and sells it in the same form, sells the goods it buys without changing the basic form. Note, however, that a merchandising company has only one inventory, while a manufacturing company has three inventories: raw materials, work in process, and finished goods.

The work-in-process inventory account is used to accumulate all factory costs. Direct materials are usually recorded into work-in-process inventory from material requisitions. Direct labor is accumulated into work-in-process inventory from payroll records. All other factory costs (factory overhead) are generally applied into work-in-process inventory based on a predetermined denominator base (discussed in Chapter 3). These inputs into work-in-process inventory (direct materials, direct labor and factory overhead) are called manufacturing costs. The credit to the work-in-process inventory account represents the cost of goods manufactured.

EXAMPLE 3

In the Cost of goods sold section of the Augusta Manufacturing Company's income statement, there is a caption *Cost of goods manufactured*. On the comparable line of the Locust Valley Merchandising Company's statement is the caption *Purchases*. The latter caption indicates that goods similar to those in the opening and closing merchandise inventory have been bought during the accounting period. The caption *Costs of goods manufactured* represents the total of materials, labor, and overhead used in manufacturing the product and is detailed in the supporting schedule of cost of goods manufactured. As can be seen, the schedule shows the direct materials, the direct labor, and the various components of factory overhead that apply. The term cost of goods manufactured relates to the cost of products which have been *fully completed and transferred to finished goods.* The products which have not been completed will remain in the work-in-process inventory at the end of the period.

Augusta Manufacturing Company
Income Statement
for year ended December 31, 19X1

Sales		$2,100,000
Less: Cost of goods sold		
Finished goods, Jan. 1, 19X1	$ 180,000	
Cost of goods manufactured (see Schedule of Cost of Goods Manufactured)	1,500,000	
	$1,680,000	
Finished goods, Dec. 31, 19X1	150,000	
Cost of goods sold	$1,530,000	
Gross profit	$ 570,000	
Less: Selling and administrative expense	250,000	
Net income	$ 320,000	

Locust Valley Merchandising Company
Income Statement
for year ended December 31, 19X1

Sales	$2,150,000
Less: Costs of goods sold	
Merchandise inventory Jan. 1, 19X1	$ 150,000
Purchases	1,550,000
	$1,700,000
Merchandise inventory Dec. 31, 19X1	175,000
Cost of goods sold	$1,525,000
Gross profit	$ 625,000
Less: Selling and administrative expense	275,000
Net income	$ 350,000

Augusta Manufacturing Company
Schedule of Cost of Goods Manufactured
for year ended December 31, 19X1

Direct Materials:		
Inventory, Jan. 1, 19X1	$ 170,000	
Purchase of direct materials	1,050,000	
	$1,220,000	
Inventory, Dec. 31, 19X1	120,000	
Direct materials used		$1,100,000
Direct labor		250,000
Factory overhead		
Indirect labor	$ 70,000	
Supplies	15,000	
Heat, light and power	23,000	
Depreciation, plant	20,000	
Depreciation, equipment	30,000	
Miscellaneous	7,000	165,000
Manufacturing costs		$1,515,000
Add: Work in process, Jan. 1, 19X1		90,000
		$1,605,000
Less: Work in process, Dec. 31, 19X1		105,000
Cost of goods manufactured (to Income Statement)		$1,500,000

Solved Problems

1.1 Centralization vs. Decentralization. The Georgia Atlantic Paper Company, which has its headquarters and manufacturing operations in the southeast, has as its principal product kraft wrapping paper. The company recently increased its production substantially and, for product outlets, acquired four corrugated box plants located in Canton, Massillon, Akron, and Springfield, Ohio. Two bag manufacturing plants, located in Hempstead and Locust Valley, New York, were also acquired. This expansion required decentralization of much of the manufacturing operations, and there has been considerable discussion of decentralization of the accounting operations as well.

Your firm has been performing this company's audit for years and you have been asked to carry out a Management Services Survey. Prepare a report covering the following points:

(a) Should the accounting and cost functions be decentralized?

(b) If so, to whom should the accountant report? Should the local accountant have line, staff or functional responsibilities?

(c) What are some of the advantages of decentralization?

SOLUTION

(a) When manufacturing operations are decentralized, it is generally desirable to decentralize the accounting function in order to better serve the newly diversified and widespread operations. It would not be practical to expect a plant manager to wait for cost accounting answers to the many everyday cost problems which arise. Instead, there should be a trained accountant at each plant or available at a nearby plant to answer cost questions promptly.

(b) The local accountant should report on a *line* basis or administratively to the local plant manager. He or she would have *staff* responsibility with respect to other departments. The accountant could advise but not command departments other than his or her own. The local accountant is a member of the plant unit or organization and is thus subject to the jurisdiction of the plant manager in all areas except accounting. Thus, the accountant and his or her staff would be expected to observe the working conditions established for the plant.

However, the chart of accounts, the preparation and filing of financial statements and reports would be a *functional* matter established by the controller in accordance with authority delegated by the president. Uniformity in accounting reports is required since consolidated financial data are submitted to stockholders, government agencies, etc. The local accountant would also prepare the many studies, analyses, and other cost information essential to local management. With the greater diversity and geographic distribution of operations and the greater need for lateral command, there is now a far greater understanding of the functional authority necessary in a large company with widespread operations.

(c) The advantages of decentralization include the following:

(1) Company accounting policies and procedures established by the corporate controller can be interpreted, implemented, and enforced by the local accountant.

(2) Decision making at the local level provides good management training for advancement within the company.

(3) An alert accountant can provide information needed by management in controlling and reducing costs and improving operations. The accountant can also greatly enhance the value of the department and increase the appreciation of the contribution that accounting can make.

1.2 Corporate Responsibilities. You have just been appointed Controller of the Fulton Company, which has grown rapidly in recent years. This expansion has brought about the need to reorganize various corporate responsibilities. The present responsibilities are as follows:

Name	**Present Responsibilities**
Helen L. Johnson	President and Production Manager
Lloyd Smith	Vice-President in Charge of Production
Alfred Knowles	Manager of Accounting
Roberta Harter	Vice-President in Charge of Sales
Jennifer Lyons	Chief Accountant
Thomas Reilly	Manager of Design
Frank Weag	Purchasing Agent
Ray Lanuto	Manager of Maintenance
Georgina Kuezek	Vice-President of Engineering

(a) Prepare an organization chart showing the proper arrangement of functions, and *(b)* describe the proposed changes in duties and titles.

SOLUTION

(a) See Fig. 1-3.

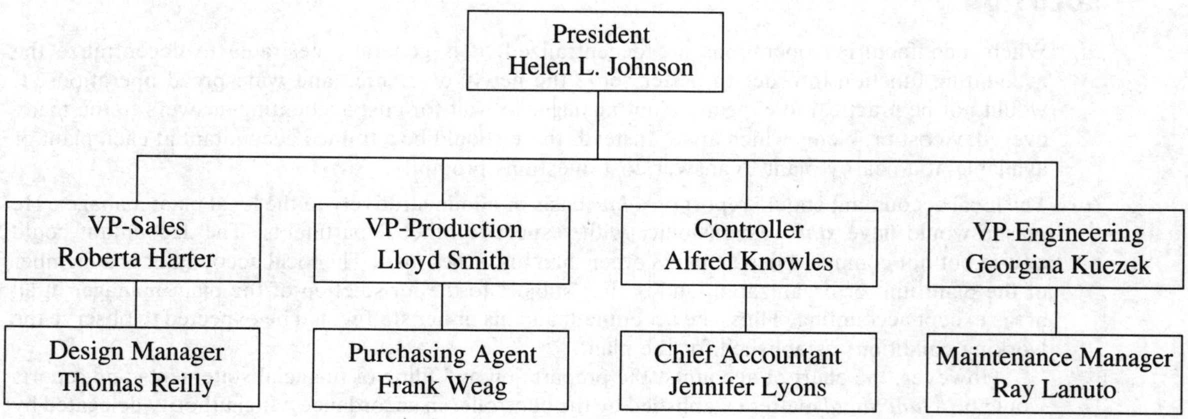

Fig. 1-3

(b) In order to avoid confusion regarding the direct responsibility for production, Lloyd Smith, the Vice-President, should be given the direct responsibility commensurate with his ability for the production function. Of course, he would be responsible to the President and perhaps a limit might be placed on contracts which the Vice-President could approve. Contracts for higher amounts would have to be approved by the President.

The title of Alfred Knowles as Manager in Charge of Accounting should be changed to Controller, the currently accepted terminology for the chief accounting officer.

The title of Roberta Harter as Vice-President in Charge of Sales might be changed to VP-Sales to be consistent with the titles of the other Vice-Presidents.

1.3 Organization Chart. The Samson Manufacturing Company has the following job classifications:

Vice-President, Marketing	Manager, Production Control Department
Manager, Costs	Supervisor, Drilling Department
Manager, Purchasing Department	Manager, Inspection Department
Supervisor, Finishing Department	

President	Supervisor, Assembly Department
Manager, Shipping Room	Manager, New Products
Vice-President, Personnel	Manager, Basic Research
Manager, Branch Sales	Manager, Product Improvement
Vice-President, Research and Development	Manager, Job Evaluation
	Manager, Engineering Services
Manager, Budgets	Treasurer
Controller	Manager, Engineering Design
Manager, Employment	Assistant Treasurer
Vice-President, Finance	Manager, Systems
Manager, Receiving Department	Vice-President, Manufacturing
Corporate Secretary	Manager, General Accounting
Manager, Market Research	Superintendent of Production
Vice-President, Engineering	Manager, Receiving Department
Manager, Internal Auditing	Manager, Stores Department
Supervisor, Machining Department	Manager, Maintenance Department

Prepare an organization chart showing the relationship among the various areas of responsibilities.

SOLUTION

See Fig. 1-4.

1.4 Indicate whether the relationship of the first individual to the second in the following pairs is of a line (L) or staff (S) nature. (*a*) VP-Finance, Controller; (*b*) VP-Manufacturing, Controller; (*c*) Controller, Cost Accountant; (*d*) Controller, Production Superintendent; (*e*) VP-Finance, Employment Manager; (*f*) VP-Finishing Dept., Manufacturing Supervisor; (*g*) Cost Accountant, Cost Clerk; (*h*) Cost Accountant, General Accountant; (*i*) Treasurer, Assistant Treasurer.

SOLUTION

(*a*) L, (*b*) S, (*c*) L, (*d*) S, (*e*) S, (*f*) L, (*g*) L, (*h*) S, (*i*) L.

1.5 **Cost Elements.** Indicate whether the cost element for each of the following cost components is direct materials (DM), direct labor (DL) or factory overhead (FO).

(*a*) Fire insurance on equipment
(*b*) Machine operator's wages
(*c*) Bags in cement mills
(*d*) Cutting tools
(*e*) Machinery repairs
(*f*) Supervisor's wages
(*g*) Bottles for product
(*h*) Cost Accountant's salary

SOLUTION

(*a*) FO, (*b*) DL, (*c*) DM, (*d*) FO, (*e*) FO, (*f*) FO, (*g*) DM, (*h*) FO.

1.6 **Fixed and Variable Costs.** Indicate whether each of the following items represents a fixed (F), variable (V) or semivariable (S) cost.

(*a*) Rent
(*b*) Production department supervisors
(*e*) Production executive salaries
(*f*) Factory power (No minimum fee)

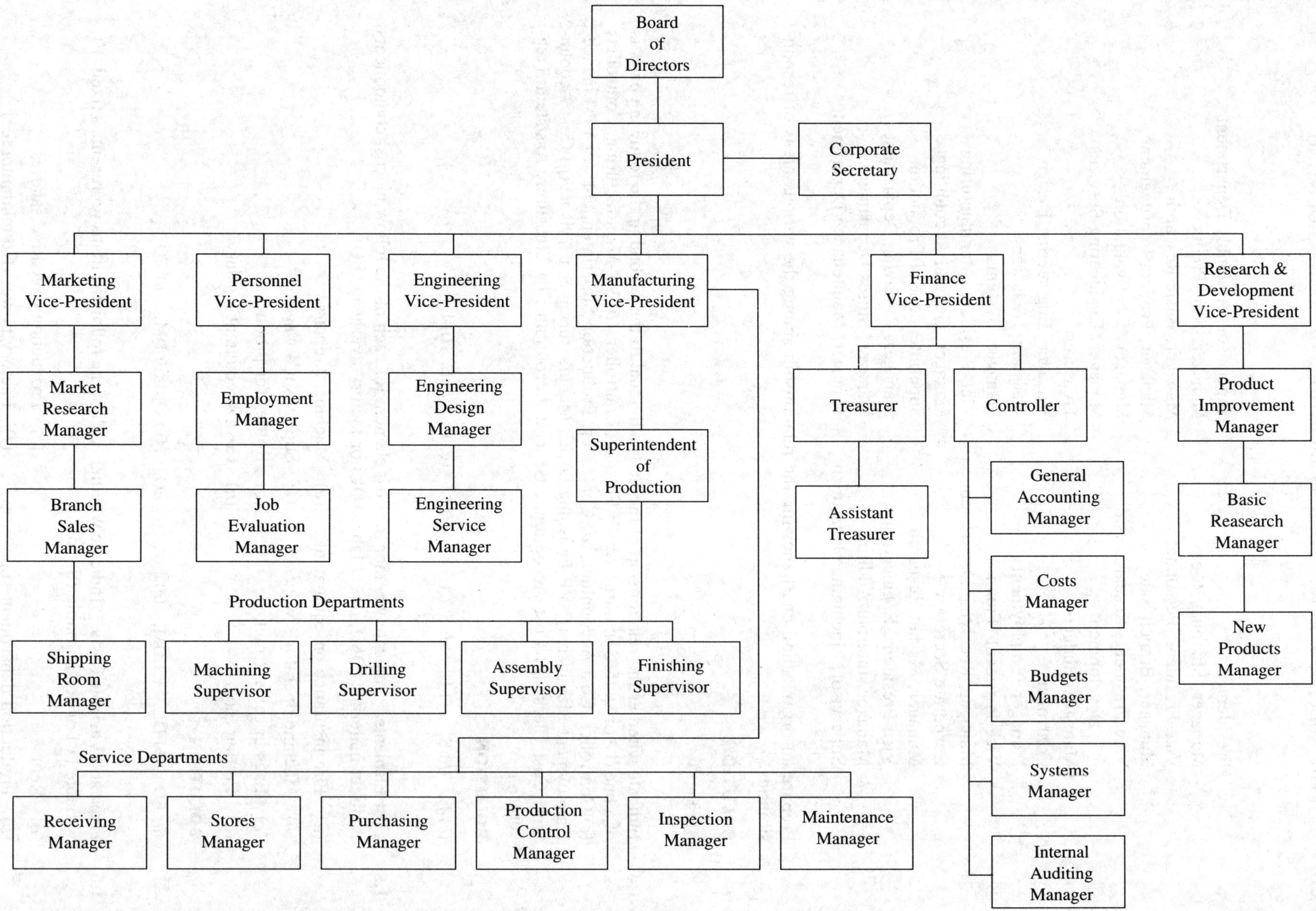
Board of Directors
President
Corporate Secretary
Marketing Vice-President
Personnel Vice-President
Engineering Vice-President
Manufacturing Vice-President
Finance Vice-President
Research & Development Vice-President
Market Research Manager
Employment Manager
Engineering Design Manager
Superintendent of Production
Treasurer
Controller
Product Improvement Manager
Branch Sales Manager
Job Evaluation Manager
Engineering Service Manager
Assistant Treasurer
General Accounting Manager
Basic Reasearch Manager
Costs Manager
New Products Manager
Production Departments
Shipping Room Manager
Machining Supervisor
Drilling Supervisor
Assembly Supervisor
Finishing Supervisor
Budgets Manager
Systems Manager
Service Departments
Receiving Manager
Stores Manager
Purchasing Manager
Production Control Manager
Inspection Manager
Maintenance Manager
Internal Auditing Manager

Fig. 1-4

(*c*) Cutting tools (*g*) Factory manager
(*d*) Property taxes (*h*) Machinery repairs

SOLUTION

(*a*) F, (*b*) S, (*c*) V, (*d*) F, (*e*) F, (*f*) V, (*g*) F, (*h*) S.

1.7 Income Statement. The records of Folk, Incorporated show the following data for November, 19X7.

Inventory Balances	November 1	November 30
Raw materials	$12,000	$13,500
Work in process	15,100	17,600
Finished goods	19,500	21,200

Operating data:

Direct labor cost	$ 50,000
Factory overhead	62,500
Purchases	43,200
Sales	250,000
Selling expenses	23,000
General and administrative expenses	25,000

Prepare (*a*) a schedule showing the cost of goods sold, and (*b*) an Income Statement.

SOLUTION

(*a*)

Folk, Incorporated
Schedule of Cost of Goods Sold
for month of November, 19X7

Raw materials cost		
Raw materials inventory, November 1	$12,000	
Purchases	43,200	
Goods available	$55,200	
Less: Raw materials inventory, November 30	13,500	
Raw materials cost		$ 41,700
Direct labor cost		50,000
Factory overhead		62,500
Total manufacturing cost		$154,200
Add: Work in process, November 1		15,100
		$169,300
Less: Work in process, November 30		17,600
Cost of goods manufactured		$151,700
Add: Finished goods inventory, November 1		19,500
		$171,200
Less: Finished goods inventory, November 30		21,200
Cost of goods sold		$150,000

(*b*)

Folk, Incorporated
Income Statement
for month of November, 19X7

Sales		$250,000
Less: Cost of goods sold (see schedule)		150,000
Gross profit on sales		$100,000
Operating expenses		
Selling expenses	$23,000	
General and administrative expenses	25,000	48,000
Net income from operations		52,000

1.8 Fixed and Variable Costs. The Englewood Company produces a large excavator selling for $400 per unit, of which cost of goods sold amounts to $320 and selling and administrative expenses, $25. During 19X5, 2,500 units were sold. The breakdown of cost of goods sold was: materials, 50%; labor, 25%; factory overhead, 25%.

The following cost increases are expected in 19X6: materials, 15%; labor, 20%. The selling price is to be raised to $460, but management anticipates an accompanying 20% decrease in the number of units sold.

(*a*) Prepare an Income Statement for 19X5, including costs per unit.

(*b*) Prepare an Income Statement for 19X6, including unit costs. Material and labor costs are to be held to 75% of cost of goods sold; selling and administrative expenses increase to $35 per unit.

(*c*) It was later found that 19X5 factory overhead consisted of $125,000 in fixed expenses and $75,000 in variable expenses. Prepare a revised Income Statement for 19X6, ignoring the previous relationship of materials and labor to cost of goods sold. Fixed costs will remain constant despite the decrease in units sold.

SOLUTION

(*a*)

Englewood Company
Income Statement
Year 19X5

	Total	Per Unit
Sales (2,500 units)	$1,000,000	$400.00
Cost of goods sold		
Materials (50%)	$ 400,000	$160.00
Labor (25%)	200,000	80.00
Factory overhead (25%)	200,000	80.00
Total cost of goods sold	$ 800,000	$320.00
Gross profit	$ 200,000	80.00
Selling and administrative expenses	62,500	25.00
Net profit	$ 137,500	$ 55.00

(*b*)

Englewood Company
Income Statement
Year 19X6

	Total	Per Unit
Sales (2,000 units)	$920,000	$460.00
Cost of goods sold		
Materials ($160 × 115%)	$368,000	$184.00
Labor ($80 × 120%)	192,000	96.00
Factory overhead (25% of cost of goods sold)	186,667*	93.33
Total cost of goods sold	$746,667	$373.33
Gross profit	$173,333	$ 86.67
Selling and administrative expenses	70,000	35.00
Net profit	$103,333	$ 51.67

* *Computation of factory overhead:*
Total cost of goods sold = ($368,000 + $192,000) ÷ 75% = $746,667
Factory overhead = $746,667 × 25% = $186,667

(*c*)

Englewood Company
Income Statement
Year 19X6 Revised

	Total		Per Unit	
Sales (2,000 units)		$920,000		$460.00
Cost of goods sold				
Materials		$368,000		$184.00
Labor		192,000		96.00
Factory overhead				
Fixed	$125,000		$62.50	
Variable	60,000*	185.000	30.00	92.50
Total cost of sales		$745,000		$372.50
Gross profit		$175,000		$ 87.50
Selling and administrative expenses		70,000		35.00
Net profit		$105,000		$ 52.50

* The factory overhead in 19X5 was $200,000, made up of $125,000 fixed expense and $75,000 variable expense. The variable expense per unit is $30 ($75,000 ÷ 2,500 units). The variable portion of factory overhead in 19X6, therefore, is 2,000 units times $30, or $60,000.

1.9 Cost of Goods Manufactured. The Hempstead Company, which manufactures a single product, shows the following ledger balances for the month of January, 19X6.

Direct labor	$180,000
Indirect labor	65,000
Factory rent	11,000
Heat, light and power	3,500

Miscellaneous factory overhead	16,500
Interest expenses	4,500
Office salaries	11,000
Sales commissions	4,000
Sales returns and allowances	5,000
Freight-out	5,500

Other data:

Purchases of raw materials: 16,000 units at $3.00 each; 10,000 units at $2.50 each.

Production: 25,000 units.

Sales: 20,000 units at $12.

Raw materials inventory, January 1: 2,000 units at $3.50 each.

The first-in, first-out method is used in valuing raw materials inventory.

Each unit of finished goods requires one unit of raw material.

Work-in-process inventory: January 1, 3,000 units costing $12,000; at January 31, 5,000 units costing $17,000.

Finished goods inventory, January 1: 5,000 units at $9 each.

Factory machinery: cost $30,000, depreciation 10% per year.

Office equipment: cost $10,000, depreciation 8% per year.

Prepare a Statement of Cost of Goods Manufactured for the month of January, 19X6.

SOLUTION

The Hempstead Company
Statement of Cost of Goods Manufactured
for month of January, 19X6

Raw materials		
Inventory, January 1	$ 7,000	
Purchases	73,000	
Raw materials available	$80,000	
Less: Inventory, January 31*	7,500	
Cost of raw materials used		$ 72,500
Direct labor		180,000
Factory overhead		
Indirect labor	$65,000	
Factory rent	11,000	
Heat, light and power	3,500	
Depreciation, machinery	250	
Miscellaneous	16,500	96,250
Total manufacturing costs		$348,750
Add: Work in process, January 1		12,000
Balance		$360,750
Deduct: Work in process, January 31		17,000
Cost of goods manufactured		$343,750

* *Raw Materials Used*

Inventory, January 1	2,000
Purchases (16,000 + 10,000)	26,000
Units available	28,000
Used in production	25,000
Inventory, January 31	3,000

Chapter 2

Costing and Control of Materials and Labor

2.1 CHARACTERISTICS OF MATERIALS AND LABOR

Materials are the basic substances that are transformed into finished goods. Materials costs may be either *direct* or *indirect*.

Direct Materials. There are three characteristics of direct materials:

(1) They are easily traced to the product.
(2) They represent a major material of the finished product.
(3) They can be identified directly with production of the product.

Indirect Materials. These include all other materials used in production (i.e., nails in furniture manufacturing) and are considered to be a factory overhead cost.

Labor is the physical and/or mental effort expended to manufacture products. *Labor cost* is the price paid for using human resources. Labor cost may be either *direct* or *indirect*.

Direct Labor. There are also three characteristics of direct labor:

(1) It is easily traced to the product.
(2) It is a major cost of producing the product.
(3) It can be identified directly with production of the product.

Indirect Labor. This includes all other labor costs related to production (e.g., salary of plant supervisor). Like indirect materials, this is considered a factory overhead cost.

Materials

2.2 SYSTEMS OF ACCOUNTING FOR THE PURCHASE OF MATERIALS

There are two systems that may be used to account for the purchase of materials.

Under a *periodic inventory system,* the purchase of both direct and indirect materials is recorded in an account entitled Purchases of Raw Materials. If a beginning materials inventory exists, it is recorded in a separate account entitled Materials Inventory—Beginning.

Under a *perpetual inventory system,* the purchase of materials is recorded in an account labeled Materials Inventory, rather than in a purchases account. If a beginning materials inventory exists, it is already included in the materials inventory account.

In this book the journal entries were prepared under the perpetual cost accumulation system. Because of the use of computers for cost accumulation, the periodic system is rarely employed.

EXAMPLE 1

Construction Company receives 1,000 feet of tubing (direct) and 2 cases of assorted screws (indirect). The tubing is $20 per foot and the screws are $25 per case. The journal entry under the perpetual inventory system follows:

Materials Inventory	*20,050*	
Accounts Payable		*20,050*

2.3 ISSUANCE OF MATERIALS

(1) A material requisition must be prepared by the production department requesting the goods. The requisition should contain the job order number and/or the name of department making the request, the quantity and description of the goods, and the unit and total costs.

(2) Recording materials issued also differs, depending on whether a periodic or perpetual system is used. No entry is made under a periodic cost accumulation system when materials are issued; however, under a perpetual cost accumulation system, a debit is made to a work-in-process account and a credit is made to the materials inventory account.

EXAMPLE 2

Construction Company places 500 feet of tubing in production ($20 per foot). The entry to record this is:

Work-in-Process Inventory	*10,000*	
Materials Inventory		*10,000*

2.4 COSTING MATERIALS ISSUED AND ENDING MATERIALS INVENTORY

Under the perpetual inventory system, materials issued are charged to the work-in-process inventory account as they are used (see above). Thus, the ending materials inventory can be readily determined from the materials inventory account.

Periods of changing prices pose problems for the valuation of inventory. For example, what price should be charged for materials placed into production during such a period; what price should be charged for materials still on hand at the end of the period (ending materials inventory); and should the cost of materials issued be determined by the beginning unit price of materials, the average unit price for the period, or the ending unit price? Because the answers to these questions vary, four methods have been developed to value ending inventories and cost of materials issued during periods of changing prices:

(1) Specific identification
(2) Average cost—simple and weighted
(3) First-in, first-out (FIFO)
(4) Last-in, first-out (LIFO)

Use of each method under both the periodic and the perpetual inventory systems is illustrated in Examples 3 to 7. For convenience, BI and EI are used to denote Beginning Inventory and Ending Inventory, respectively. All these examples are based on the following data:

Sweet Dreams Company's inventory and purchases of brass tubing are as follows:

	Date	Units Purchased	Cost per Unit ($ per ft)	Units Issued
(BI)	1/1	1,500	$1.75	—
	1/7	1,000	1.80	—
	1/9	—	—	1,000 (from BI)
	1/15	—	—	500 (from BI)
	1/21	2,000	2.00	—
	1/25	500	2.10	—
	1/30	—	—	2,000 (from 1/7 & 1/21 purchase)

Ending Inventory 1/31: 1,500 units

(1) ***Specific Identification.*** Under this method each item is placed into inventory with a price tag. Both ending inventory and materials issued are valued at the prices tagged on each unit. This technique is generally used for expensive items.

EXAMPLE 3

Periodic and Perpetual Inventory Systems

When specific identification is used, both the application of the technique and the results are *identical* under *either* the periodic or the perpetual inventory system, as illustrated below:

Cost of materials issued:

(BI)	1,000 × $1.75 =	$1,750
(BI)	500 × $1.75 =	875
(1/7)	1,000 × $1.80 =	1,800
(1/21)	1,000 × $2.00 =	2,000
		$6,425

Ending inventory:

(1/21)	1,000 × $2.00 =	$2,000
(1/25)	500 × $2.10 =	1,050
		$3,050

(2) ***Average Cost.*** This method is more appropriate for small, homogeneous items (i.e., brass tubing) and when specific identification is impossible (i.e., peanuts). There are two ways to compute average cost—simple average and weighted average.

(*a*) *Simple Average.* The *unit price* of the items in beginning inventory is added to the *unit price* of each purchase, and the sum is divided by the number of purchases plus one (for beginning inventory). This method is most accurate when purchases are of the same quantity. The object is to compute the average purchase (unit) price.

EXAMPLE 4

Periodic Inventory System

Because inventory and materials issued are not valued until the end of the period under periodic inventory systems, the average cost is calculated only once, at the end of the period.

$$\text{Simple average unit cost} = \frac{\text{BI unit price} + \text{Unit price of each purchase}}{\text{Number of purchases} + 1 \text{ (for BI)}}$$

$$= \frac{\$1.75 + \$1.80 + \$2.00 + \$2.10}{3 + 1} = \frac{\$7.65}{4} = \$1.9125$$

Cost of materials issued:	3,500 × $1.9125 =	$6,693.75
Ending inventory:	1,500 × $1.9125 =	$2,868.75

Note: The actual cost of materials available differs from $9,475 because of the unequal number of units purchased at each price.

Perpetual Inventory System

Under perpetual inventory systems an average must be calculated *each time* a purchase is made because a running inventory is being kept. Materials are issued at the last average cost at their date of issuance. This is called a *simple moving average*. See Table 2-1.

Table 2-1 Simple Moving Average

Date	Purchases			Issued			Balance		
	Units	Unit Cost	Cost of Materials Avail. for Use	Units	Unit Cost	Cost of Materials Issued	Units	Unit Cost	Total Cost
(BI) 1/1	1,500	$1.75	$2,625	—	—	—	1,500	$1.75	$2,625.00
1/7	1,000	1.80	1,800	—	—	—	2,500	1.775(a)	4,437.50
1/9	—	—		1,000	$1.775	$1,775.00	1,500	1.775	2,662.50
1/15	—	—		500	1.775	887.50	1,000	1.775	1,775.00
1/21	2,000	2.00	4,000	—	—	—	3,000	1.85(b)	5,550.00
1/25	500	2.10	1,050	—	—	—	3,500	1.9125(c)	6,693.75
1/30	—	—		2,000	1.9125	3,825.00	1,500	1.9125	$2,868.75 (EI)
			$9,475			$6,487.50			

Computations:

(a) $\frac{\$1.75 + \$1.80}{2} = \$1.775$

(b) $\frac{\$1.75 + \$1.80 + \$2.00}{3} = \$1.85$

(c) $\frac{\$1.75 + \$1.80 + \$2.00 + \$2.10}{4} = \$1.9125$

Cost of materials issued	$6,487.50
Ending inventory	2,868.75
Actual cost of materials available	$9,356.25

Note: The actual cost of materials available differs from $9,475 (Table 2-1, column 4) because of the unequal number of units purchased at each price. This problem is overcome by the weighted average method (Example 5).

(*b*) *Weighted Average.* This method overcomes the limitations of simple average by considering the purchase quantity as well as the price. Under this method each purchase (including beginning inventory) is calculated by multiplying the quantity purchased by the respective unit cost to get a total purchase cost. The purchase costs are summed and divided by the units of materials available for use. The implementation of this method differs depending on whether a periodic or perpetual system is under use.

EXAMPLE 5

Periodic Inventory System

Under a periodic system the weighted average is calculated only once, at the end of the period.

$$\text{Weighted average} = \frac{\text{Total purchase cost}}{\text{Materials available for use}}$$

$$= \frac{(1{,}500 \times \$1.75) + (1{,}000 \times \$1.80) + (2{,}000 \times \$2.00) + (500 \times \$2.10)}{5{,}000} = \$1.895$$

Cost of materials issued: 3,500 × $1.895 = $6,632.50

Ending inventory: 1,500 × $1.895 = $2,842.50

Perpetual Inventory System

Under a perpetual system an average is calculated at the time of each purchase (hence it is called a weighted *moving* average) and is used to issue materials until a new purchase is made, at which time the average cost must be recalculated. See Table 2-2.

Table 2-2 Weighted Moving Average

Date	Purchases			Issued			Balance		
	Units	Unit Cost	Cost of Materials Avail. for Use	Units	Unit Cost	Cost of Materials Issued	Units	Unit Cost	Total Cost
(BI) 1/1	1,500	$1.75	$2,625	—	—	—	1,500	$1.75	$2,625.00
1/7	1,000	1.80	1,800	—	—	—	2,500	1.77(a)	4,425.00
1/9	—	—		1,000	$1.77	$1,770.00	1,500	1.77	2,655.00
1/15	—	—		500	1.77	885.00	1,000	1.77	1,770.00
1/21	2,000	2.00	4,000	—	—	—	3,000	1.9233(b)	5,769.90
1/25	500	2.10	1,050	—	—	—	3,500	1.9485(c)	6,819.75
1/30	—	—		2,000	1.9485	3,897.00	1,500	1.9485	$2,922.75 (EI)
			$9,475			$6,552.00			

Computations:

(a) $\frac{(1{,}500 \times \$1.75) + (1{,}000 \times \$1.80)}{2{,}500} = \$1.77$

(b) $\frac{(1{,}000 \times \$1.77) + (2{,}000 \times \$2.00)}{3{,}000} = \$1.9233$

(c) $\frac{(3{,}000 \times \$1.9233) + (500 \times \$2.10)}{3{,}500} = \$1.9485$

Cost of materials issued	$6,552.00
Ending inventory	2,922.75
Rounding difference	0.25
Cost of materials available	$9,475.00

(3) ***FIFO (First-in, first-out).*** Materials issued for use under this method come from beginning inventory and then the earlier purchases. The ending inventory here is considered to be the last materials purchased and therefore reflects current costs.

EXAMPLE 6

Periodic and Perpetual Inventory Systems

Both inventory systems yield identical results for materials issued and ending inventory when FIFO is used.

Cost of materials issued: The 3,500 units issued come from the earliest purchases, so we start with beginning inventory and work forward.

	Date	Units	Unit Cost ($)	Cost of Materials Issued
(BI)	1/1	1,500	$1.75	$2,625
	1/7	1,000	1.80	1,800
	1/21	1,000	2.00	2,000
		3,500		$6,425

Ending inventory: To get the ending inventory we start with the last purchase and work backward.

Date	Units	Unit Cost ($)	Total	
1/25	500	$2.10	$1,050	
1/21	1,000	2.00	2,000	
	1,500		$3,050	EI

Cost of materials available: $6,425 + $3,050 = $9,475

(4) ***LIFO (Last-in, first-out).*** Under this method we assume that the last goods received will be the first issued (exactly the opposite of FIFO). Therefore, our ending inventory will include the period's beginning inventory and the early purchases. Results of LIFO application differ, depending on whether a periodic or perpetual system is used.

EXAMPLE 7

Periodic Inventory System

The calculation of materials issued and ending inventory is done at the end of the period, as is normal with periodic systems.

Cost of materials issued: To value the 3,500 units issued, we begin with the last purchase and work backward.

Date	Units	Unit Cost ($)	Cost of Materials Issued
1/25	500	$2.10	$1,050
1/21	2,000	2.00	4,000
1/7	1,000	1.80	1,800
	3,500		$6,850

Ending inventory: To arrive at a value for the ending inventory, we begin with the beginning inventory and work forward.

	Date	Units	Unit Cost ($)	Total	
(BI)	1/1	1,500	$1.75	$2,625	EI

Cost of materials available: $6,850 + $2,625 = $9,475

Perpetual Inventory System

The ending inventory and the value of materials issued will differ from those calculated under a periodic system because costs are assigned as materials are issued and *not* at the end of the period. Our ending inventory value will be greater here for this reason.

Table 2-3 LIFO in Perpetual Inventory System

Date	Purchases			Issued			Balance		
	Units	Unit Cost	Cost of Materials Avail. for Use	Units	Unit Cost	Cost of Materials Issued	Units	Unit Cost	Total Cost
(BI) 1/1	1,500	$1.75	$2,625	—	—	—	1,500	$1.75	$2,625
1/7	1,000	1.80	1,800	—	—	—	2,500	*(a)*	4,425
1/9	—	—		1,000	$1.80	$1,800	1,500	1.75	2,625
1/15	—	—		500	1.75	875	1,000	1.75	1,750
1/21	2,000	2.00	4,000	—	—	—	3,000	*(b)*	5,750
1/25	500	2.10	1,050	—	—	—	3,500	*(c)*	6,800
1/30	—	—		2,000	*(e)*	4,050	1,500	*(d)*	$2,750(EI)
			$9,475			$6,725			

Computations:

(a) (1,500 × $1.75) + (1,000 × $1.80) = $4,425

(b) (1,000 × $1.75) + (2,000 × $2.00) = $5,750

(c) (1,000 × $1.75) + (2,000 × $2.00) + (500 × $2.10) = $6,800

(d) (1,000 × $1.75) + (500 × $2.00) = $2,750

(e) (500 × $2.10) + (1,500 × $2.00) = $4,050

Cost of materials issued	$6,725
Ending inventory	2,750
Cost of materials available	$9,475

2.5 COMPARISON OF INVENTORY METHODS

The method selected determines the values of materials issued and ending inventory. The inventory system used also has an effect on these values. A firm should select its method of inventory valuation carefully since the *principle of consistency* states that the method chosen should be adhered to each period. A change can be made only if it can be shown that doing so would improve the accuracy of the firm's financial statements.

2.6 LOWER OF COST OR MARKET (LCM)

LCM is a rule which states that inventory should be valued at the lower of its historical cost (time of purchase) or current market value (usually replacement cost).

(1) Generally, in inflationary times, historical cost is lower than market, so no adjustment is necessary.

(2) If market is lower than cost, the ending inventory must be reported at market. This is based on the *principle of conservatism,* which requires applying the accounting treatment that results in the lowest estimate of assets and income for the current period.

(3) If inventory is reduced under LCM, the resulting loss is generally added to the cost of goods manufactured.

LCM can be computed two ways:

(1) Applied to the total inventory value

(2) Applied on an item-by-item basis to ending inventory

EXAMPLE 8

Using the ending inventory calculated under LIFO (perpetual) in Example 7, assume the replacement cost of brass tubing decreased to $1.80 per foot.

(a) LCM applied to the total inventory value:

	Date	Units	Unit Cost ($)	Total
(BI)	1/1	1,000	$1.75	$1,750
	1/21	500	2.00	1,000
		1,500		$2,750

Applying LCM to ending inventory, we get 1,500 × $1.80 = $2,700.

Ending inventory before LCM adjustment	$2,750
Ending inventory after LCM adjustment	2,700
Loss (to be added to Cost of Goods Manufactured)	$ 50

(b) LCM applied item-by-item to ending inventory:

	Date	Units	Unit Cost ($)	Replacement Cost	Adjusted Total	
(BI)	1/1	1,000	$1.75	$1.80	(1,000 × 1.75)	$1,750
	1/21	500	2.00	1.80	(500 × 1.80)	900
		1,500				$2,650

Ending inventory before LCM adjustment	$2,750
Ending inventory after LCM adjustment	2,650
Loss (to be added to Cost of Goods Manufactured)	$ 100

Note: The application of LCM on an item-by-item basis results in the *most conservative* ending inventory value.

There are several criticisms of LCM:

(1) It violates the principle of consistency because inventories may be valued one way at one time and another way at another time.

(2) It is also inconsistent because the technique recognizes losses in inventory value before inventory is sold but doesn't recognize increases in replacement cost until goods are sold.

2.7 CONTROL PROCEDURES

Because inventory represents a major investment to a firm, adequate control is essential. The level of raw materials inventory is based on scheduled production, which is in turn based on sales forecasts. Four control procedures are commonly used:

(1) ***Order cycling.*** Materials are reviewed on a regular cycle, and orders are placed to maintain a desired inventory level.

(2) ***Min-max method.*** Minimum and maximum inventory levels are determined. Goods are reordered when the minimum level is reached.

(3) ***Two-bin method.*** This is used for inexpensive items. When the first bin is empty, an order is placed. The second bin provides coverage until the order is received.

(4) ***Automatic order system.*** An order is automatically placed when the inventory reaches a predetermined level. This system works best when a computer is used to keep track of inventory, ordering, etc.

In addition to the four control procedures, the *ABC plan* is used by many companies to monitor inventory levels. The inventory is separated into three categories. Category A represents the most expensive items, which require the most careful monitoring, and would utilize a method such as order cycling. Category B items are moderate in price and quantity. The min-max method is appropriate in this case. Category C items are inexpensive and kept in large quantities. The two-bin method may be used for these items. In each of these categories, the automatic order system is useful in companies that employ computers.

Labor

2.8 LABOR COSTS

Labor costs usually represent a significant cost of production and are steadily increasing in proportion to other costs. Much of the increase is due to fringe benefits such as vacations, insurance, bonuses, etc., included in an employee's compensation. The single major component of employee compensation is usually the wage or salary.

Wages are payments made on an hourly, daily, or piecework basis, whereas *salaries* are fixed payments for managerial services. Other terms necessary for any discussion of labor costs are best defined by equations, as follows:

Gross earnings = Regular wages + Overtime premium

Regular wage = *Total* hours worked (including overtime) × *Regular* hourly rate

Overtime premium = Overtime hours worked × Extra hourly compensation for overtime

2.9 OVERTIME AND SHIFT PREMIUM

Overtime Premium

The additional compensation paid for overtime is separated from regular wages and charged to factory overhead. The effect of this is to charge all units produced with the same rate of labor (regular rate).

EXAMPLE 9

An employee worked 45 hours this week. His regular wage is $10.00 per hour, and he is paid time and a half for overtime hours (i.e., hours beyond 40 per week).

Regular wage = $10.00/hour
Overtime wage = $15.00/hour
Overtime premium = $5.00/hour

Work-in-Process Inventory	*450**	
Factory Overhead Control—Overtime Premium	*25***	
Payroll Payable		*475*

* 45 hours × $10.00

** 5 hours × $5.00

Note: As with direct materials, direct labor is charged to work-in-process inventory as incurred under a perpetual cost accumulation system. All additional compensation (above regular wage rates) is charged to *one* account, called Factory Overhead Control.

Shift Premium or Differential

Often an above-normal wage is paid for undesirable shifts (e.g., night shifts). Like the overtime premium, this *extra* portion is charged to factory overhead.

EXAMPLE 10

Employees who work days are paid $5.00 per hour. Those who work nights are paid $5.50 per hour. All employees work 40 hours per week. Record the weekly wages for one night employee.

Regular wage = $5.00/hour
Night wage = $5.50/hour
Shift premium = $0.50/hour

Work-in-Process Inventory	*200**	
Factory Overhead Control—Shift Premium	*20***	
Payroll Payable		*220*

* 40 hours × $5.00
** 40 hours × $0.50

2.10 BONUS

A bonus is additional compensation generally given in recognition of exceptional productivity. Bonuses may be a set amount, a percentage of profits, or a percentage of an employee's salary. Theoretically, a bonus is a direct cost of production. However, because the purpose of cost accumulation is the establishment of a standard unit cost, bonuses are charged to factory overhead. Ideally, a bonus should be charged to a liability each week the eligible employee works. In practice this can rarely be done, so a single entry at the end of the period is made.

EXAMPLE 11

Each of ABC's employees is entitled to receive a bonus of 1% of the company's prior year's profits. Record the weekly payroll of one assembly-line employee, including accrual of the bonus, if weekly pay is $500. Assume that profits for the prior year were $260,000. The entry is:

Work-in-Process Inventory	*500*	
Factory Overhead Control—Bonuses	*50**	
Bonuses Payable		*50*
Payroll Payable		*500*

* $260,000 × 1% = $2,600
$2,600 ÷ 52 weeks = $50

2.11 VACATION AND HOLIDAY PAY

After a certain length of service, an employee generally receives paid vacations and holidays. Compensation of this sort is called nonproductive pay because an employee is receiving wages while making no contribution to output. Vacation and holiday pay are charged to factory overhead. As a result, we are able to charge each week of service equally with a portion of vacation pay.

EXAMPLE 12

Marlene has worked for the Long Life Battery Company for five years and is therefore entitled to two weeks paid vacation. Her weekly pay is $500. Make the entry to accrue Marlene's vacation pay for the week, assuming she is not on vacation now.

Total vacation pay: $500 per week × 2 weeks = $1,000

Weeks over which vacation pay is to be accrued: 52 weeks − 2-week vacation = 50 weeks

Weekly accrual: $1,000 ÷ 50 weeks = $20 per week

Work-in-Process Inventory	*500*	
Factory Overhead Control—Vacation Pay	*20*	
Vacation Pay Payable		*20*
Payroll Payable		*500*

Some major points to remember about paid holidays and vacations are:

(1) Like vacations, the number of company paid holidays is subject to policy and known in advance. These two are often combined in one account called Vacation and Holiday Pay and accrued together.

(2) Vacations are often taken in the summer, so any necessary corrections in the accruals can be spread over the remainder of the year. In reality, employees leave or are hired or terminated, so adjustments are continually required. Many companies charge off vacation and holiday pay monthly to reduce the number of entries.

(3) For salaried employees, vacation and holiday pay is charged to the period when the absence occurs rather than being accrued.

2.12 PENSIONS

Pension accounting is a separate field in itself due to the complex nature and enormous expense of pension plans. Actuaries, experts in life expectancies, determine a company's pension costs through a series of complicated formulas. To arrive at a cost for a pension plan, the following factors must be considered:

(1) Number of employees retiring each year.

(2) Amount of benefits paid to each retired employee.

(3) Length of time that benefits will be paid.

(4) Amount of income earned from pension fund investments.

(5) Amount of administrative expenses.

(6) Benefits for employees who leave before retirement age.

After pension costs have been established, those costs associated with production employees are debited to factory overhead control.

2.13 FRINGE COSTS

Wages and salaries plus any fringe benefits constitute the employer's payroll expense. Vacation pay and pension plans are only two of a number of employee benefits. Other common fringe costs are listed below.

(1) ***Federal Insurance Contribution Act (FICA)***, also known as the ***Social Security Act***. Employees *and* employers contribute *equal* percentages based on employee wages.

(2) ***Federal Unemployment Tax Act (FUTA).*** This tax is paid *only* by employers as a percentage of employee wages.

(3) ***State Unemployment Tax Act (SUTA).*** This tax is also a percentage based on employee wages and generally is fully paid by the employer.

(4) ***State Workers' Compensation.*** Again, a percentage based on employee wages is contributed by the employer. Rates vary depending on occupational hazards.

(5) ***Other.*** There are also a variety of optional plans an employer may provide, such as health or life insurance. Often the cost of these plans is shared by the employee.

The majority of companies treat the expenses of fringe costs as charges to factory overhead.

Incentive Plans

Some companies adopt incentive plans to encourage increases in production. Employees are not penalized for producing less than the specified amount but are paid extra for producing more. Wages paid but not earned on a piecework basis are charged to factory overhead.

EXAMPLE 13

Muffler Ltd. manufactures scarves. The average salary is $200 per week. To increase production, the company adopted an incentive plan. The piecework rate per scarf is $1.00. Any employee who produces fewer than 200 scarves per week will still receive his or her original pay. Production above this amount will earn the employee $1.00 for each additional scarf. One week after the plan was implemented, the following data were collected:

Employee	**Scarves Produced**	**Wages Paid**
Bob	200	$200
Carol	215	215
Ted	190	200
Alice	205	205

Bob:	200 scarves × $1 per unit = $200	No adjustment necessary
Carol:	215 scarves × $1 per unit = $215	Entire amount is direct labor
Ted:	190 scarves × $1 per unit = $190	$190 is direct labor $10 is charged to factory overhead control
Alice:	205 scarves × $1 per unit = $205	Entire amount is direct labor

Provided a unit is produced for each wage increment, the entire amount is considered direct labor. When an employee is paid for *more* than he or she actually produces, the difference is charged to factory overhead to avoid distorting the unit cost.

Note: Since in theory no single unit is any more expensive to produce than any other, all additional compensation above regular wage rates and all nonproductive pay are charged to factory overhead. This is then distributed over all units produced.

2.14 ACCOUNTING FOR LABOR

Three activities are involved in accounting for labor: (1) timekeeping, (2) computation of total payroll, and (3) allocation of payroll cost.

(1) ***Timekeeping.*** In a manufacturing concern, two forms of timekeeping are commonly used.

 (a) *Time card.* This is used for punching a time clock to record all hours spent at work.

 (b) *Labor job ticket.* This is a record prepared by an employee showing how the hours at work were spent (i.e. jobs that were worked on and hours spent on each). Any time *not* allocated to a particular job is charged to factory overhead.

(2) ***Computing Total Payroll.*** The function of determining each employee's pay, taking the appropriate deductions, and issuing the pay checks is generally done by the payroll department.

(3) ***Allocating Payroll Costs.*** This function is generally performed by the cost accounting department. The total payroll expense, including fringe costs, is allocated to particular jobs or departments. The *entire* payroll cost must be allocated.

Journalizing Payroll

Once the preceding three steps have been completed, the payroll is entered into a journal. The basic journal entries to record factory labor costs are as follows:

(1) To record the payroll:

Work-in-Process Inventory (direct labor)	*X*	
Factory Overhead Control (indirect labor)	*X*	
Payroll Payable		*X*

(2) To record employee withholdings and pay the payroll:*

Payroll Payable	*X*	
Employee Withholdings Payable		*X*
Cash (to employees)		*X*

* These withholdings include FICA, state and federal taxes, union dues, insurance, savings, etc.

(3) To record employer taxes and fringe benefit costs (pensions, insurance, etc.):

Factory Overhead Control	*X*	
Employer Taxes and Benefits Payable		*X*

In addition to accounting for employee payroll taxes (FICA and federal and state withholdings), employers are required to account for and pay certain employer payroll taxes, such as an amount equal to the FICA tax withheld from each employee's salary, and federal and state unemployment taxes. Employees are not responsible for paying unemployment taxes. In addition, many employers contribute to a pension plan for the benefit of employees.

In the examples in this book we will assume the following tax rates and fringe benefit contributions:

FICA: 7% paid by employer AND employee
Federal unemployment taxes (FUTA): 0.8%
State unemployment taxes (SUTA): 4%
Pension fund contribution: 5%

EXAMPLE 14

Using the data above and the following payroll information, prepare the journal entries to (1) record the payroll, (2) record employee taxes and pay the payroll, and (3) record employer taxes and fringe benefit cost.

Direct labor	$40,000	Federal and state income	
Indirect labor	15,000	taxes payable	$4,500

(1) To record the payroll:

Work-in-Process Inventory	*40,000*	
Factory Overhead Control	*15,000*	
Payroll Payable		*55,000*

(2) To record employee taxes and pay the payroll:

Payroll Payable	*55,000*	
Employee Income Taxes Payable		*4,500*
Employee FICA Taxes Payable		*3,850**
Cash		*46,650*

* $55,000 × 7%

(3) To record employer taxes and fringe benefits:

Factory Overhead Control	*9,240(a)*	
Employer FICA Taxes Payable		*3,850(b)*
Employer FUTA Taxes Payable		*440(c)*
Employer SUTA Taxes Payable		*2,200(d)*
Employer Pension Fund Payable		*2,750(e)*

Computations:

(a)

FICA tax rate	7.0%
FUTA tax rate	.8%
SUTA tax rate	4.0%
Pension contribution	5.0%
Total	16.8% × $55,000 = $9,240

(b) $55,000 × 7% = $3,850

(c) $55,000 × 0.8% = $ 440

(d) $55,000 × 4% = $2,200

(e) $55,000 × 5% = $2,750

Solved Problems

2.1 Tepee Ltd., a tent manufacturer, recorded the following transactions for the month of May:

	Date	Units Purchased	Unit Cost ($)	Units Issued
(BI)	5/1	10	$15	—
	5/5	20	20	—
	5/15	—	—	15
	5/19	—	—	10
	5/24	15	18	—
	5/30	—	—	15

Assume the company uses a periodic inventory system and compute the ending materials inventory and cost of materials issued under (*a*) specific identification (materials issued on 5/15 came from the 5/5 purchase, materials issued on 5/19 came from beginning inventory, and those issued on 5/30 came from the 5/5 and 5/24 purchases); (*b*) weighted average cost; (*c*) FIFO; (*d*) LIFO.

SOLUTION

(*a*) **Specific identifcation**

Date of Issue	Purchase Lot	Units × Cost		Cost of Materials Issued
5/15	5/5	15 × $20	=	$300
5/19	BI	10 × $15	=	150
5/30	5/5 & 5/24	(5 × $20) + (10 × $18)	=	280
				$730

Ending inventory: 5 (from 5/24 purchase) × $18 = $90

(*b*) **Weighted average cost**

$$\frac{(10 \times \$15) + (20 \times \$20) + (15 \times \$18)}{45} = \$18.222$$

Cost of materials issued: 40 × $18.222 = $728.88

Ending inventory: 5 × $18.222 = $91.11

(*c*) **FIFO**

Date	Units	Unit Cost ($)	Cost of Materials Issued
BI	10	$15	$150
5/5	20	20	400
5/24	10	18	180
	40		$730

Ending inventory: 5 × $18 = $90

(*d*) **LIFO**

Date	Units	Unit Cost ($)	Cost of Materials Issued
5/24	15	$18	$270
5/5	20	20	400
BI	5	15	75
	40		$745

Ending inventory: 5 (from BI) × $15 = $75

2.2 Assume the same set of facts as presented in Problem 2.1 except that Tepee Ltd. now uses a perpetual inventory system. Compute the cost of materials issued and ending inventory under (*a*) specific identification, (*b*) weighted average cost, (*c*) FIFO, and (*d*) LIFO.

SOLUTION

(a) **Specific identification**
The solution is the same as for Problem 2.1(*a*).

(b) **Weighted (moving) average cost**

	Purchases			Issued			Balance			
	Date	Units	Unit Cost ($)	Units	Unit Cost ($)	Cost of Materials Issued	Units	Unit Cost ($)	Total Cost	
(BI)	5/1	10	$15	—	—	—	10	$15.000	$150.00	
	5/5	20	20	—	—	—	30	18.333*(a)*	550.00	
	5/15	—	—	15	$18.333	$275.00	15	18.333	275.00	
	5/19	—	—	10	18.333	183.33	5	18.333	91.67	
	5/24	15	18	—	—	—	20	18.083*(b)*	361.66	
	5/30	—	—	15	18.083	271.25	5	18.083	90.42	EI
						$729.58				

Computations:

(a) $\frac{(10 \times \$15) + (20 \times \$20)}{30} = \$18.333$

(b) $\frac{(5 \times \$18.333) + (15 \times \$18)}{20} = \$18.083$

(c) **FIFO.** The solution is the same as for Problem 2.1(*c*).

(d) **LIFO**

	Purchases			Issued			Balance			
	Date	Units	Unit Cost $	Units	Unit Cost $	Cost of Materials Issued	Units	Unit Cost $	Total	
(BI)	5/1	10	$15	—	—	—	10	$15	$150	
	5/5	20	20	—	—	—	30	*(a)*	550	
	5/15	—	—	15	$20	$300	15	*(b)*	250	
	5/19	—	—	10	*(c)*	175	5	15	75	
	5/24	15	18	—	—	—	20	*(d)*	345	
	5/30	—	—	15	18	270	5	15	$ 75	EI
						$745				

Computations:

(a) $(10 \times \$15) + (20 \times \$20) = \$550$

(b) $(10 \times \$15) + (5 \times \$20) = \$250$

(c) $(5 \times \$20) + (5 \times \$15) = \$175$

(d) $(5 \times \$15) + (15 \times \$18) = \$345$

2.3 The Rainy Day Pool Company is preparing for the upcoming season. The following data relate to the company's inventory of pool liners for the month of March:

(BI)	3/1	1,000 liners at $100 ea.
	3/4	Purchased 1,500 at $90 ea.

3/10	Issued 1,200 liners
3/16	Issued 800 liners
3/20	Purchased 2,000 liners at $75 ea.
3/25	Issued 1,000 liners
3/28	Issued 900 liners
3/30	Purchased 1,000 liners at $110 ea.

Prepare the journal entries to record these transactions under the perpetual inventory system. The company uses the LIFO method to record inventory.

SOLUTION

3/4	*Materials Inventory (1,500 × $90)*	*135,000*	
	Cash		*135,000*
3/10	*Work-in-Process Inventory (1,200 × $90)*	*108,000*	
	Materials Inventory		*108,000*
3/16	*Work-in-Process Inventory (300 × $90) + (500 × $100)*	*77,000*	
	Materials Inventory		*77,000*
3/20	*Materials Inventory (2,000 × $75)*	*150,000*	
	Cash		*150,000*
3/25	*Work-in-Process Inventory (1,000 × $75)*	*75,000*	
	Materials Inventory		*75,000*
3/28	*Work-in-Process Inventory (900 × $75)*	*67,500*	
	Materials Inventory		*67,500*
3/30	*Materials Inventory (1,000 × $110)*	*110,000*	
	Cash		*110,000*

2.4 The following information relates to the ending inventory of the Four Seasons Coat Company:

Materials	Quantity	Cost per Unit	Replacement Cost
Sleeves	50	$2.00	$1.95
Collars	32	1.50	1.60
Linings	25	2.50	2.25
Belts	41	1.75	1.80

(a) Compute the ending inventory before any LCM adjustment. Apply the LCM rule to the inventory *(b)* as a whole and *(c)* on an item-by-item basis.

SOLUTION

(a) **Before LCM adjustment**

Materials	Quantity		Cost per Unit		Total Cost
Sleeves	50	×	2.00	=	$100.00
Collars	32	×	1.50	=	48.00
Linings	25	×	2.50	=	62.50
Belts	41	×	1.75	=	71.75
					$282.25 EI

(b) **LCM applied to inventory in total**

Materials	Quantity		Replacement Cost		Total Replacement Cost
Sleeves	50	×	$1.95	=	$ 97.50
Collars	32	×	1.60	=	51.20
Linings	25	×	2.25	=	56.25
Belts	41	×	1.80	=	73.80
					$278.75

Ending inventory before LCM adjustment	$282.25
Ending inventory after LCM adjustment	278.75
Loss (to be entered in Cost of Goods Manufactured)	$ 3.50

(c) **LCM applied to inventory item-by-item**

Materials	Quantity		Lower of Cost or Replacement Cost		Total
Sleeves	50	×	$1.95	=	$ 97.50
Collars	32	×	1.50	=	48.00
Linings	25	×	2.25	=	56.25
Belts	41	×	1.75	=	71.75
					$273.50

Ending inventory before LCM adjustment	$282.25
Ending inventory after LCM adjustment	273.50
Loss (to be entered in Cost of Goods Manufactured)	$ 8.75

2.5 Dippin' Donuts has six bakers and a bakery supervisor on each of its two shifts. Bakers working from 8 a.m.–5 p.m. (with a 1-hour break) are paid $6.00 per hour. Bakers working the 10 p.m.–7 a.m. shift (with a 1-hour break) are paid $6.75 per hour. The supervisors are paid a salary of $300 per week. Due to the large volume of business, two of the daytime bakers worked until 8 p.m. three evenings this week; they both received time and a half for the extra hours worked. Prepare journal entries to distribute the weekly payroll.

SOLUTION

Day Shift

Wages: $6/hour × 40 hours/week = $240/week for each baker
6 bakers × $240/week = $1,440/week for all bakers (direct labor)

Overtime: ($6/hour × 3 hours/evening) × 2 bakers = $36/evening × 3 evenings
= $108 (direct labor)

Overtime premium: ($3/hour × 3 hours/evening) × 2 bakers = $18/evening × 3 evenings
= $54 (overtime premium)

Night Shift

Wages: $6/hour × 40 hours/week = $240/week for each baker
6 bakers × $240/week = $1,440/week for all bakers (direct labor)

Shift premium: $0.75/hour × 40 hours/week = $30/week for each baker
6 bakers × $30/week = $180/week for all bakers (shift premium)

Supervisors

Salary: $300/week × 2 supervisors = $600/week, both supervisors (indirect labor)

Distribution

	Days	Nights	
Direct labor:	($1,440 + $108) +	$1,440	= $2,988
Overtime premium:	$54		
Shift premium:		$180	
Indirect labor:	$600		

Work-in-Process Inventory	*2,988*	
Factory Overhead Control	*834*	
Payroll Payable		*3,822*

Shift premium, overtime premium, and indirect labor are all elements of factory overhead. Under a perpetual system, these are all posted to one control account. A *control account* is a master balance for a subsidiary ledger. The reason the Factory Overhead Control account appears with subtitles earlier in this chapter (e.g., Factory Overhead Control—Shift Premium) is to denote the account in the *subsidiary ledger* in which the entry is made. It does not mean that separate Factory Overhead Control accounts appear in the general ledger.

2.6 The Lion's Den fur coat factory has a bonus plan with the following structure:

(a) The fur cleaners (direct labor) receive one week's salary as a bonus at year-end. There are 20 workers in this category; each earns $273 per week.

(b) The tailors (direct labor) are paid 5% of their yearly salary as a bonus at year-end. The company has 10 tailors, each making $350 per week.

Prepare separate journal entries to accrue the bonuses each week for each of the above categories of employees and distribute the weekly payroll in the same entry. Assume the company uses a perpetual cost accumulation system.

SOLUTION

(a)

Work-in-Process Inventory ($273 × 20)	*5,460*	
Factory Overhead Control—Bonus	*105**	
Bonus Payable		*105*
Payroll Payable		*5,460*

* $273 ÷ 52 weeks = $5.25 × 20 fur cleaners = $105

(b)

Work-in-Process Inventory ($350 × 10)	*3,500*	
Factory Overhead Control—Bonus	*175**	
Bonus Payable		*175*
Payroll Payable		*3,500*

* $350/week × 5% = $17.50 × 10 tailors = $175

2.7 The Billings Industrial Supply Corporation has the following vacation policy:

1 to 3 years of service: 1 week paid vacation
4 to 7 years of service: 2 weeks paid vacation

8 to 10 years of service:	3 weeks paid vacation
Over 10 years of service:	4 weeks paid vacation

Examination of the payroll data on the company's 10 assembly line workers revealed the following:

Name	Years of Service	Weekly Salary
J. Adams	5	$210
O. White	10	355
A. McFinny	6	250
F. Vasquez	8	300
R. Rubin	12	390
E. Cheshire	1/2	150
K. Quentin	4	190
D. Mancini	2	175
L. Johnson	15	425
Y. Flynn	1	160

(*a*) Determine the weekly accrual for each employee.

(*b*) Prepare the journal entry to distribute the payroll and accrue the vacation pay.

SOLUTION

(*a*)

Name	Weeks of Vacation	Total Vacation Pay	Weekly Accrual*
J. Adams	2	$ 420	$ 8.40
O. White	3	1,065	21.73
A. McFinny	2	500	10.00
F. Vasquez	3	900	18.37
R. Rubin	4	1,560	32.50
E. Cheshire	0	0	0
K. Quentin	2	380	7.60
D. Mancini	1	175	3.43
L. Johnson	4	1,700	35.42
Y. Flynn	1	160	3.14
			$140.59

* Total vacation pay/[52 weeks − week(s) of vacation due]

(*b*)

Work-in-Process Inventory	*2,605.00*	
Factory Overhead Control—Vacation Pay	*140.59*	
Vacation Pay Payable		*140.59*
Payroll Payable		*2,605.00*

2.8 Payroll is being prepared at Morgan Manufacturing, Inc. Examination of the labor job tickets for the week ending August 20 produced the following data:

		Labor Hours	
Employee	**Hourly Wage**	**Direct**	**Indirect**
Howard	$4.50	32	8
Peabody	5.25	38	2
Lancer	4.25	29	11
Cahill	4.30	40	0
Barnes	5.05	34	6
Williams	4.75	39	1
Thomas	4.90	28	12
Greene	5.15	36	4

Total FICA (employee)	$102.24
Total FICA (employer)	102.24
Total Federal and State Income Tax	350.26
Federal Unemployement Tax (FUTA)	10.68
State Unemployment Tax (SUTA)	41.20

Prepare journal entries for a periodic cost accumulation system to *(a)* record payroll, *(b)* record employee taxes and payment of payroll, and *(c)* record the employer's payroll taxes.

SOLUTION

		Payroll				
Employee	**Hourly Wage**	**Direct Labor**		**Indirect Labor**		**Total**
Howard	$4.50	(32 hr)	$ 144.00	(8 hr)	$ 36.00	$ 180.00
Peabody	5.25	(38 hr)	199.50	(2 hr)	10.50	210.00
Lancer	4.25	(29 hr)	123.25	(11 hr)	46.75	170.00
Cahill	4.30	(40 hr)	172.00	(0)	0	172.00
Barnes	5.05	(34 hr)	171.70	(6 hr)	30.30	202.00
Williams	4.75	(39 hr)	185.25	(1 hr)	4.75	190.00
Thomas	4.90	(28 hr)	137.20	(12 hr)	58.80	196.00
Greene	5.15	(36 hr)	185.40	(4 hr)	20.60	206.00
			$1,318.30		$207.70	$1,526.00

(a)	*Work-in-Process Inventory*	*1,318.30*	
	Factory Overhead Control	*207.70*	
	Payroll Payable		*1,526.0*
(b)	*Payroll Payable*	*1,526.00*	
	Employee FICA Payable		*102.24*
	Employee Income Taxes Payable		*350.26*
	Cash		*1,073.50*
(c)	*Factory Overhead Control*	*154.12*	
	Employer FICA Payable		*102.24*
	Employer FUTA Payable		*10.68*
	Employer SUTA Payable		*41.20*

Chapter 3

Factory Overhead and the Factory Ledger

3.1 FACTORY OVERHEAD DEFINED

The cost of direct labor and direct materials can easily be identified and charged to specific jobs. All other costs, such as indirect materials, indirect labor, and other factory expenses which cannot be identified with or charged directly to specific jobs, are called *factory overhead*. These *indirect* costs are categorized below.

Variable Costs. Total costs that vary in direct proportion to production volume are called variable overhead costs. If 20 gallons of glue are needed to produce 100,000 units and 40 gallons of glue are needed to produce 200,000 units, glue is considered a variable cost.

Fixed Costs. Total costs that do not vary in proportion to production volume within a relevant range are called fixed overhead. Rent is one example. Whether 100 or 1,000 units are produced, the rent for the use of a factory remains the same.

At the same time, fixed overhead *per unit* varies with production. If rent were $10,000 a year and 100,000 units were produced in a year, rent per unit would be $0.10. If 200,000 units were produced in a year, rent per unit would be only $0.05.

Semivariable Costs. Total costs that will change, but *not in direct proportion* to production volume. An example of this would be factory utilities which often are comprised of a basic fee (fixed amount) plus a usage fee (variable).

3.2 APPLIED FACTORY OVERHEAD

An estimate of the next period's factory overhead costs is made which is then divided by a base, such as labor hours, machine hours, etc., and expressed as a predetermined rate. This predetermined rate helps management measure unit costs. If no predetermined rate is used, management would have to wait until the end of the period to know the amount of factory overhead costs and, therefore, the total cost per unit. Thus, it would be more difficult to quote selling prices to customers since costs would be less exact.

3.3 BASE TO BE USED

The base used to compute the predetermined factory overhead rate should be closely related to functions represented by the factory overhead cost being applied. Note that the base, like the total factory overhead costs, is an estimate of the future period's production quantity or cost. The five bases generally used to calculate the factory overhead rate are described below.

Units of Production. This method is considered the most efficient means of applying factory overhead. The equation is:

$$\frac{\text{Estimated factory overhead}}{\text{Estimated units of production}} = \text{Factory overhead rate per unit}$$

EXAMPLE 1

Based on the units of production method, if 20,000 units are to be manufactured and the estimated factory overhead for the period is $100,000, the factory overhead rate would be $5 per unit ($100,000 ÷ 20,000).

Direct Materials Cost. This method uses estimated total direct materials cost as a base, and the rate is expressed as a percentage. The equation is:

$$\frac{\text{Estimated factory overhead}}{\text{Estimated direct materials cost}} \times 100 = \begin{array}{l}\text{Percentage of factory overhead}\\ \text{per direct materials cost}\end{array}$$

EXAMPLE 2

Suppose that estimated direct materials cost is $50,000 and estimated factory overhead for the period is $100,000. Using direct materials cost as the base, the factory overhead rate is computed as follows:

$$\frac{\$100{,}000}{\$50{,}000} \times 100 = 200\% \text{ of direct materials cost}$$

Direct Labor Cost. This base is widely used because of the high degree of correlation found in most cases between direct labor cost and factory overhead. The following equation is used:

$$\frac{\text{Estimated factory overhead}}{\text{Estimated direct labor cost}} \times 100 = \text{Percentage of direct labor cost}$$

EXAMPLE 3

Based on direct labor hours, an estimated direct labor cost of $400,000 and estimated factory overhead per period of $100,000 would result in an overhead rate of 25% of direct labor cost, since

$$\frac{\$100{,}000}{\$400{,}000} \times 100 = 25\%$$

Direct Labor Hours. When labor rates vary widely, direct labor hours may be more suitable than direct labor cost as a base. The equation in this case is:

$$\frac{\text{Estimated factory overhead}}{\text{Estimated direct labor hours}} = \text{Rate per direct labor hour}$$

EXAMPLE 4

If direct labor hours are estimated at 8,000 and estimated factory overhead per period is $100,000, the factory overhead rate based on direct labor hours is calculated as follows:

$$\frac{\$100{,}000}{8{,}000} = \$12.50 \text{ per direct labor hour}$$

Machine Hours. When production is largely by machine, an appropriate basis would be the time required by a machine or group of machines to perform production operations. The base used is total estimated machine hours for the period. The equation is:

$$\frac{\text{Estimated factory overhead}}{\text{Estimated machine hours}} = \text{Rate per machine hour}$$

EXAMPLE 5

Assume that estimated machine hours equal 10,000 and estimated factory overhead per period is $100,000. The factory overhead rate based on machine hours would be calculated as follows:

$$\frac{\$100{,}000}{10{,}000} = \$10 \text{ per machine hour}$$

In summary, the reader should note that in the above five methods the numerator is always the estimated factory overhead cost. The denominator changes with each method.

Note also that when costs or dollars are used as a base, a percentage rate is developed and therefore the fraction is multiplied by 100. When units or hours are used as a base, a dollar rate is developed.

3.4 ACTIVITY LEVEL TO BE USED

Normal or Long-run Capacity. This concept assumes a stable rate or capacity level of production over a period of time long enough to even out high and low levels of production. Therefore, the expected or estimated capacity used each period to compute factory overhead rates does not change.

Expected Actual or Short-run Capacity. The capacity expected for the next period may be used as a base to determine a factory overhead rate. Therefore, factory overhead rates may vary each period, depending on estimated changes in capacity levels, whereas the factory overhead rates based on normal capacity will remain constant even if expected actual capacity fluctuates.

Which Activity Level to Use. The use of normal capacity will result in a uniform cost per unit for different periods (assuming all other factors are constant), whereas the use of expected actual capacity may result in varying unit costs for different periods (if expected actual capacity changes). Therefore, the use of normal capacity is preferred because it eliminates the possible manipulation of unit costs by changing production levels. Expected actual capacity is generally used only when the normal production activity is difficult to determine.

3.5 JOURNALIZING FACTORY OVERHEAD

The journal entries to record factory overhead costs will depend on the cost accumulation system used and the amount of information desired by management. Actual factory overhead costs are basically recorded the same way under both periodic and perpetual systems (debit Factory Overhead Control and credit Cash, Vouchers Payable, Accumulated Depreciation, etc.) When a perpetual cost accumulation system is used, both actual and applied factory overhead costs are commonly recorded, whereas in a periodic cost accumulation system, only actual costs are recorded. The remaining examples in this chapter are presented on the assumption that a perpetual cost accumulation system is in use.

As was previously stated, actual factory overhead costs incurred during a period are debited to a Factory Overhead Control account. Ideally, the balance in the Factory Overhead Control account should equal the amount of factory overhead applied for the period. This rarely occurs in actual situations because of the difficulty in accurately estimating the extent of involvement of various factors (see Section 3.6). Only applied (not actual) factory overhead is charged to work-in-process inventory.

The Factory Overhead Applied account is closed out to the Factory Overhead Control account at the end of the period. The Factory Overhead Control account debit balance and the Applied Factory Overhead account credit balance are compared to arrive at a net debit or credit balance. Some companies do not use a separate Factory Overhead Applied account; instead they credit factory overhead control for factory overhead applied.

EXAMPLE 6

Assume the following account balances:

Factory Overhead Control

Date	Debit	Credit
1/5	7,000	
1/8	9,000	
1/12	10,000	
1/28	6,000	

Work-in-Process Inventory

Date	Debit	Credit
1/15	15,000	
1/31	25,000	

Accounts Payable

		1/5	7,000
		1/8	9,000
		1/12	10,000
		1/28	6,000

Factory Overhead Applied

		1/15	15,000
		1/31	25,000

The entries to record rent of $8,000 payable on January 31, 19X5 and to close out the Factory Overhead Control and Applied accounts are

January 31	*Factory Overhead Control—Rent*	*8,000*	
	Accounts Payable		*8,000*
January 31	*Factory Overhead Applied*	*40,000*	
	Factory Overhead Control		*40,000*

The entries are posted to the accounts as follows:

Factory Overhead Control

1/5	7,000	1/31	40,000
1/8	9,000		
1/12	10,000		
1/28	6,000		
1/31	8,000		
	40,000		40,000

Work-in-Process Inventory

1/15	15,000		
1/31	25,000		

Accounts Payable

		1/5	7,000
		1/8	9,000
		1/12	10,000
		1/28	6,000
		1/31	8,000

Factory Overhead Applied

1/31	40,000	1/15	15,000
		1/31	25,000
	40,000		40,000

3.6 OVER- OR UNDERAPPLIED OVERHEAD

The balance in the factory overhead control account will usually not equal the balance in the Factory Overhead Applied account because of incorrect estimates of one or more of the following:

(1) Estimated factory overhead cost for the period

(2) Estimated production (did not equal normal capacity)

(3) Labor or machine hour efficiency

EXAMPLE 7

Assume that the normal amount of time to complete a job is 100 direct labor hours and that factory overhead is $5 per direct labor hour (applied on the basis of direct labor hours). If a specific job took 105 direct labor hours (the 5 extra hours due to labor inefficiency), factory overhead would be overapplied by $25 (5 extra hours × $5 per direct labor hour).

When factory overhead is over- or underapplied and a variance or difference results, either of the following two methods is acceptable to account for the difference in closing the account:

(1) *To Cost of Goods Sold and Ending Inventories (if difference is significant)*

The over- or underapplied factory overhead may be debited or credited to Cost of Goods Sold and Ending Inventories. This would change cost per unit.

(2) *To Cost of Goods Sold (if difference is insignificant)*

The over- or underapplied factory overhead may be debited or credited to Cost of Goods Sold. This has no effect on unit cost and treats the entire variance as a period cost.

EXAMPLE 8

Assume the following data:

Underapplied factory overhead	$12,000	
Units sold	80,000	(80%)
Units in ending work-in-process inventory	20,000	(20%)

The journal entries to close the Factory Overhead Applied account according to the two acceptable methods are shown below.

(*1*) *To Cost of Goods Sold and Work-in-Process Inventory:*

Cost of Goods Sold		
($12,000 × 80%)	*9,600*	
Work-in-Process Inventory		
($12,000 × 20%)	*2,400*	
Factory Overhead Control		*12,000*

(2) *To Cost of Goods Sold:*

Cost of Goods Sold	*12,000*	
Factory Overhead Control		*12,000*

3.7 ALLOCATION OF SERVICE DEPARTMENT COSTS TO PRODUCING DEPARTMENTS

There are two basic types of factory departments in a manufacturing company: producing departments and service departments. A producing department is one where the conversion or production takes place. A service department (e.g., personnel or maintenance) provides support to the producing departments. Since the producing departments are directly benefited by service departments, the expenses of a service department should be allocated to the appropriate producing departments (as part of factory overhead costs). One of the following methods may be used to allocate service department costs to producing departments:

(1) Direct method
(2) Step method
(3) Algebraic method

Direct Method

This is the most common method of allocating service department costs to producing departments because of its mathematical simplicity and ease of application. It involves allocation of service department costs directly to producing departments and ignores any services provided by one service department to another.

EXAMPLE 9

Assume the following data for R. Mirador Rattan Industries:

Service Departments:	
Dept. N, Maintenance	$12,000
Dept. I, Cafeteria	5,500
Producing Departments:	
Dept. C, Machinery	42,000
Dept. K, Assembly	78,700

The cost of the maintenance department is allocated to the producing departments based on the number of square feet; the cost of the cafeteria department is allocated based on the number of employees.

Department	Direct Labor Hours	Square Feet	Number of Employees
N, Maintenance	—	250	15
I, Cafeteria	—	900	12
C, Machinery	4,500	2,250	35
K, Assembly	20,000	5,700	150
Total	24,500	9,100	212

The service departments' costs allocation under the direct method and the calculation of factory overhead rate per direct labor hours is shown below:

Allocation of Costs
Direct Method

	Service Departments		Producing Departments	
	N, Maintenance	**I, Cafeteria**	**C, Machinery**	**K, Assembly**
Total Cost	$12,000	$5,500	$42,000	$78,700
Allocated to Producing Depts. C and K	<12,000> *(c)*		3,396 *(a)*	8,604 *(b)*
,		<5,500> *(f)*	1,041 *(d)*	4,459 *(e)*
Balance after Allocation	0	0	$46,437	$91,763
Factory Overhead Rates per direct labor hour			$10.319 *(g)*	$ 4.588 *(h)*

Computations:

Allocation of Department N, Maintenance:

$$\frac{\text{Total cost}}{\text{Total square feet—Departments C and K}} = \text{Allocation rate}$$

$$\frac{\$12{,}000}{7{,}950 \text{ sq ft}} = \$1.50943/\text{sq ft}$$

				Square Feet × Rate/Sq Ft
(a)	To Dept. C, Machinery	$ 3,396	=	2,250 × $1.50943
(b)	To Dept. K, Assembly	8,604	=	5,700 × $1.50943
(c)	Total	$12,000		

Allocation of Department I, Assembly:

$$\frac{\text{Total cost}}{\text{Total number of employees—Departments C and K}} = \text{Allocation rate}$$

$$\frac{\$5{,}500}{185 \text{ employees}} = \$29.72973/\text{employee}$$

				Number of Employees	× Rate/Employee
(d)	To Dept. C, Machinery	$1,041	=	35	× $29.72973
(e)	To Dept. K, Assembly	4,459	=	150	× $29.72973
(f)	Total	$5,500			

Factory overhead rates (based on direct labor hours) for producing departments:

				Total Cost After Allocation	÷	Direct Labor Hours
(g)	For Dept. C, Machinery	$10.319	=	$46,437	÷	4,500
(h)	For Dept. K, Assembly	$4.588	=	$91,763	÷	20,000

Step Method

This method is more accurate than the direct method when services are provided to other service departments. The allocation of service department costs is performed by a series of steps:

(1) The costs of the service department that provides services to the greatest number of other service departments are usually allocated first.

(2) The costs of the service department that provides services to the next greatest number of service departments are then allocated. Any costs added to this department from step 1 are included. Note that under this method, the costs of subsequent service departments will not be allocated to the preceding service departments; thus any reciprocal services among service departments are ignored.

(3) The sequence outlined above is continued, step by step, until all the service department costs have been allocated to producing departments.

EXAMPLE 10

Using the same data as in Example 9, assume that the cost of the maintenance department is allocated first. The allocation of service department costs and the calculation of factory overhead rate per direct labor hour under the step method is as follows:

Allocation of Costs
Step Method

	Service Departments		Producing Departments	
	N, Maintenance	I, Cafeteria	C, Machinery	K, Assembly
Total Cost	$12,000	$5,500	$42,000	$78,700
Allocated to Service Dept. I and Producing Depts. C and K	<12,000>	1,220 *(a)*	3,051 *(b)*	7,729 *(c)*
Subtotal		$6,720	$45,051	$86,429
Allocated to Producing Depts. C and K		<6,720>	1,271 *(d)*	5,449 *(e)*
Balance after Allocation	0	0	$46,322	$91,878
Factory Overhead Rates per direct labor hour			$10.294 *(f)*	$ 4.594 *(g)*

Computations:

Allocation of Department N, Maintenance:

$$\frac{\text{Total cost}}{\text{Square feet—Departments I, C, and K}} = \frac{\$12{,}000}{8{,}850} = \$1.35593/\text{sq ft}$$

				Square Feet	× Rate/Sq Ft
(a)	To Dept. I, Cafeteria	$ 1,220	=	900	× $1.35593
(b)	To Dept. C, Machinery	3,051	=	2,250	× $1.35593
(c)	To Dept. K, Assembly	7,729	=	5,700	× $1.35593
	Total	$12,000			

Allocation of Department I, Cafeteria:

$$\frac{\text{Total cost}}{\text{Total number of employees—Departments C and K}} = \frac{\$6{,}720}{185} = \$36.32432/\text{employee}$$

				Number of Employees	× Rate/Employee
(d)	To Dept. C, Machinery	$1,271	=	35	× $36.32432
(e)	To Dept. K, Assembly	5,449	=	150	× $36.32432
	Total	$6,720			

Factory overhead rates (based on direct labor hours) for producing departments:

				Total Cost After Allocation	÷	Direct Labor Hours
(f)	For Dept. C, Machinery	$10.294	=	$46,322	÷	4,500
(g)	For Dept. K, Assembly	$4.594	=	$91,878	÷	20,000

Algebraic Method

This is the most accurate of the three methods when reciprocal services are provided among the service departments. With the algebraic method, simultaneous equations are used to allocate service department costs to service departments and producing departments. The number of simultaneous equations is proportional to the number of service departments. The use of a computer facilitates the computations when many service departments exist.

EXAMPLE 11

In addition to the data from Example 9, assume the following:

	Services Provided by Department N	Services Provided by Department I
Service Departments:		
Dept. N, Maintenance	—	10%
Dept. I, Cafeteria	15%	—
Producing Departments:		
Dept. C, Machinery	25%	20%
Dept. K, Assembly	60%	70%
Total	100%	100%

Using the algebraic method and the above percentages, the allocation of service department costs to the producing departments is computed as follows:

The cost to be allocated by Department N, Maintenance: $N = \$12{,}000 + 0.10I$

The cost to be allocated by Department I, Cafeteria: $I = \$5{,}500 + 0.15N$

By substituting the above value for I (i.e., $\$5{,}500 + 0.15N$) for the unknown I in the first equation, we can solve for N:

$$N = \$12{,}000 + 0.10(\$5{,}500 + 0.15N)$$
$$N = \$12{,}000 + \$550 + 0.015N$$
$$N - 0.015N = \$12{,}000 + \$550$$
$$0.985N = \$12{,}550$$
$$N = \$12{,}741$$

3.8 THE FACTORY LEDGER

It is often practical for a manufacturing concern to include a factory ledger in its accounting system. Generally, this procedure is used when manufacturing operations are far from the main office, or when the nature of such operations requires a great number of accounts.

Most firms maintain cash and other factory assets on the general office records. Thus, the General Ledger includes such accounts as Sales, Cost of Goods Sold, Factory Equipment, Accumulated-Depreciation (depreciation expense for the period kept in the factory journal), and Liabilities. It also includes the control account, Factory Ledger.

Entries relating to the General Ledger and Factory Ledger are first recorded in the general journal and factory journal. The control accounts Factory Ledger and General Ledger are reciprocal in nature (i.e., a debit to one is an automatic credit to the other). They are used whenever a transaction affects both journals, should always equal each other, and cancel out for financial statement purposes. In essence, they permit each ledger to be self-balancing.

Because of the widespread use of computers in cost accounting and the ability to link computers through modems, use of the Factory Ledger has greatly decreased.

Solved Problems

3.1 Factory Overhead Rates. The Myriad Corporation estimates the following for the next period:

Factory overhead	$250,000
Units produced	50,000
Materials cost of units produced	$500,000

Production will require 50,000 labor hours at an estimated direct labor cost of $100,000. The machine is estimated to run about 40,000 hours.

Determine the factory overhead rate to be used in applying factory overhead to production on each of the following bases: *(a)* units of production, *(b)* direct labor cost, *(c)* direct materials cost, *(d)* direct labor hours, and *(e)* machine hours.

SOLUTION

(*a*) Units of production

$$\frac{\text{Estimated factory overhead}}{\text{Estimated units of production}} = \frac{\$250{,}000}{50{,}000} = \$5 \text{ factory overhead per unit}$$

(*b*) Direct labor cost

$$\frac{\text{Estimated factory overhead}}{\text{Estimated direct labor cost}} \times 100 = \frac{\$250{,}000}{\$100{,}000} \times 100 = 250\% \text{ of direct labor cost}$$

(*c*) Materials cost

$$\frac{\text{Estimated factory overhead}}{\text{Estimated materials cost}} \times 100 = \frac{\$250{,}000}{\$500{,}000} \times 100 = 50\% \text{ of direct materials cost}$$

(*d*) Direct labor hours

$$\frac{\text{Estimated factory overhead}}{\text{Estimated direct labor hours}} = \frac{\$250{,}000}{50{,}000} = \$5 \text{ per direct labor hour}$$

(*e*) Machine hours

$$\frac{\text{Estimated factory overhead}}{\text{Estimated machine hours}} = \frac{\$250{,}000}{40{,}000} = \$6.25 \text{ per machine hour}$$

3.2 Factory Overhead: Journal Entries. Mint Airlines has factory overhead to be allocated. It maintains a work-in-process inventory account and a factory overhead control account. The amounts are:

July 3:	Indirect materials	$ 500
July 5:	Indirect labor	1,000
July 10:	Other expenses	3,000

During the month, 4,000 direct labor hours were worked. Factory overhead is applied at a rate of $1.10 per direct labor hour at the end of the month.

Prepare the journal entries for factory overhead. Assume a perpetual cost accumulation system.

SOLUTION

July 3	*Factory Overhead Control,*	*500*	
	Accounts Payable		*500*
July 5	*Factory Overhead Control,*	*1,000*	
	Payroll Payable		*1,000*
July 10	*Factory Overhead Control,*	*3,000*	
	Accounts Payable		*3,000*
July 31	*Work-in-Process Inventory*		
	($1.10 × 4,000)	*4,400*	
	Factory Overhead Applied		*4,400*

3.3 Over- and Underapplied Overhead. The Overbrook Company manufactures widgets using a job order cost system with a predetermined factory overhead application rate based on direct labor hours. For the year ended June 30, 19X8, there were 200,000 direct labor hours used at the established rate of $1.75 per direct labor hour. Actual factory overhead for the period amounted to $360,000, composed of $190,000 of indirect materials and $170,000 of indirect labor. Overbrook Company uses a perpetual cost accumulation system.

Prepare journal entries to *(a)* record the total factory overhead costs to be applied to jobs, *(b)* close out the factory overhead applied to the Factory Overhead Control account, *(c)* accumulate total actual factory overhead, and *(d)* close out the underapplied factory overhead balance to Cost of Goods Sold.

SOLUTION

(*a*)	*Work-in-Process Inventory*	*350,000*	
	Factory Overhead Applied (200,000 × $1.75)		*350,000*
(*b*)	*Factory Overhead Applied*	*350,000*	
	Factory Overhead Control		*350,000*
(*c*)	*Factory Overhead Control*	*360,000*	
	Materials Inventory		*190,000*
	Payroll Payable		*170,000*
(*d*)	*Cost of Goods Sold*	*10,000*	
	Factory Overhead Control		*10,000*

3.4 Factory Overhead: Service Departments' Cost Allocation. The Val Aur Company has two service departments and two producing departments.

Service Departments:	**Total Cost**
Dept. N, Factory Administration	$12,900
Dept. J, Building and Grounds	10,500
Producing Departments:	
Dept. G, Machinery	41,600
Dept. P, Assembly	38,000

Additional Information:

Department	Estimated Total Labor Hours	Square Footage
N, Factory Administration	2,900	1,200
J, Building and Grounds	1,100	1,500
G, Machinery	2,000	1,900
P, Assembly	1,600	3,200
	7,600	7,800

The costs of factory administration are allocated based on estimated labor hours; building and grounds costs are allocated based on square footage. The producing departments compute these factory overhead rates based on machine hours, with 30,000 for machinery and 22,800 for assembly.

Allocate the costs of the service departments to the producing departments by using the following: *(a)* Direct Method, *(b)* Step Method (allocate the costs of factory administration first), and *(c)* Algebraic Method. Include the factory overhead rates for each producing department.

SOLUTION

(a)

Allocation of Costs
Direct Method

	Service Departments		Producing Departments	
	N, Factory Admin.	**J, Bldg. and Grounds**	**G, Machinery**	**P, Assembly**
Total Cost	$12,900	$10,500	$41,600	$38,000
Allocate to Producing Depts. G and P	<12,900>		7,167 *(a)*	5,733 *(b)*
		<10,500>	3,912 *(c)*	6,588 *(d)*
Balance after allocation	0	0	$52,679	$50,321
Factory overhead rates per machine hour			$1.75597 *(e)*	$2.20706 *(f)*

Computations:

Allocation of Department N, Factory Administration:

$$\frac{\text{Total cost}}{\text{Total estimated labor hours—Departments G and P}} = \frac{\$12,900}{3,600} = \$3.58333/\text{labor hour}$$

				Labor Hours	×	Rate/Labor Hour
(a)	To Dept. G, Machinery	$ 7,167	=	2,000	×	$3.58333
(b)	To Dept. P, Assembly	5,733	=	1,600	×	$3.58333
	Total	$12,900				

Allocation of Department J, Building and Grounds:

$$\frac{\text{Total cost}}{\text{Total square feet—Departments G and P}} = \frac{\$10,500}{5,100} = \$2.05882/\text{sq ft}$$

				Square Feet	×	Rate/Sq Ft
(c)	To Dept. G, Machinery	$ 3,912	=	1,900	×	$2.05882
(d)	To Dept. P, Assembly	6,588	=	3,200	×	$2.05882
	Total	$10,500				

Factory overhead rates (based on machine hours) for producing departments:

				Total Cost After Allocation	÷	Machine Hours
(e)	For Dept. G, Machinery	$1.75597	=	$52,679	÷	30,000
(f)	For Dept. P, Assembly	$2.20706	=	$50,321	÷	22,800

(*b*)

Allocation of Costs
Step Method

	Service Departments		**Producing Departments**	
	N, Factory Admin.	**J, Bldg. and Grounds**	**G, Machinery**	**P, Assembly**
Total cost	$12,900	$10,500	$41,600	$38,000
Allocated to Service Dept. J and Producing Depts. G and P	<12,900>	3,019 (*a*)	5,489 (*b*)	4,392 (*c*)
Subtotal		$13,519	$47,089	$42,392
Allocated to Producing Depts. G and P		<13,519>	5,036 (*d*)	8,483 (*e*)
Balance after allocation	0	0	$52,125	$50,875
Factory overhead rates per machine hour			$1.738 (*f*)	$2.231 (*g*)

Computations:

Allocation of Department N, Factory Administration:

$$\frac{\text{Total cost}}{\text{Total estimated labor hours—Departments J, G, and P}} = \frac{\$12{,}900}{4{,}700} = \$2.74468/\text{labor hour}$$

				Labor Hours	×	Rate/Labor Hour
(a)	To Dept. J, Building and Grounds	$ 3,019	=	1,100	×	$2.74468
(b)	To Dept. G, Machinery	5,489	=	2,000	×	$2.74468
(c)	To Dept. P, Assembly	4,392	=	1,600	×	$2.74468
	Total	$12,900				

Note: The cost allocated to Department P, Assembly includes the corrected rounding difference.

Allocation of Department J, Buildings and Grounds:

$$\frac{\text{Total cost}}{\text{Total square feet—Departments G and P}} = \frac{\$13{,}519}{5{,}100} = \$2.65078/\text{sq ft}$$

				Square Feet	×	Rate/Sq Ft
(d)	To Dept. G, Machinery	$ 5,036	=	1,900	×	$2.65078
(e)	To Dept. P, Assembly	8,483	=	3,200	×	$2.65078
	Total	$13,519				

Factory overhead rates (based on machine hours) for producing departments:

				Total Cost After Allocation	÷	Machine Hours
(f)	For Dept. G, Machinery	$1.738	=	$52,125	÷	30,000
(g)	For Dept. P, Assembly	$2.231	=	$50,875	÷	22,800

(*c*)

	Services Provided by	
Department	**Factory Administration (Labor Hours)**	**Building and Grounds (Square Feet)**
N, Factory Administration	—	1,200
J, Building and Grounds	1,100	—
G, Machinery	2,000	1,900
P, Assembly	1,600	3,200
Total	4,700	6,300

Let N = Total cost of factory administration and J = Total cost of building and grounds. The cost to be allocated to each department is then

$$N = \$12{,}900 + \frac{1{,}200}{6{,}300}J \quad \text{and} \quad J = \$10{,}500 + \frac{1{,}100}{4{,}700}N$$

By substitution we get

$$N = \$12{,}900 + \frac{1{,}200}{6{,}300}\left(\$10{,}500 + \frac{1{,}100}{4{,}700}N\right)$$

$$N = \$12{,}900 + \$2{,}000 + 0.04458N$$

$$0.95542N = \$14{,}900$$

$$N = \$15{,}595$$

By inserting the value for N in the equation for Department J, we get

$$J = \$10{,}500 + \frac{1{,}100}{4{,}700}(\$15{,}595) = \$10{,}500 + \$3{,}650 = \$14{,}150$$

Allocation of Costs
Algebraic Method

	Service Departments		Producing Departments	
	N, Factory Admin.	**J, Bldg. and Grounds**	**G, Machinery**	**P, Assembly**
Total cost	$12,900	$10,500	$41,600	$38,000
Allocated to Service Dept. J and Producing Depts. G and P	<15,595>	3,650 *(a)*	6,636 *(b)*	5,309 *(c)*
Allocated to Service Dept. N and Producing Depts. G and P	2,695 *(d)*	<14,150>	4,268 *(e)*	7,187 *(f)*
Balance after allocation	0	0	$52,504	$50,496
Factory overhead rates per machine hour			$1.750 *(g)*	$2.215 *(h)*

Computations:

Allocation of Department N, Factory Administration:

				Proportionate Labor Hours	× Total Cost
(a)	To Dept. J, Building and Grounds	$ 3,650	=	(1,100 ÷ 4,700) ×	$15,595
(b)	To Dept. G, Machinery	6,636	=	(2,000 ÷ 4,700) ×	$15,595
(c)	To Dept. P, Assembly	5,309	=	(1,600 ÷ 4,700) ×	$15,595
	Total	$15,595			

Allocation of Department J, Building and Grounds:

				Proportionate Square Feet	× Total Cost
(d)	To Dept. N, Factory Administration	$ 2,695	=	(1,200 ÷ 6,300) ×	$14,150
(e)	To Dept. G, Machinery	4,268	=	(1,900 ÷ 6,300) ×	$14,150
(f)	To Dept. P, Assembly	7,187	=	(3,200 ÷ 6,300) ×	$14,150
	Total	$14,150			

Note: The cost allocated to Department G, Machinery includes corrected rounding difference.

Factory overhead rates (based on machine hours) for producing departments

				Total Cost After Allocation	÷	Machine Hours
(g)	For Dept. G, Machinery	$1.750	=	$52,504	÷	30,000
(h)	For Dept. P, Assembly	$2.215	=	$50,496	÷	22,800

3.5 Factory Overhead Entries. The Wilson Company assembles and sells one product, the Speedy Blender. The costs per unit are: direct materials, $15; direct labor, $17. Production for year 19X8 is estimated to be 20,000 units; estimated factory overhead is: indirect labor, $22,000; indirect materials, $16,000; depreciation, $7,000; light and power, $5,000; miscellaneous, $10,000. Wilson Company uses a perpetual cost accumulation system.

Completed production for year 19X8 was 18,000 units, and actual factory overhead cost included indirect materials of \$26,000, indirect labor of \$18,000, depreciation of \$7,000, light and power of \$5,000, and no miscellaneous expenses. There were no beginning or ending work-in-process inventories.

Prepare (*a*) the journal entries for direct materials, direct labor and factory overhead, and (*b*) the entry to close over- or underapplied factory overhead to Cost of Goods Sold.

SOLUTION

		Debit	Credit
(*a*)	*Work-in-Process Inventory*	*270,000*	
	Materials Inventory (18,000 units × \$15)		*270,000*
	Work-in-Process Inventory	*306,000*	
	Payroll Payable (18,000 units × \$17)		*306,000*
	Work-in-Process Inventory	*54,000*	
	Factory Overhead Applied (18,000 × \$3)*		*54,000*
	Factory Overhead Applied	*54,000*	
	Factory Overhead Control		*54,000*
	Factory Overhead Control	*56,000*	
	Materials Inventory		*26,000*
	Payroll Payable		*18,000*
	Accumulated Depreciation		*7,000*
	Accounts Payable		*5,000*
(*b*)	*Cost of Goods Sold (\$56,000 − \$54,000)*	*2,000*	
	Factory Overhead Control		*2,000*

* Predetermined Factory Overhead Application Rate (\$22,000 + \$16,000 + \$7,000 + \$5,000 + \$10,000) ÷ 20,000 = \$3

Chapter 4

Job Order Cost System

4.1 JOB ORDER COST SYSTEM

The job order cost system is most suitable when the products differ in types of material and work performed. Thus, each product is made according to the customer's specifications and the price quoted is closely tied to estimated cost. Examples of types of companies which might use job order costing are printing companies and shipbuilding firms.

Under a job order cost system, the three basic elements of cost—direct materials, direct labor and factory overhead—are accumulated according to assigned job numbers. The unit cost for each job is obtained by dividing the total units for the job into the total cost. Selling and administrative costs are *not* considered part of the cost of the job and are shown separately on the cost sheet and income statement.

In order for a job order cost system to function properly, it is necessary to identify each job and segregate its related costs. Each individual order or batch is assigned a job number. Material requisitions, labor costs, and other charges carry the particular job number, and a cost sheet is used to summarize the applicable job costs. The profit or loss can be computed for each job and the unit cost can be computed for purposes of inventory costing.

EXAMPLE 1

Power Manufacturing Corporation uses a job order cost system during 19X1, these costs were incurred on the following open jobs:

Direct Materials

Job #	Cost
H 702	$16,872
G 901	10,980
B 168	5,670

Direct Labor

Job #	Hours	Cost
L 1670	200	$ 800
J 1901	3,000	9,600
H 702	500	1,575
G 901	600	1,200
B 168	90	180

Factory Overhead

Applied at $2.00 per direct labor hour.

Work-in-Process Inventory—January 1, 19XX

Job #	Direct Materials	Direct Labor	Factory Overhead	Total
L 1670	$1,500	$6,000	$8,000	$15,500
J 1901	5,000	8,000	4,000	17,000

Sales

Job #	Selling Price
L 1670	$ 18,000
J 1901	45,000
H 702	28,000
G 901	25,000
	$116,000

Jobs Completed during the Year: #L 1670, #J 1901, #H 702, #G 901
Selling and Administrative Expenses: $25,510

Computed below are (1) the cost of completed jobs, (2) the ending work-in-process inventory, and (3) the net income for the year.

(1) *Cost of Completed Jobs*

Job #	Opening W.I.P.	Direct Materials	Direct Labor	Factory Overhead	Total Cost
L 1670	$15,500		$ 800	$ 400	$16,700
J 1901	17,000		9,600	6,000	32,600
H 702		$16,872	1,575	1,000	19,447
G 901		10,980	1,200	1,200	13,380
	$32,500	$27,852	$13,175	$8,600	$82,127

(2) *Work-in-Process Inventory-Ending*

Job #	Opening W.I.P.	Direct Materials	Direct Labor	Factory Overhead	Total Cost
B 168	0	$5,670	$180	$180	$6,030

(3) *Net Income*

Sales	$116,000
Cost of goods sold	82,127
Gross profit	$ 33,873
Selling and administrative expenses	25,510
Net income	$ 8,363

4.2 JOURNAL ENTRIES FOR JOB ORDER COST SYSTEM

The appropriate journal entries for a job order cost system are illustrated in Example 2.

EXAMPLE 2

Sloane Manufacturing Company uses a job order cost system and compiled the following data during 19X1 for Job 1:

Materials and Supplies Purchased	$242,000
Direct Material Used	190,000
Supplies Used (indirect materials)	20,000
Direct Labor	150,000
Indirect Labor	35,000
Utility Costs for Year Payable	65,000
Miscellaneous Overhead Payable	40,000
Depreciation, Equipment	22,000
Depreciation, Buildings	8,000
Applied Factory Overhead (120% of direct labor costs)	
Cost of Goods Manufactured	520,000
Sales	600,000
Cost of Goods Sold	326,000
Selling and Administrative Expenses	110,000

Shown below are (1) the appropriate journal entries and (2) the computation of net income.

(1) Journal Entries

Jan 3	Materials Inventory	242,000	
	Accounts Payable		242,000
Jan 10	Work-in-Process Inventory—Job 1	190,000	
	Factory Overhead Control	20,000	
	Materials Inventory		210,000
Jan 17	Work-in-Process Inventory—Job 1	150,000	
	Factory Overhead Control	35,000	
	Payroll Payable		185,000
Jan 19	Payroll Payable	185,000	
	Cash		185,000
Jan 24	Factory Overhead Control	135,000	
	Accounts Payable ($65,000 + $40,000)		105,000
	Accumulated Depreciation—Equipment		22,000
	Accumulated Depreciation—Building		8,000
Feb 1	Work-in-Process Inventory—Job 1	180,000	
	Factory Overhead Applied		180,000
	($150,000 direct labor × 120% = $180,000)		
Feb 15	Finished Goods	520,000	
	Work-in-Process Inventory—Job 1		520,000
Mar 1	Cost of Goods Sold	326,000	
	Finished Goods		326,000
Mar 1	Accounts Receivable	600,000	
	Sales		600,000

(2) Net Income

Sales	$600,000
Cost of goods sold	326,000
Gross profit	$274,000
Selling and administrative expenses	110,000
Net income	$164,000

4.3 JOB ORDER COST SHEET

This form is used to summarize the direct materials, direct labor, and factory overhead charged to a particular job. The form varies according to the needs of the particular company.

The materials cost and labor cost may be obtained from materials and labor summaries or may be recorded directly from materials requisitions and time tickets. Factory overhead is applied on the basis of a predetermined rate. The rate may be based on direct labor hours, direct labor cost, machine hours, etc. When there are two or more departments, it is usually desirable to have separate factory overhead rates for each department, or separate bases may be used. For example, factory overhead may be applied in Department A on the basis of machine hours and in Department B on the basis of direct labor hours.

In order to have additional information for the particular job readily available, many companies provide a summary on the cost sheet that includes the selling price as well as estimated selling and administrative expenses so that the estimated profit can be shown.

EXAMPLE 3

The Pompano Company received an order from the Bayville Company on July 13, 19X1 for 1,000 tea pots, model #6. The price is $2.50 each, and delivery is promised in three months. Job No. 1201 was assigned to the order.

Direct Materials. Direct materials costs for the job, obtained from materials requisitions, are as follows:

Department A:	August 5, 500 bases at $0.80	$400
	August 10, 500 bases at $0.90	450
Department B:	September 8, 600 handles at $0.30	$180
	September 20, 400 handles at $0.50	200

Direct Labor. Direct labor costs obtained from time tickets are as follows:

Department A:	August 15, Forming, 12 hours at $10	$120
	August 20, Polishing, 10 hours at $11	110
Department B:	September 12, Assembly, 14 hours at $8	112
	September 25, Assembly, 13 hours at $9	117

Factory Overhead. Factory overhead is applied when the job is completed or at the end of a period for jobs in process. The predetermined factory overhead rate is based on direct labor hours for each department as follows: Department A, $5.00 per hour; Department B, $6.00 per hour.

Selling and Administrative Expenses are based on 10% of selling price

The completed Job Cost Sheet for Job No. 1201 is shown in Fig. 4-1.

4.4 SPOILED AND DEFECTIVE UNITS

Spoiled units are those that do not meet production standards and are either sold for their salvage value or discarded. *Defective units* do not meet production standards but are further processed to be sold as good units or as irregular units.

Normal spoilage is that which is expected to occur despite efficient production. Normal spoilage can be applied to all jobs by including an estimate for normal spoilage in the factory overhead

POMPANO COMPANY
Job Order Cost Sheet

Customer:	Bayville Company	Job No:	1201
Date Ordered:	July 13, 19X1	Product:	Copper Pot #6
Date Completed:	October 13, 19X1	Quantity:	1,000

Direct Materials

Date	Description	Quantity	Cost	Amount
8/5	Bases, Dept. A	500	.80	$ 400
8/10	Bases, Dept. A	500	.90	450
9/8	Handles, Dept. B	600	.30	180
9/20	Handles, Dept. B	400	.50	200
			Total	$1,230

Factory Overhead

Month	Dept.	Hours	Rate	Amount
Aug.	A	22	$5.00	$110
Sept.	B	27	6.00	162
			Total	$272

Summary

Selling price		$2,500
Factory Costs		
Direct Materials	$1,230	
Direct Labor	459	
Factory Overhead	272	
(Unit Cost: $1.96)		1,961
Gross Profit (21.56%)		$ 539
Selling & Admin. (10%)		250
Profit (11.56%)		$ 289

Direct Labor

Date	Description	Hours	Rate	Amount
8/15	Forming, Dept. A	12	$10	$120
8/20	Polishing, Dept. A	10	11	110
9/12	Assembly, Dept. B	14	8	112
9/25	Assembly, Dept. B	13	9	117
			Total	$459

Fig. 4-1

application rate, or it can be allocated only to the job in which it occurs by transferring the salvage value out of work-in-process inventory into a spoiled units inventory.

Abnormal spoilage is that which is in excess of what is acceptable; therefore, the total cost of the abnormal spoiled units should be removed from work-in-process inventory, and any salvage value should be recorded in a Spoiled Units Inventory account.

The rework costs for *normal defective units* are treated in a manner similar to those for spoiled units: either applied to all jobs by including an estimate in the factory overhead application rate, or applied only to the affected job.

Costs incurred to rework *abnormal defective units* are charged to an account called Loss from Abnormal Defective Units and are thus treated as a period cost.

Solved Problems

4.1 Journal Entries. The J. Nelson Company maintains its cost records under the job order system. Selected cost data pertaining to Job A for the month of July, 19X1 are as follows:

Work-in-Process Inventory, July 1, 19X1	$35,000
Transactions for July:	
(1) Raw materials purchased on credit	45,000
(2) Materials issued (indirect, $5,000)	35,000
(3) Payroll (indirect, $10,000)	50,000
(4) Factory overhead, actual	60,000
(5) Factory overhead is applied to production at 120% of direct labor.	
(6) Jobs with a cost of $110,000 were completed in July.	
(7) Jobs costing $140,000 were shipped out and billed at a markup of 25% on cost.	

(*a*) Prepare the general journal entries for the above transactions. (*b*) Compute the work-in-process inventory amount at July 31, 19X1.

SOLUTION

(*a*) **General Journal Entries**

(1)	Materials Inventory	45,000	
	Accounts Payable		45,000
(2)	Work-in-Process Inventory—Job A	30,000	
	Factory Overhead Control	5,000	
	Materials Inventory		35,000
(3)	Work-in-Process Inventory—Job A	40,000	
	Factory Overhead Control	10,000	
	Payroll Payable		50,000
	Payroll Payable	50,000	
	Cash		50,000
(4)	Factory Overhead Control	60,000	
	Accounts Payable		60,000
(5)	Work-in-Process Inventory—Job A	48,000	
	Factory Overhead Applied (120% × $40,000)		48,000
(6)	Finished Goods	110,000	
	Work-in-Process Inventory—Job A		110,000
(7)	Cost of Goods Sold	140,000	
	Finished Goods		140,000
(8)	Accounts Receivable	175,000	
	Sales (125% × $140,000)		175,000

(*b*) **Work-in-Process Inventory, July 31, 19X1**

Work-in-Process Inventory

Balance 7/1	35,000	Completed in July	110,000
Direct Materials, July	30,000	Balance 7/31	43,000
Direct Labor, July	40,000		
Factory Overhead, July	48,000		
	153,000		153,000
Balance 7/31	43,000		

4.2 Job Order Cost Sheet. The Liebman Manufacturing Company produces expensive furniture by special order. One order was started and completed during August. There was no other production. Factory overhead is applied at a rate of $4.00 per direct labor hour. Cost information for the month was as follows:

	Job 201
Direct materials	$11,500
Direct labor	
Cost	$10,500
Hours	3,500
Factory overhead	
Indirect materials	$10,000
Other factory overhead	3,000
Total	$13,000

Job 201 was ordered by the Binderman Company. They requested 1,000 rocking chairs. The selling price was $40 per chair, and selling and administrative expenses relating to Job 201 were $1,500.

Prepare a Job Order Cost Sheet. (Assume the order was placed on August 1 and the job was completed on August 31.)

SOLUTION

LIEBMAN MANUFACTURING CO.
Job Order Cost Sheet

Customer: Binderman Co. Job No: 201
Date Ordered: 8-1-XX Product: Rocking Chairs
Date Completed: 8-31-XX Quantity: 1,000

Direct Materials

Date	Description	Quantity	Cost	Amount
8/31	Lumber			$ 11,500
			Total	$11,500

Direct Labor

Date	Description	Hours	Rate	Amount
8/31		3,500	$3.00	$10,500
			Total	$10,500

Factory Overhead

Month	Dept.	Hours	Rate	Amount
Aug.		3,500	$4.00	$14,000
			Total	$14,000

Summary

Selling price		$40,000
Factory Costs		
Direct Materials	$11,500	
Direct Labor	10,500	
Factory Overhead	14,000	36,000
Gross Profit		$ 4,000
Selling & Admin.		1,500
Profit		$ 2,500

Fig. 4-2.

4.3 **Profit on Jobs.** The Green Engineering Company produces specialized machine parts according to customer specifications. At January 1, 19X1, the following jobs were in process:

	Job #20	**Job #28**	**Job #48**
Direct Materials	$4,000	$ 8,000	$3,300
Direct Labor	2,000	4,000	2,200
Factory Overhead	1,000	2,000	1,100
Totals	$7,000	$14,000	$6,600

Additional costs to complete:

Direct materials: $20,000, allocated as follows: Job #20, 40%; Job #28, 40%; and Job #48, 20%.

Direct labor: $4,000 per job.

Factory overhead: 20% of direct labor.

Unit selling prices: Job #20, $2.20; Job #28, $2.50; Job #48, $1.80.

Assuming the total unit cost for each job is $2.00, (*a*) calculate the number of units completed on each job. (*b*) Compute the profit or loss on each job.

SOLUTION

Before unit costs can be computed, it is necessary to determine the total cost for each job, as follows:

Job #20	January 1	Additional	Total
Direct Materials	$ 4,000	$ 8,000	$12,000
Direct Labor	2,000	4,000	6,000
Factory Overhead	1,000	800	1,800
Total	$ 7,000	$12,800	$19,800

Job #28	January 1	Additional	Total
Direct Materials	$ 8,000	$ 8,000	$16,000
Direct Labor	4,000	4,000	8,000
Factory Overhead	2,000	800	2,800
Total	$14,000	$12,800	$26,800

Job #48	January 1	Additional	Total
Direct Materials	$ 3,300	$ 4,000	$ 7,300
Direct Labor	2,200	4,000	6,200
Factory Overhead	1,100	800	1,900
Total	$ 6,600	$ 8,800	$15,400

(*a*) **Units Completed**

	Total Cost		Unit Cost		Total Units
Job #20	$19,800	÷	$2.00	=	9,900
Job #28	26,800	÷	2.00	=	13,400
Job #48	15,400	÷	2.00	=	7,700
Totals	$62,000				31,000

(*b*) **Profit or Loss on Each Job**

		Unit Price				
	Units	Selling	Cost	Selling Price	Total Cost	Profit (Loss)
Job #20	9,900	$2.20	$2.00	$21,780	$19,800	$1,980
Job #28	13,400	2.50	2.00	33,500	26,800	6,700
Job #48	7,700	1.80	2.00	13,860	15,400	(1,540)
Totals				$69,140	$62,000	$7,140

4.4 **Factory Overhead Rates and Job Costs.** The Tableau Manufacturing Company has been in business for one month. At the end of the month the company had the following account balances on its books:

Direct materials used	$ 5,000
Direct labor	10,000
Indirect labor	3,000
Indirect materials	2,000
Labor fringe costs	1,000
Supervisor's salary	1,000
Depreciation of machinery	2,000
Miscellaneous factory overhead	1,000
Heat and light	500
Insurance on plant	1,500

The company processed two jobs during the month as follows:

	Job 101	Job 102
Direct materials cost	$3,000	$2,000
Direct labor cost	6,000	4,000
Direct labor hours	4,000	3,000
Machine hours	2,000	1,000

The company does not use a predetermined rate for factory overhead. The rate is computed at the end of each month.

In terms of both direct labor hours and machine hours, compute (*a*) the factory overhead rates for the month, (*b*) the factory overhead cost of each job, and (*c*) the total cost for each job.

SOLUTION

(*a*) The factory overhead rates for the month are as follows:

$$\frac{\text{Factory overhead costs}}{\text{Total direct labor hours}} = \frac{\$12{,}000}{7{,}000} = \$1.71$$

$$\frac{\text{Factory overhead costs}}{\text{Total machine hours}} = \frac{\$12{,}000}{3{,}000} = \$4.00$$

(*b*) Factory overhead charged to jobs is as follows. For Job 101:

Factory overhead rate × direct labor hours = $1.71 × 4,000 = $6,840
Factory overhead rate × machine hours = $4.00 × 2,000 = $8,000

For Job 102:

Factory overhead rate × direct labor hours = $1.71 × 3,000 = $5,130
Factory overhead rate × machine hours = $4.00 × 1,000 = $4,000

(c) Total cost:

	Job 101		Job 102	
Component Costs	**Direct Labor Hours**	**Machine Hours**	**Direct Labor Hours**	**Machine Hours**
Direct materials	$ 3,000	$ 3,000	$ 2,000	$ 2,000
Direct labor	6,000	6,000	4,000	4,000
Factory overhead	6,840	8,000	5,130	4,000
Total cost	$15,840	$17,000	$11,130	$10,000

4.5 FILL-INS

(1) Units which must be sold for their salvage value are known as ______________________________.

(2) ______________________________units are further processed in order to be sold as good units.

(3) ______________________________spoilage is expected to occur despite efficient production.

(4) The total cost of abnormal spoiled units should be (a)______________________________ and any salvage value should be (b)______________________________.

(5) Rework costs for normal defective units can be (a)______________________________ or (b)______________________________.

SOLUTION

(1) spoiled units
(2) defective
(3) normal
(4) (a) removed from work-in-process inventory
(b) recorded in a Spoiled Units Inventory Account
(5) (a) applied to all jobs
(b) allocated to the job in which it occurs

Chapter 5

Process Cost System

5.1 INTRODUCTION

Under a process cost system, costs are accumulated according to each department, cost center, or process. For simplicity, this discussion of cost accumulation will refer to departments rather than to cost centers or processes. Note, however, that there may be two or more processes performed in one department (and therefore, more than one cost center in a department). In such cases, costs may vary significantly between cost centers, so it is desirable in practice to accumulate costs according to cost center or process rather than by department.

The average unit cost for a day, week, or year is obtained by dividing the department cost by the number of units (tons, gallons, etc.) produced during the particular period.

The process cost system is commonly used where products are manufactured under mass production methods or by continuous processing. Industries using process costs are paper, steel, chemicals, and textiles. Assembly-type processes such as washing machines and electrical appliances would also use process costs.

5.2 ACCUMULATION OF COSTS

In a process cost system procedures must be developed to:

(1) Accumulate direct materials, direct labor, and factory overhead costs by department.

(2) Determine the unit cost for each department.

(3) Transfer costs from one department to the next.

(4) Assign costs to work-in-process inventory.

The procedure to record the accumulation of costs is described below.

(1) ***Direct Materials Costs.*** In a process cost system the number of requisitions or charges for direct materials is far lower than in a job order cost system, since charges are made to departments rather than to individual jobs. In some industries the type and quantity of direct materials may be specified by formulas or engineering specifications. When there is continuous use of the same direct materials, the usage each day or week is obtained from consumption reports rather than individual requisitions. The journal entry for recording direct materials would be

Work-in-Process Inventory—Department A	*10,500*	
Materials Inventory		*10,500*

(2) ***Direct Labor Costs.*** The detail of accumulating direct labor costs by departments is also less than accumulating the same costs by individual jobs under the job order cost system. Direct labor costs to departments may be summarized in the payroll distribution entry as follows:

Work-in-Process Inventory—Department A	*6,000*	
Work-in-Process Inventory—Department B	*2,000*	
Payroll Payable		*8,000*

(3) ***Factory Overhead Costs.*** There is a greater difference between job order costing and process costing with respect to factory overhead than with direct materials or direct labor

costs. Generally, production is more stable for process costing from month to month, since products are made for stock rather than to order. The entry to record factory overhead is

Work-in-Process Inventory—Department A	*9,000*	
Work-in-Process Inventory—Department B	*4,000*	
Factory Overhead Applied		*13,000*

When factory overhead costs accumulate fairly evenly throughout the year, or at a reasonably normal rate each month, many companies apply actual factory overhead to Work-in-Process Inventory. However, substantial fluctuation in production between months can distort the factory overhead charged to production. Thus, a predetermined factory overhead application rate based on a year's operation is frequently used to eliminate the difficulties of allocating factory overhead based on month-to-month differences in production.

5.3 DEPARTMENTAL TRANSFERS

Process costing is ordinarily used when products require a number of different production operations which are performed in two or more departments or cost centers. For example, the first operation may be performed in Department A, such as a machining or mixing process. After completion the units are transferred to Department B for an assembly or refining process. When this is completed, the units are transferred to finished goods inventory.

EXAMPLE 1

The Sunshine Company manufactures Product X, which requires processing in Departments A and B. During July 19X1, 5,000 units were placed in production and completed during the month. The costs were as follows: direct materials, $10,000; direct labor, $9,000; and factory overhead, $6,000. The computations are:

Work-in-Process Inventory—Department A

	Total Cost	**Unit Cost**
Direct materials placed into production	$10,000	$2.00
Direct labor	9,000	1.80
Factory overhead	6,000	1.20
Total cost	$25,000	$5.00

The unit cost in each case is found by dividing the total cost by the number of units produced. When the process in Department A is completed, the 5,000 units and their total cost of $25,000 are transferred to Department B.

5.4 FLOW OF UNITS

The flow of units (in terms of quantity) through a process cost system can be summarized by the following equation:

Units in process at beginning + Units started in process or transferred in (Units to account for)
= Units transferred out + Units completed and on hand
+ Units still in process (Units accounted for)

When any four terms in the equation are known, the missing component can be computed from the equation. Note that all the components are not necessarily present in each situation (i.e., there may not always be units in process at the beginning of the period or units completed and still on hand at the end of the period).

EXAMPLE 2

Assume that the Bickerman Company had 1,500 units in work in process at the beginning of the month, put 5,000 units into process and had 1,000 units in work in process at the end of the month. All units completed were transferred out to Department B. The number of units transferred is computed as follows:

1,500	Units in process at beginning
+5,000	Units started in process
6,500	Total units in process
−1,000	Units still in process
5,500	Units completed and transferred to Department B

5.5 EQUIVALENT UNITS OF PRODUCTION

Rarely are all units placed in production during the month completed and sent to the next department by the end of the month. In most cases there will be beginning and ending inventories of work in process at different stages of completion each month.

To allocate costs when inventories of partially finished goods exist, all units (beginning work-in-process inventory and ending work-in-process inventory) must be expressed in terms of completed units. This is done by means of a common denominator, known as *equivalent units of production* or *equivalent production*. By using the equivalent production figure, the unit cost for the month would include the cost of completing any work in process at the beginning of the month and the cost to date of work in process at the end of the month.

Two separate equivalent production computations are usually needed, one for *direct materials* and another for direct labor and factory overhead, known as *conversion costs*.

There are two principal methods for costing work-in-process inventories: *average costing* and *first-in, first-out* (FIFO) *costing*. There are minor differences in cost report format or procedure; the major difference relates to the way in which the work-in-process inventories are treated.

Average Costing. Under this method, also known as weighted average costing, the opening work-in-process inventory costs are *merged* with the costs of the new period and a new average cost is obtained. Thus, there is only one average cost for goods completed.

Equivalent units under average costing may be computed as follows:

Units Completed (Transferred out plus still on hand) + [Ending Work in Process × Degree of Completion (%)]

This method is based on the assumption that *all* units in beginning work-in-process inventory were completed during the current period.

EXAMPLE 3

The following data relate to the activities of Department A during the month of May:

	Units
Beginning work-in-process inventory (100% complete as to direct materials, 70% complete as to conversion costs)	8,000
Goods started in process	86,000
Units transferred to Dept. B	80,000
Units completed and on hand	4,000
Ending work in process inventory (100% complete as to direct materials, 60% complete as to conversion costs)	10,000

Equivalent production in Department A for the month, using average costing, is computed as follows.

	Direct Materials	Conversion Costs
Units completed		
Transferred to Dept. B	80,000	80,000
Completed and on hand	4,000	4,000
Ending inventory units, amount completed:		
Direct materials (100%)	10,000	
Conversion costs (60%)		6,000
Equivalent production	94,000	90,000

This method adds the portion of beginning work-in-process inventory that was completed in the previous month to the current month's production. The result is that the portion of beginning work-in-process inventory completed during the previous period is counted twice, in this case once as last April's ending work-in-process inventory and again as May's beginning work-in-process inventory.

FIFO Costing. Under this method, the opening work-in-process inventory costs are *separated* from additional costs applied in the new period. Thus, there are two unit costs for the period: (1) opening work-in-process units completed and (2) units started and finished in the same period.

Under FIFO, the beginning work-in-process inventory is assumed to be completed and transferred first. The ending work-in-process inventory is then assumed to be from the goods put into production during the period. Thus, ending work-in-process inventory is calculated from current period unit costs according to degree of completion.

Equivalent units under FIFO Costing may be computed as follows:

Units Completed (Transferred out plus still on hand)

− Beginning Work-in-Process Inventory (regardless of stage of completion)

\+ Amount needed to complete Beginning Work-in-Process Inventory

\+ Amount completed in Ending Work-in-Process Inventory

EXAMPLE 4

Using the same data as in Example 3, we compute the equivalent production for Department A under the FIFO method as follows.

	Units	
	Direct Materials	Conversion Costs
Units completed and transferred		
Transferred to Dept. B	80,000	80,000
Completed and on hand	4,000	4,000
Less: Beginning work-in-process inventory	⟨ 8,000⟩	⟨ 8,000⟩
Started and completed during this period	76,000	76,000
Completion of beginning work-in-process inventory		
Direct materials (0%)	0	
Conversion costs (30%)		2,400
	76,000	78,400
Ending inventory units, amount completed		
Direct materials (100%)	10,000	
Conversion costs (60%)		6,000
Equivalent production	86,000	84,400

Equivalent production under FIFO may also be computed by subtracting the portion of beginning work in process inventory that was completed during the previous month from equivalent production under average costing.

	Units	
	Direct Materials	**Conversion Costs**
Equivalent production, average costing (from Example 3)	94,000	90,000
Less: Beginning work-in-process inventory (portion completed last month)		
Direct materials (100%)	⟨ 8,000⟩	
Conversion costs (70%)		⟨ 5,600⟩
Equivalent production, FIFO costing	86,000	84,400

The FIFO method is superior to the average costing method in that it corrects the double count resulting from the carry-over of the previous month's work-in-process inventory. Even with this inherent inaccuracy in the average method, it is still commonly used in business because the double count usually represents an insignificant portion of the total units produced.

5.6 COST OF PRODUCTION REPORT

The Cost of Production Report shows all costs chargeable to a department or cost center for the period. Since its principal objective is the control of costs, detailed data relating to total and unit costs must be provided. Typically, the cost breakdown is made by cost elements for each department (or cost center). This report is also a good source for summary journal entries prepared at the end of the month.

The cost of production report generally contains four sections:

(1) ***Quantities.*** This section accounts for the physical flow of *units* into and out of a department.

(2) ***Equivalent Production.*** This section shows the sum of: (1) units still in process, restated in terms of completed units, and (2) total units actually completed. Section 5.5 illustrated the computation of equivalent units of production under both average costing and FIFO costing.

(3) ***Costs to Account For.*** This section accounts for the *incurrence* of costs that were: (1) *in process* at the beginning of the period, (2) *transferred in* from previous departments, and (3) *added* by the department.

(4) ***Costs Accounted For.*** This section accounts for the *disposition* of costs charged to the department. Were the costs: (1) *transferred out* to another department or to finished goods? (2) *completed* and on *hand*? (3) *still in process* at the end of the period? It should be noted that the total of the *Costs to Account For* must equal the total of the *Costs Accounted For*.

The Cost of Production Report may be greatly detailed (i.e., item by item) or may show only totals, depending on the needs of the business and the desire of management. In our presentation we will show the breakdown according to cost elements in each of the cost categories.

EXAMPLE 5

The Vogel Manufacturing Corporation uses the first-in, first-out method of process costing. The following data relate to the operations of Department A during the month of July, 19X1:

Production (in units)

Beginning work-in-process inventory (100% complete as to direct materials; 60% complete as to conversion costs)	1,500
Started in process	5,000
Transferred to Dept. B	5,500
Ending work-in-process inventory (100% complete as to direct materials; 60% complete as to conversion costs)	1,000

Costs in Beginning Inventory		Costs Added during the Month	
Direct materials	$1,680	Direct materials	$10,000
Direct labor	1,400	Direct labor	8,500
Factory overhead	1,120	Factory overhead	6,800
Total	$4,200	Total	$25,300

The July Cost of Production Report for Department A is shown below.

The Vogel Manufacturing Corporation
Cost of Production Report, Department A
FIFO Costing Method
for the month of July, 19X1

(Section 1)	Quantities	
Units to account for:		
Beginning units in process	1,500	
Units started in process	5,000	6,500
Units accounted for:		
Units transferred to next department	5,500	
Ending units in process	1,000	6,500

(Section 2)	Equivalent Production		
	Direct Materials	Conversion Costs	(Computations)
Units completed and transferred	5,500	5,500	
− Beginning units in process	1,500	1,500	
= Units started and completed	4,000	4,000	
+ Amount needed to complete beginning work-in-process inventory	0	600	(1,500 × 40%)
+ Ending units in process	1,000	600	(1,000 × 60%)
Total equivalent units	5,000	5,200	

(Section 3)	Costs to Account For				
	Total Cost	÷	Equivalent Production	=	Equivalent Unit Cost
Work-in-process inventory—beginning	$ 4,200				
Costs added during the period:					
Direct materials	10,000		5,000		$2.000
Direct labor	8,500		5,200		1.635
Factory overhead	6,800		5,200		1.308
Total costs to account for	$29,500				$4.943

(Section 4)	Costs Accounted For	
Transferred to next department:		
From beginning inventory:		
Inventory cost	$4,200	
Direct labor (1,500 × $1.635 × 40%)	981	
Factory overhead (1,500 × $1.308 × 40%)	785	$ 5,966
From current production:		
Units started and completed (4,000 × $4.943)		19,772
Total transferred		$25,738
Work-in-process inventory—ending:		
Direct materials (1,000 × $2.000)	$2,000	
Direct labor (1,000 × $1.635 × 60%)	981	
Factory overhead (1,000 × $1.308 × 60%)	785	3,766
Total		$29,504
Less: Rounding difference		⟨4⟩
Total costs accounted for		$29,500

EXAMPLE 6

If the Vogel Manufacturing Corporation had used the average costing method instead of FIFO, its Cost of Production Report for the month of July would have appeared as shown below. The data are the same as in Example 5.

The Vogel Manufacturing Corporation
Cost of Production Report, Department A
Average Costing Method
for the month of July, 19X1

(Section 1)	Quantities	
Units to account for:		
Beginning units in process	1,500	
Units started in process	5,000	6,500

Units accounted for:		
Units transferred to next department	5,500	
Ending units in process	1,000	6,500

(Section 2) Equivalent Production

	Direct Materials	Conversion Costs	(Computations)
Units completed and transferred	5,500	5,500	
Ending units in process	1,000	600	(1,000 × 60%)
Total equivalent units	6,500	6,100	

(Section 3) Costs to Account For

	Total Cost	÷	Equivalent Production	=	Equivalent Unit Cost
Costs added by department:					
Direct materials					
Work-in-process inventory—beginning	$ 1,680				
Added during the period	10,000				
Total	$11,680		6,500		$1.797
Direct labor					
Work-in-process inventory—beginning	$1,400				
Added during the period	8,500				
Total	$ 9,900		6,100		1.623
Factory overhead					
Work-in-process inventory—beginning	$ 1,120				
Added during the period	6,800				
Total	$ 7,920		6,100		1.299
Total costs to account for	$29,500				$4.719

(Section 4) Costs Accounted For

Transferred to next department: (5,500 × $4.719)		$25,954
Work-in-process inventory—ending:		
Direct materials (1,000 × $1.797)	$1,797	
Direct labor (1,000 × $1.623 × 60%)	974	
Factory overhead (1,000 × $1.299 × 60%)	779	3,550
Less: Rounding difference		(4)
Total costs accounted for		$29,500

5.7 JOURNAL ENTRIES

Two sets of journal entries are needed to record the information developed in the Cost of Production Report.

(1) ***Entry for Costs to Account For.*** The following entry is needed to record the costs put into process in the current period:

Work-in-Process Inventory—Department A	*XX*	
Materials Inventory		*XX*
Payroll Payable		*XX*
Factory Overhead Applied		*XX*

(2) ***Entry for Costs Accounted For.*** The following entry is needed to record the costs transferred out:

Work-in-Process Inventory—Department B	*XX*	
Work-in-Process Inventory—Department A		*XX*

EXAMPLE 7

Continuing with the Vogel Manufacturing Corporation data in Examples 5 and 6, the journal entry to record costs put into the process in Department A is as follows, whether average costing or FIFO is used:

Work-in-Process Inventory—Department A	*25,300*	
Materials Inventory		*10,000*
Payroll Payable		*8,500*
Factory Overhead Applied		*6,800*

Under FIFO, the entry to record transfer of costs to Department B is

Work-in-Process Inventory—Department B	*25,738*	
Work-in-Process Inventory—Department A		*25,738*

5.8 SECOND DEPARTMENT AND INTRODUCTION OF ADDITIONAL MATERIALS

While in many cases all direct materials are introduced at the beginning of the process, it is sometimes necessary to include additional direct materials in departments subsequent to the first. In such instances, there are two possible effects on units and related costs:

(1) The number of final units *remains the same while the unit cost increases*. In this case, the treatment of the additional direct materials cost is identical to that for the inclusion of all direct materials in the first department (i.e., it is included in "Cost Added by Department"; that total is divided by the appropriate equivalent units figure to derive the periodic unit cost).

(2) The number of final units *increases* while unit cost *decreases*. When this occurs, an adjustment of the preceding department's unit cost becomes necessary, because the same total cost will be allocated over a greater number of units.

EXAMPLE 8

Assume the following information for Department 2:

Costs transferred in from Dept. 1	$50,000
Units transferred in from Dept. 1	20,000
Additional units put into process in Dept. 2	5,000

The preceding department's unit cost to be used in Department 2 is computed as follows:

$50,000 (cost transferred in) ÷ 25,000 units = $2 per unit

5.9 COST OF PRODUCTION REPORT—SECOND DEPARTMENT

The Cost of Production Report for a subsequent department is generally the same as that for the first department except that it contains a section for units and costs transferred in.

EXAMPLE 9

The Cost of Production Report prepared in Example 6 will be used as the basis for this example. There was no beginning work-in-process inventory in Department B, and no additional direct materials were added in this department.

Of the 5,500 units transferred in from Department A, 4,000 were transferred to finished goods. The ending work-in-process inventory was 80% complete as to conversion costs.

Direct labor of $6,000 and factory overhead of $4,500 were added by Department B.

The August Cost of Production Report for Department B follows:

The Vogel Manufacturing Corporation
Cost of Production Report, Department B
Average Costing Method
for the month of August, 19X1

Quantities

Units to account for:		
Units received from Department A		5,500
Units accounted for:		
Units transferred to finished goods	4,000	
Ending units in process	1,500	5,500

Equivalent Production

	Conversion Costs	
Units transferred to finished goods	4,000	
Ending units in process	1,200	(1,500 × 80%)
Total equivalent units	5,200	

Costs to Account For

	Total Cost	÷	Equivalent Production	=	Equivalent Unit Cost
Costs from preceding department:					
Transferred in during the period	$25,954		5,500		$4.719
Costs added by department:					
Direct labor					
Added during the period	6,000		5,200		1.154
Factory overhead					
Added during the period	4,500		5,200		.865
Total costs to account for	$36,454				$6.738

Costs Accounted For	
Transferred to finished goods inventory (4,000 × $6.738)	$26,952
Work-in-process inventory—ending:	
Costs from preceding department (1,500 × $4,719)	7,079
Direct labor (1,500 × $1.154 × 80%)	1,385
Factory overhead (1,500 × $.865 × 80%)	1,038
Total costs accounted for	$36,454

5.10 SPOILED UNITS (GOODS)

Units that do not meet production standards and are either sold for their salvage value or discarded are called spoiled units. When spoiled units are discovered, they are immediately taken out of production, and no further work is performed on them. The amount of spoilage for a period can be considered either normal or abnormal.

Normal. Spoilage that results from an efficient production process is called normal spoilage. It is the unavoidable cost of producing good units.

Abnormal. Spoilage that exceeds what is considered normal for a particular production process is called abnormal spoilage. It is controllable and results from inefficient operations.

5.11 ACCOUNTING FOR SPOILED UNITS

(1) *Spoilage in the First Department*

Method 1—Theory of Neglect. Spoiled units are considered as not put into production at all. Equivalent unit cost increases as costs are allocated over fewer units. This method is used because of its simplicity, but it is not the preferred method because it does not distinguish between normal and abnormal spoilage.

Method 2—Spoilage as a Separate Element of Cost. This method establishes a separate cost for spoiled units. The spoiled units are included in the computation of equivalent production up to the point at which they were removed from production (usually the point of inspection). Once the cost is recognized, it can be further allocated between normal and abnormal spoilage. Abnormal spoilage cost is considered to be a period cost, while normal spoilage is considered to be a product cost.

(2) *Spoilage in Subsequent Departments*

Method 1—Theory of Neglect. Spoiled units after the first department are also considered as never having been put in production. The transferred-in cost is higher because spoiled units were not removed from production in the first department. The number of transferred-in units is reduced by the number of spoiled units, thereby allocating transferred-in costs to fewer units. The unit cost for units started and completed is also greater as the cost of spoiled units is absorbed.

Method 2—Spoilage as a Separate Element of Cost. Total spoilage cost is equal to the sum of transferred-in cost of spoiled units plus spoilage costs in the current department. Computed as follows:

$$\text{Total spoilage cost} = \left(\begin{array}{c}\text{Number of}\\ \text{spoiled units}\end{array} \times \begin{array}{c}\text{Transferred-}\\ \text{in cost}\end{array}\right) + \left(\begin{array}{c}\text{Equivalent}\\ \text{production of}\\ \text{spoiled units}\end{array} \times \begin{array}{c}\text{Equivalent}\\ \text{unit cost}\end{array}\right)$$

EXAMPLE 10

To illustrate the computation of spoilage costs, assume the following:

Units transferred in from Department 1	5,000
Normal spoilage in Department 2 (units)	40
Cost per unit of units transferred in	$8
Unit costs for Department 2:	
Direct materials	$2.00
Direct labor	.60
Factory overhead applied	.90

There was no beginning work-in-process inventory, and spoiled units were removed when conversion costs were 50% complete. All the direct materials were added at the beginning of the process.

Method 1—Theory of Neglect

	Units	Total Cost	÷	Equivalent Production	=	Equivalent Unit Cost
Costs from preceding dept.:						
Transferred in during period (5,000 × $8.00)	5,000	$40,000		4,960		$8.06
Less: Total spoiled units	−40					
Adjusted units and unit cost	4,960					

Note that the equivalent unit cost increased from $8.00 to $8.06 because the costs are spread over the remaining good units.

Method 2—Spoilage as a Separate Element of Cost

Transferred-in equivalent unit cost from Department 1 (40 × $8.00)		$320
Costs added by department 2:		
Direct materials (40 × $2 × 100%)	$80.00	
Direct labor (40 × $0.60 × 50%)	12.00	
Factory overhead (40 × $0.90 × 50%)	18.00	110
Total spoilage cost		$430

Note that with this method, actual spoilage cost is computed. Management can identify the units and further allocate the cost between normal and abnormal spoilage.

Solved Problems

5.1 Flow of Units; Quantity Schedules. The Katz Supply Company manufactures door knobs. The products pass through two departments. Department A had 5,500 door knobs in process on July 1, and 2,500 in process on July 31. During the month, 6,000 door knobs were transferred to Department B for further processing. There were no completed units on hand at the end of the month.

(*a*) Compute the number of door knobs started in process during July and (*b*) prepare a quantity schedule for Department A.

SOLUTION

(*a*) Let $x =$ the number of units started in process.

$$5{,}500 + x = 6{,}000 + 0 + 2{,}500$$
$$x = 8{,}500 - 5{,}500$$
$$x = 3{,}000$$

(*b*) **Quantity Schedule**

Units to account for		
Units in process at beginning of period	5,500	
Units started in process	3,000	8,500
Units accounted for		
Units transferred to next department	6,000	
Units still in process at end of period	2,500	8,500

5.2 Flow of Units; Quantity Schedules. The Meyer Manufacturing Company manufactures woolen mittens that require processing in two departments, A and B. During the month of October, Department A completed 10,500 mittens, of which 8,000 were transferred to Department B. There were 500 mittens in process in Department A and 300 in Department B on October 1. During the month, 15,000 additional mittens were started in production in Department A; no additional units were added by Department B. All 7,000 mittens completed during the month were transferred from Department B to the finished goods storeroom. The remaining units for Departments A and B were still in process on October 31.

For each department (*a*) compute the number of units still in process on October 31, and (*b*) prepare a quantity schedule.

SOLUTION

(*a*) Let $x =$ the number of units still in process.

Department A

$$500 + 15{,}000 + 0 = 8{,}000 + 2{,}500 + x$$
$$15{,}500 = 10{,}500 + x$$
$$5{,}000 = x$$

Department B

$$300 + 0 + 8{,}000 = 7{,}000 + 0 + x$$
$$8{,}300 = 7{,}000 + x$$
$$1{,}300 = x$$

(*b*) **Quantity Schedules**

	Department A	Department B
Units to account for		
Units in process at beginning	500	300
Units started in process	15,000	
Units from preceding department		8,000
	15,500	8,300
Units accounted for		
Units transferred to next department	8,000	7,000
Units completed and on hand	2,500	
Units still in process	5,000	1,300
	15,500	8,300

5.3 Equivalent Production—Average Costing. The following information is available for the Blutter Manufacturing Company:

	Units	
Work in process, January 1 (75% complete as to direct materials and conversion costs)	4,000	
Units started in process	46,000	50,000
Units transferred out	36,000	
Units completed and on hand	8,000	
Units still in process, January 31 (100% direct materials; 40% conversion costs)	6,000	50,000

Compute the equivalent units for the Blutter Manufacturing Company using the average costing method.

SOLUTION

	Direct Materials	Conversion Costs	(Computations)
Units completed			
Transferred to next department	36,000	36,000	
Still on hand	8,000	8,000	
Ending units in process			
Direct materials	6,000		(6,000 × 100%)
Conversion costs		2,400	(6,000 × 40%)
Total equivalent units	50,000	46,400	

5.4 **Equivalent Production—FIFO.** Using the data in Problem 5.3, compute the equivalent units under the FIFO costing method.

SOLUTION

	Direct Materials	Conversion Costs	(Computations)
Units completed			
Transferred out	36,000	36,000	
Still on hand	8,000	8,000	
Less: Beginning work-in-process inventory	⟨4,000⟩	⟨4,000⟩	
	40,000	40,000	
Amount needed to complete beginning work in process	1,000	1,000	(4,000 × 25%)
	41,000	41,000	
Ending units in process			
Direct materials	6,000		(6,000 × 100%)
Conversion costs		2,400	(6,000 × 40%)
Total equivalent units	47,000	43,400	

5.5 **Cost of Production Report: Average Costing.** The Nan Corporation manufactures typewriters and uses a process cost system to account for the costs. Production is done in two departments and the average costing method is used. The following information is available for you to prepare a cost of production report (*a*) for Department 1 and (*b*) for Department 2.

Units	Dept. 1	Dept. 2
Beginning units in process		
Department 1:		
100% direct materials; 20% complete as to conversion costs	6,000	
Department 2:		
100% direct materials; 70% complete as to conversion costs		8,000
Started in process during the period	45,000	—
Received in from Department 1	—	42,000
Transferred to finished goods	—	45,000
Ending units in process		
Department 1:		
100% direct materials; 75% complete as to conversion costs	9,000	
Department 2:		
100% direct materials; 40% complete as to conversion costs		5,000

Costs	Dept. 1	Dept. 2
Beginning work-in-process inventory		
From preceding department	$ 0	$ 57,720
Direct materials	8,000	0
Direct labor	5,000	18,000
Factory overhead	3,000	8,000
	$ 16,000	$ 83,720

Added during the period		
Direct materials	$200,000	$ 0
Direct labor	100,000	150,000
Factory overhead	90,000	120,000
	$390,000	$270,000

SOLUTION

(*a*)

Nan Corporation
Cost of Production Report, Department 1
Average Costing Method

Quantities

Units to account for:		
Beginning units in process	6,000	
Units started in process	45,000	51,000
Units accounted for:		
Units transferred to Department 2	42,000	
Ending units in process	9,000	51,000

Equivalent Production

	Direct Materials	Conversion Costs	(Computations)
Units completed and transferred	42,000	42,000	
Ending units in process	9,000	6,750	(9,000 × 75%)
Total equivalent units	51,000	48,750	

Costs to Account For

	Total Cost	÷	Equivalent Production	=	Equivalent Unit Cost
Costs added by department:					
Direct materials					
Work-in-process inventory—beginning	$ 8,000				
Added during the period	200,000				
Total	$208,000		51,000		$4.078
Direct labor:					
Work-in-process inventory—beginning	5,000				
Added during the period	100,000				
Total	$105,000		48,750		2.154
Factory overhead:					
Work-in-process inventory—beginning	3,000				
Added during the period	90,000				
Total	$ 93,000		48,750		1.908
Total costs to account for	$406,000				$8.140

Costs Accounted For	
Transferred to Department 2: (42,000 × $8.140)	$341,880
Work-in-process inventory—ending:	
Direct materials (9,000 × $4.078)	36,702
Direct labor (9,000 × $2.154 × 75%)	14,540
Factory overhead (9,000 × $1.908 × 75%)	12,879
Less: rounding difference	⟨1⟩
Total costs accounted for	$406,000

(*b*)

Nan Corporation
Cost of Production Report, Department 2
Average Costing Method

Quantities		
Units to account for:		
Beginning units in process	8,000	
Received from preceding department	42,000	50,000
Units accounted for:		
Units transferred to finished goods inventory	45,000	
Ending units in process	5,000	50,000

Equivalent Production	Direct Materials	Conversion Costs	(Computations)
Transferred to finished goods inventory	45,000	45,000	
Ending units in process	5,000	2,000	(5,000 × 40%)
Total equivalent units	50,000	47,000	

Costs to Account For	Units	Total Cost	÷	Equivalent Production	=	Equivalent Unit Cost
Costs from preceding department:						
Work-in-process inventory—beginning	8,000	$ 57,720				
Transferred in during the period:	42,000	341,880				
	50,000	$399,600		50,000		$ 7.99200

Costs added by department:			
Direct labor			
Work-in-process inventory—beginning	$ 18,000		
Added during the period	150,000		
Total	$168,000	47,000	3.57446
Factory overhead:			
Work-in-process inventory—beginning	$ 8,000		
Added during the period	120,000		
Total	$128,000	47,000	2.72340
Total costs to account for	$695,600		$14.28986

Costs Accounted For

Transferred to finished goods inventory (45,000 × $14.28986)	$643,044
Work-in-process inventory—ending:	
Costs from preceding department (5,000 × $7.992)	39,960
Direct labor (5,000 × $3.57446 × 40%)	7,149
Factory overhead (5,000 × $2.72340 × 40%)	5,447
Total costs accounted for	$695,600

5.6 Cost of Production Report: FIFO. Recompute Problem 5.5 under FIFO costing.

SOLUTION

(*a*)

Nan Corporation
Cost of Production Report, Department 1
FIFO Costing Method

Quantities

Costs to account for:		
Beginning units in process	6,000	
Units started in process	45,000	51,000
Costs accounted for:		
Units transferred to Department 2	42,000	
Ending units in process	9,000	51,000

Equivalent Production

	Direct Materials	Conversion Costs	(Computations)
Units completed and transferred	42,000	42,000	
− Beginning units in process	6,000	6,000	
= Units started and completed	36,000	36,000	
+ Amount needed to complete beginning work-in-process inventory	0	4,800	(6,000 × 80%)
+ Ending units in process	9,000	6,750	(9,000 × 75%)
Total equivalent units	45,000	47,550	

Costs to Account For

	Total Cost	÷	Equivalent Production	=	Equivalent Unit Cost
Work-in-process inventory—beginning	$ 16,000				
Costs added during period:					
Direct materials	200,000		45,000		$4.44444
Direct labor	100,000		47,550		2.10305
Factory overhead	90,000		47,550		1.89274
Total costs to account for	$406,000				$8.44023

Costs Accounted For

Transferred to Department 2:		
From beginning inventory:		
Inventory cost	$16,000	
Direct labor (6,000 × $2.10305 × 80%)	10,095	
Factory overhead (6,000 × $1.89274 × 80%)	9,085	$ 35,180
From current production:		
Units started and completed		
Total transferred (36,000 × $8.44023)		303,848
Work-in-process inventory—ending:		
Direct materials (9,000 × $4.44444)	$40,000	
Direct labor (9,000 × $2.10305 × 75%)	14,196	
Factory overhead (9,000 × $1.89274 × 75%)	12,776	66,972
Total costs accounted for		$406,000

(*b*)

Nan Corporation
Cost of Production Report, Department 2
FIFO Costing Method

Quantities

Units to account for:		
Beginning units in process	8,000	
Received from preceding department	42,000	50,000
Units accounted for:		
Units transferred to finished goods inventory	45,000	
Ending units in process	5,000	50,000

Equivalent Production

	Direct Materials	Conversion Costs	(Computations)
Units completed and transferred	45,000	45,000	
− Beginning units in process	8,000	8,000	
= Units started and completed	37,000	37,000	
+ Amount needed to complete beginning work-in-process inventory	0	2,400	(8,000 × 30%)
+ Ending units in process	5,000	2,000	(5,000 × 40%)
Total equivalent units	42,000	41,400	

Costs to Account For

	Units	Total Cost	÷	Equivalent Production	=	Equivalent Unit Cost
Costs from preceding department and prior period:						
Work-in-process inventory—beginning	8,000	$ 83,720				
Transferred in during period:	42,000	339,028*		42,000		$ 8.0721
	50,000					
Costs added by department:						
Direct materials		0				
Direct labor		150,000		41,400		3.6232
Factory overhead		120,000		41,400		2.8986
Total costs to account for		$692,748				$14.5939

* Costs transferred in:

From beginning inventory:	$ 35,180
From current production:	303,848
	$339,028

Costs Accounted For		
Transferred to finished goods inventory:		
From beginning inventory		
Inventory cost	$83,720	
Direct labor (8,000 × $3.6232 × 30%)	8,696	
Factory overhead (8,000 × $2.8986 × 30%)	6,956	$ 99,372
From current production:		
Units started and completed (37,000 × $14.5939)		539,974
Total transferred		$639,346
Work-in-process inventory—ending:		
Costs from preceding department (5,000 × $8.0721)	$40,361	
Direct labor (5,000 × $3.6232 × 40%)	7,246	
Factory overhead (5,000 × $2.8986 × 40%)	5,797	53,404
Less: rounding difference		⟨2⟩
Total costs accounted for		$692,748

5.7 Normal Spoilage. At the Stalle Pretzel Co., inspection for spoilage occurs when units are complete. Company policy is to treat spoilage as a separate element of cost. Using the following information, compute spoilage cost for Department 2.

Units transferred in from Department 1	50,000
Normal spoilage	500
Unit cost of units transferred in	$1.20
Unit costs for Department 2:	
Direct materials	$1.50
Direct labor	.75
Factory overhead applied	.50

SOLUTION

Computation of spoilage cost:

Transferred-in equivalent unit cost from Department 1 (500 × $1.20)	$600
Cost added by Department 2:	
Direct materials (500 × $1.50)	750
Direct labor (500 × $0.75)	375
Factory overhead (500 × $0.50)	250
Total spoilage cost	$1,975

Chapter 6

By-Product and Joint Product Costing

6.1 JOINT COSTS

The nature of by-products and joint products is such that they contain an element called joint costs. *Joint costs* are those incurred up to the point in a given process where individual products can be identified. In the case of by-products, this is the point at which the main product and its associated by-products emerge. For joint products, it is the point at which separate products having relatively equal sales values can be identified. In both cases, the stage of production at which separate products are identifiable is known as the *split-off point*.

6.2 DIFFICULTIES ASSOCIATED WITH JOINT COSTS

The two major difficulties inherent in joint costs are as follows:

(1) *True joint costs are indivisible*; that is, they are not specifically identified with any of the products being simultaneously produced. Thus, the total of these costs must be allocated to individual products on some logical basis. For example, a sample of ore usually contains a variety of minerals (i.e., iron, lead, zinc, etc.). These minerals are joint products in their raw state; until they are extracted by ore reduction, the costs of locating, mining, and processing are properly considered joint costs.

(2) *Joint costs are frequently confused with common costs*. Common costs are those incurred to produce products simultaneously, but each of the products could have been produced separately. The difference here is that joint costs are indivisible while common costs are divisible. That is, the various products resulting from common costs could have each been obtained separately, so common costs can be allocated on the basis of relative usage.

6.3 BY-PRODUCTS DEFINED

By-products are products of limited sales value produced simultaneously with a product of greater sales value. The *main product*, as it is called, is generally produced in much greater quantities than the by-products.

By-products generally fall into one of two categories: (1) those that are sold in the same form as originally produced (revenue recognized when sold), and (2) those that undergo further processing before sale (revenue recognized when produced).

6.4 ACCOUNTING FOR BY-PRODUCTS

By-products are of secondary importance; therefore, cost allocation differs from that of joint products.

The costing of by-products falls into one of two categories:

(1) ***Category 1—By-Products Are Recognized When "Sold."*** By-products are considered to be of little importance, so no production costs are allocated to them. However, net by-product income (which is by-product income less actual additional processing costs and marketing and administration expenses) is shown on the income statement in one of two ways:

(A) As an *addition to income*, either
  (1) as part of other sales or
  (2) as other income

(B) As a *deduction from cost of goods sold* of the main product

(2) ***Category 2—By-Products Are Recognized When "Produced."*** By-products are considered important and the net by-product income is significant. Therefore, production costs are allocated to by-products.

On the income statement, the production costs of the main products *produced* are reduced by the expected value of the by-products *produced*. (*Note:* the calculations are performed on units produced, not units sold.)

The amount deducted from production costs is computed in one of two ways:

(A) *Net Realizable Value Method*. The expected sales value of the by-product produced is reduced by the expected additional processing costs and marketing and administrative expenses.

(B) *Reversal Cost Method*. The expected sales value of the by-product is reduced by the expected additional processing costs and normal gross profit of the by-product (or by the marketing and administrative expenses and net income).

In doing this computation (revenue less additional costs less gross profit), the amount remaining represents the portion of joint costs allocated to the by-product.

Upon the sale of the by-product, the inventory account must be reduced and the cost of by-products sold must be recognized.

This is the only method where a portion of the joint costs is actually allocated to the by-product. Management should utilize this method when a by-product is considered significant.

EXAMPLE 1

Costs

	Production Costs	**Marketing and Administrative**	**Sales Revenue**
Main product and by-product—Department 1	$150,000	$21,000	$300,000
By-product—Department 2 (additional processing costs)	4,500	3,000	21,000
Total	$154,500	$24,000	$321,000

Units

	Produced	**Sold**	**Ending**
Main product	40,000	35,000	5,000
By-product	20,000	10,000	10,000

The expected gross profit rate for by-products is 40%. The by-product emerges at the end of processing in Department 1 (split-off point) and is transferred to Department 2, where additional processing is performed.

Category 1

(A) *Addition to income*
(1) *As part of other sales*

Sales:		
Main product		$300,000
By-product		13,500 (*a*)
Total sales		$313,500
Cost of main product sold:		
Total production costs (Dept. 1)	$150,000	
Less: Ending inventory	18,750 (*b*)	
Total cost of main product sold		131,250
Gross profit		$182,250
Less: Marketing and administrative expenses of main product		21,000
Net income		$161,250

(2) *As other income*

Sales (main product)		$300,000
Cost of main product sold:		
Total production costs (Dept. 1)	$150,000	
Less: Ending inventory	18,750 (*b*)	
Total cost of main product sold		131,250
Gross profit		$168,750
Less: Marketing and administrative expenses of main product		21,000
Income from operations		$147,750
Other income:		
Net by-product income		13,500 (*a*)
Net income		$161,250

(B) *Deduction from cost of goods sold of main product*

Sales (main product)		$300,000
Cost of main product sold:		
Total production costs (Dept. 1)	$150,000	
Less: Ending inventory	18,750 (*b*)	
Total cost of main product sold	$131,250	
Less: Net by-product income	13,500 (*a*)	117,750
Gross profit		$182,250
Less: Marketing and administrative expenses of main product		21,000
Net income		$161,250

(a) *By-product net income* = $21,000 sales revenue − $4,500 additional processing costs − $3,000 marketing and administrative expense = $13,500.

(b) *Main product ending inventory* = $150,000 ÷ 40,000 units = $3.75 per unit × 5,000 units = $18,750.

Category 2

(A) *Net realizable value method*

Sales (main product)		$300,000
Cost of main products sold:		
Total production costs (Dept. 1)	$150,000	
Less: Value of by-product produced	34,500 (*c*)	
Net production costs	$115,500	
Less: Ending inventory	14,450 (*d*)	101,050
Gross profit		$198,950
Less: Marketing and administrative expenses of main product		21,000
Net income		$177,950

(B) *Reversal cost method*

Sales:			
Main product		$300,000	
By-product		21,000	$321,000
Cost of main product and by-product sold:			
Production costs:			
Main product	$129,300 (*e*)		
By-product	25,200 (*f*)	$154,500	
Less: Ending inventory			
Main product	$ 16,163 (*g*)		
By-product	10,350 (*h*)	26,513	127,987
Gross profit			$193,013
Less: Marketing and administrative expenses:			
Main product		$ 21,000	
By-product		3,000	24,000
Net income			$169,013

(c) *Value of by-product produced* = by-product sales of $21,000 ÷ 10,000 units sold = $2.10 per unit × 20,000 units produced = $42,000 − $4,500 additional processing costs − $3,000 marketing and administrative costs = $34,500.

(d) *Main product ending inventory* = net production costs of $115,500 ÷ 40,000 units = $2.89 per unit × 5,000 units = $14,450.

(e) *Production cost of main product*

Total production costs—Department 1			$150,000
Less: Joint costs applicable to by-products produced:			
Expected sales value ($2.10 per unit × 20,000 units)		$42,000	
Less: Additional processing costs	$ 4,500		
Expected gross profit (40% of $42,000)	16,800	21,300	20,700
Production cost of main product			$129,300

(f) *Production cost of by-product* = $20,700 joint cost applicable to by-product (above) + $4,500 additional processing costs = $25,200.

(g) *Main product ending inventory* = $129,300 production costs ÷ 40,000 units produced = $3.2325 per unit × 5,000 units = $16,163

(h) *By-product ending inventory* = $20,700 production costs ÷ 20,000 units produced = $1.035 per unit × 10,000 units = $10,350.

6.5 JOINT PRODUCTS DEFINED

The term *joint products* refers to individual products, each of significant sales value, produced simultaneously as a result of a common process or series of processes. *Joint product costs* are those which arise in the course of such common processes involving common raw materials. Note that joint product costs are inherently indivisible, having been incurred simultaneously for all products, and not for each product individually.

The basic characteristics of joint products are as follows: (1) an unavoidable physical relationship which requires simultaneous, common processing, (2) a split-off point at which separate products emerge to be sold or further processed, and (3) none of the joint products are significantly greater in value than other joint products' values. Joint products manufacturing is found in the meat-packing industry, in natural resource refining industries, and in those where raw materials must be graded before processing.

6.6 ACCOUNTING FOR JOINT PRODUCTS

A portion of joint costs must be allocated to each of the joint products. Following are the methods commonly used:

(1) *Market Value at Split-Off Point Method*

The allocation of joint costs on the basis of market or sales values of the individual products is the most popular allocation method. Advocates of this method argue that a direct relationship exists between cost and selling price, namely, that the selling price of a product is determined primarily by the production cost. This method is used when the market value is known.

$$\text{Joint cost allocation of each product} = \frac{\text{Total market value of } \textit{each} \text{ product*}}{\text{Total market value of } \textit{all} \text{ products**}} \times \text{Joint costs}$$

* Total market value of *each* product = Units produced of *each* product × Unit market value of *each* product

** Total market value of *all* products = Sum of all the total market values of *each* product

EXAMPLE 2

Joint Cost Allocation
Market Value at Split-Off Point Method
Total Joint Costs: $310,000

	Joint Products		
	A	**B**	**C**
Units produced	40,000	80,000	20,000
Market value at split-off point:			
Unit	$4.00	$5.00	$3.00
Total	$160,000	$400,000	$60,000

$$\text{Product A: } \frac{\$160{,}000}{\$620{,}000^*} \times \$310{,}000 = \$\ 80{,}000$$

$$\text{Product B: } \frac{\$400{,}000}{\$620{,}000} \times \$310{,}000 = 200{,}000$$

$$\text{Product C: } \frac{\$60{,}000}{\$620{,}000} \times \$310{,}000 = \underline{30{,}000}$$

Total Joint Costs $\underline{\underline{\$310{,}000}}$

* Total market value of all products:
$160,000 + $400,000 + $60,000 = $620,000

(2) *Net Realizable Value Method*

When the market value of a joint product cannot be readily determined at the split-off point, as, for example, when a product requires additional processing before it can be sold, a *hypothetical* market value at the split-off point is calculated. The hypothetical market value is determined by subtracting the cost of additional processing from the market value of the completed product. The total cost of each product (allocation of joint costs + after split-off processing costs) is computed as follows.

$$\text{Total cost allocation of } \textit{each} \text{ product} = \left(\frac{\text{Total hypothetical market value of } \textit{each} \text{ product at split-off point*}}{\text{Total hypothetical market value of } \textit{all} \text{ products at split-off point**}} \times \text{Joint costs}\right) + \text{After split-off processing costs of } \textit{each} \text{ product}$$

* Total hypothetical market value of *each* product at split-off point = (Units produced of *each* product × Hypothetical market value of *each* product) − After split-off processing costs of *each* product.

** Total hypothetical market value of *all* products at split-off point = Sum of all the total hypothetical market values of *each* product.

EXAMPLE 3

Joint Cost Allocation
Net Realizable Value Method
Total Joint Costs: $310,000

	Joint Products		
	A	**B**	**C**
Number of units produced	40,000	80,000	20,000
Market value *after* further processing (no market value at split-off is available)			
Unit	$4.00	$5.00	$3.00
Total	$160,000	$400,000	$60,000
Additional processing costs after split-off	$8,000	$12,000	$6,000

$$\text{Product A: } \frac{\$160{,}000 - 8{,}000}{\$594{,}000^*} \times \$310{,}000 = \$\ 79{,}327$$

$$\text{Product B: } \frac{\$400{,}000 - \$12{,}000}{\$594{,}000} \times \$310{,}000 = 202{,}492$$

$$\text{Product C: } \frac{\$60{,}000 - \$6{,}000}{\$594{,}000} \times \$310{,}000 = 28{,}182$$

Total Joint Costs $310,001**

* Total hypothetical market value of all products:
($160,000 − $8,000) + ($400,000 − $12,000) + ($60,000 − $6,000) = $594,000

** Rounding difference

(3) *Physical Output Method*

Under this method, the quantity of output (expressed in units) is used as the basis for allocating joint costs. Since the quantity of output of all the joint products must be stated in the same terms, a common denominator (for example, quantity/ton) must be determined when the measurement basis of output varies from product to product. The joint cost allocated to each product under this method is computed by using the following formula:

$$\text{Joint cost allocation of } \textit{each} \text{ product} = \frac{\text{Total units of } \textit{each} \text{ product}}{\text{Total units of } \textit{all} \text{ products*}} \times \text{Joint costs}$$

* Total units of *all* products = Sum of all units produced

EXAMPLE 4

The information presented in Example 3 is used here to illustrate the allocation of joint costs under the physical output method.

$$\text{Product A: } \frac{40{,}000}{140{,}000^*} \times \$310{,}000 = \$\ 88{,}571$$

$$\text{Product B: } \frac{80{,}000}{140{,}000} \times \$310{,}000 = 177{,}143$$

$$\text{Product C: } \frac{20{,}000}{140{,}000} \times \$310{,}000 = 44{,}286$$

Total $310,000

* Total units of all products:
40,000 + 80,000 + 20,000 = 140,000

Solved Problems

6.1 **By-product Profit Determination.** The following income statement of the Lepolstat Manufacturing Company treats revenues from sales of by-products as other income. Determine the gross profit, the profit from operations, and the net profit by recognizing revenue from sales of by-products as (*a*) other sales revenue, (*b*) a deduction from cost of goods sold, and (*c*) other income. (Round to three places.)

Sales (main product, 10,000 units @ $6)		$60,000
Cost of Goods Sold		
Production Costs (14,000 units @ $3)	$42,000	
Ending Inventory (4,000 units @ $3)	12,000	30,000
Gross Profit		$30,000
Marketing and Administrative Expenses		2,000
Income from Operations		$28,000
Other Income		
Net By-product Income		3,000
Net Income		$31,000

SOLUTION

(*a*) Other Sales Revenue

Sales:		
Main product		$60,000
By-product		3,000
Total sales		$63,000
Cost of main product sold:		
Total production costs	$42,000	
Less: Ending inventory	12,000	
Total cost of main product sold		30,000
Gross profit		$33,000
Less: Marketing and administrative expenses of main product		2,000
Net income		$31,000

(*b*) Deduction from Cost of Goods Sold

Sales (main product)		$60,000
Cost of main product sold:		
Total production costs	$42,000	
Less: Ending inventory	12,000	
Total cost of main product sold	$30,000	
Less: Net by-product income	3,000	27,000
Gross profit		$33,000
Less: Marketing and administrative expenses of main product		2,000
Net income		$31,000

(*c*) Other Income

Sales (main product)		$60,000
Cost of main product sold:		
Total production costs	$42,000	
Less: Ending inventory	12,000	
Total cost of main product sold		30,000
Gross profit		$30,000
Less: Marketing and administrative expenses of main product		2,000
Income from operations		$28,000
Other income:		
Net by-product income		3,000
Net income		$31,000

6.2 By-products: Reversal Cost Method. The Whitcomb Industrial Corporation manufactures one main product and one by-product. During one period of production, the following data were compiled:

	Main Product	By-Product X
Sales	$300,000	$11,800
Processing costs before separation	120,000	
Processing costs after separation		3,600
Marketing and administrative expenses	20,000	2,200
Units sold	30,000	1,000

There are no beginning or ending inventories. The corporation allows a 20% gross profit for Product X

Calculate net income using the reversal cost method.

SOLUTION

Sales:		
Main product	$300,000	
By-product	11,800	$311,800
Cost of main product and by-product sold:		
Production costs:		
Main product	$114,160 (*a*)	
By-product	9,440 (*b*)	123,600
Gross profit		$188,200
Less: Marketing and administrative expenses:		
Main product	$ 20,000	
By-product	2,200	22,200
Net income		$166,000

(*a*) *Production cost of main product:*

Total production costs			$120,000
Less: Joint costs applicable to by-products produced:			
Expected sales value ($11.80 per unit × 1,000 units)		$11,800	
Less: Additional processing costs	$3,600		
Expected gross profit (20% of $11,800)	2,360	5,960	5,840
Production cost of main product			$114,160

(*b*) *Production cost of by-product:*

$5,840 joint cost applicable to by-product (above) + $3,600 additional processing costs = $9,440.

6.3 By-products: Net Realizable Value Method. Using the information in Problem 6.2, compute net income using the net realizable value method.

SOLUTION

Sales (main product)		$300,000
Cost of main products sold:		
Total production costs	$120,000	
Less: Value of by-product produced	6,000 (*a*)	
Net production costs		114,000
Gross profit		$186,000
Less: Marketing and administrative expenses of main product		20,000
Net income		$166,000

(*a*) *Value of by-product produced* = $11.80 per unit × 1,000 units produced = $11,800 − $3,600 additional processing costs − $2,200 marketing and administrative expense = $6,000.

6.4 Joint Costs: Net Realizable Value Method. The Bounceback Manufacturing Company manufactures two products, Realrubber and Fakerubber, from the same material. The material costs $0.95 per pound and must pass through two departments. In Department 1, the material is split into Realrubber and Fakerubber. Realrubber requires no further processing; Fakerubber must be processed further in Department 2. The costs below pertain to the year ended December 31, 19X8.

Department	Direct Materials	Direct Labor	Factory Overhead	Total
1	$144,000	$21,000	$15,000	$180,000
2	...	10,000	18,000	28,000
Totals	$144,000	$31,000	$33,000	$208,000

Product	Pounds Sold	Pounds of Finished Goods, Ending Inventory	Sales
Realrubber	30,000	15,000	$ 52,500
Fakerubber	45,000	...	150,750

There were no materials on hand at year end.

Compute the allocation of joint costs between Realrubber and Fakerubber.

SOLUTION

$$\text{Unit price of Realrubber} = \frac{\text{Sales}}{\text{Pounds sold}} = \frac{\$52,500}{30,000} = \$1.75$$

The market value of Realrubber at the split-off point is computed as follows:

Sales	$52,500
Ending inventory (15,000 lbs @ $1.75)	26,250
Market value at split-off	$78,750

Hypothetical market value of Fakerubber:

Market value at split-off	$150,750
Additional processing costs	−28,000
Hypothetical market value	$122,750

Allocation of joint costs of $180,000:

$$\text{Realrubber: } \frac{\$78{,}750}{\$201{,}500\ (a)} \times \$180{,}000 = \$\ 70{,}347$$

$$\text{Fakerubber: } \frac{\$122{,}750}{\$201{,}500\ (a)} \times \$180{,}000 = \$109{,}653$$

(a) $78,750 + $122,750 = $201,500

6.5 Joint Costs: Market Value Method. Using the information from Problem 6.4, and assuming that the actual market value of Fakerubber is $165,000, compute the joint cost allocation.

SOLUTION

$$\text{Realrubber } \frac{\$52{,}500}{\$217{,}500} \times \$180{,}000 = \$\ 43{,}448$$

$$\text{Fakerubber } \frac{\$165{,}000}{\$217{,}500} \times \$180{,}000 = \$136{,}552$$

6.6 Joint Costs: Physical Output Method. Using the information from Problem 6.4, compute the joint cost allocation using the physical output method.

SOLUTION

$$\text{Realrubber } \frac{30{,}000}{75{,}000} \times \$180{,}000 = \$\ 72{,}000$$

$$\text{Fakerubber } \frac{45{,}000}{75{,}000} \times \$180{,}000 = \$108{,}000$$

Chapter 7

The Master Budget

7.1 NATURE OF THE BUDGET

A budget is a quantitative expression of management objectives and a tool used to analyze progress toward those objectives. An effective budget should be properly coordinated with management and accounting systems. Budgets may be short-term (1 year or less) or long-term (greater than 1 year).

7.2 DEVELOPING THE MASTER BUDGET

The master budget encompasses all functions and management levels, although the approach to formulating the budget may differ from company to company. Two opposite and extreme views of how to develop a master budget are the *top management approach* (input comes *only* from top officers) and the *grass roots approach* (all levels participate in forecasting). Irrespective of who is involved in providing input, the following sequence is generally followed in constructing a master budget:

(1) Sales budget
(2) Production budget
(3) Direct materials purchase budget
(4) Direct materials usage budget
(5) Direct labor budget
(6) Factory overhead budget
(7) Ending inventories budget
(8) Cost of goods sold budget
(9) Selling expense budget
(10) Administrative expense budget
(11) Budgeted income statement
(12) Cash budget
(13) Budgeted balance sheet

The following balance sheet and additional information will be used to prepare the master budget for the Coates Corporation for the first quarter of 19XX:

Coates Corporation
Balance Sheet
January 1, 19XX

Assets

Current			
Cash		$ 20,700	
Accounts receivable		132,930	
Materials		6,600	
Finished goods		79,800	
Total			$ 240,030
Plant			
Equipment	$ 75,000		
Less: Accumulated depreciation	7,140	$ 67,860	
Buildings	$800,000		
Less: Accumulated depreciation	48,460	751,540	
Total			819,400
Total assets			$1,059,430

Liabilities and Stockholders' Equity

Liabilities		
Accounts payable	$ 10,300	
Stockholders' Equity		
Common stock $10 par; 90,000 shares issued and outstanding	900,000	
Retained earnings	149,130	
Total liabilities and stockholders' equity		$1,059,430

Forecasted Sales by Territory

	Units		
Territory	January	February	March
1	300	450	200
2	280	500	170
3	350	550	300

Variable Expenses (% of Total Sales Dollars)

Commissions	5%
Travel	3%
Advertising	7%

Fixed Expenses per Month

Indirect materials	$2,000
Indirect labor	900
Maintenance	1,200
Heat and light	300
Power	200
Insurance	270
Depreciation (60% equipment; 40% building)	1,350
Taxes	600
Sales salaries	1,400
Executive salaries	2,000
Administrative expenses	1,500
Selling expenses	1,300

Desired Finished Goods Inventories* (Units)

January 1	950
January 31	900
February 28	980
March 31	1,100

* *Assumption:* All ending inventories are at standard cost.

Other Data

Average sales price	$150 per unit
Materials cost	$25 per unit
December purchases	$25,750
Desired direct materials ending inventory	30% of next month's production (this policy was in effect last year)
Production, April	600 units
Direct labor hours	3 per unit
Direct materials	1 unit per product
Labor cost	$12.25 per hour
Income tax rate	50%

Variable Factory Overhead Rates per Direct Labor Hour

Indirect labor	$1.20
Maintenance	1.30
Power	1.55
Payroll taxes	1.10

Construction of the master budget begins with the sales budget.

7.3 SALES BUDGET

A sales forecast is the basis upon which the sales budget and all other budgets are developed. The formula used to develop a sales budget in dollars is:

$$\text{Sales budget (units)} \times \text{Sales price per unit}$$

EXAMPLE 1

Coates Corporation
Sales Budget
First Quarter, 19XX

Territory	Jan.	Feb.	Mar.	Total
	Units			
1	300	450	200	950
2	280	500	170	950
3	350	550	300	1,200
Total	930	1,500	670	3,100
	Dollars*			
1	$ 45,000	$ 67,500	$ 30,000	$142,500
2	42,000	75,000	25,500	142,500
3	52,500	82,500	45,000	180,000
Total	$139,500	$225,000	$100,500	$465,000

* Sales price = $150 per unit

7.4 PRODUCTION BUDGET

The production budget can be developed with the information provided by the sales budget and the inventory estimates. Essentially it is the sales budget adjusted for changes in inventory. The formula used to compute the production requirement for the quarter is:

Sales budget (units) + desired ending inventory (units) − beginning inventory (units)

EXAMPLE 2

Coates Corporation
Production Budget
First Quarter, 19XX

	Units			
	Jan.	**Feb.**	**Mar.**	**Total**
Sales budget	930	1,500	670	3,100
Add: Desired ending inventory	900	980	1,100	1,100
Subtotal	1,830	2,480	1,770	4,200
Less: Beginning inventory	950	900	980	950
Production required	880	1,580	790	3,250

7.5 DIRECT MATERIALS PURCHASE BUDGET

The required purchases are a function of each period's production, beginning inventory level, and desired ending inventory level. The formulas used are:

Purchase of direct materials required (units)
= Production budget (units) + Desired ending inventory (units)
− Beginning inventory (units)
= Purchase of direct materials required (units) × Purchase cost per unit
= Direct materials purchase cost

EXAMPLE 3

Coates Corporation
Direct Materials Purchase Budget
First Quarter, 19XX

	Jan.	**Feb.**	**Mar.**	**Total**
Production units required	880	1,580	790	3,250
Add: Desired ending inventory*	474	237	180**	180
Subtotal	1,354	1,817	970	3,430
Less: Beginning inventory***	264	474	237	264
Purchases required	1,090	1,343	733	3,166
Cost per unit	× $25	× $25	× $25	× $25
Purchase cost	$27,250	$33,575	$18,325	$79,150

* Desired direct materials ending inventory is 30% of the *next* month's production.

** 600 units (April production) × 30% = 180 units.

*** Beginning direct materials inventory is 30% of the *same* month's production (the same as the desired ending inventory of the previous month).

7.6 DIRECT MATERIALS USAGE BUDGET

The usage budget (in units and usage cost) is based upon the standard costing systems requirements (specifically, the number of direct material units required to produce one unit of finished product). The formula used to determine direct materials usage cost is:

Direct materials required (units) × Materials unit cost

EXAMPLE 4

Coates Corporation
Direct Materials Usage Budget
First Quarter, 19XX

	Jan.	Feb.	Mar.	Total
Direct materials required* (units)	880	1,580	790	3,250
Materials unit cost	× $25	× $25	× $25	× $25
Direct materials usage cost	$22,000	$39,500	$19,750	$81,250

* One unit of direct materials is needed for each unit of production. Hence, the amounts are the same as the production units required (Example 2).

7.7 DIRECT LABOR BUDGET

Direct labor standards are usually based on time studies conducted by engineers. Indirect labor costs are included in the factory overhead budget. The formula used to determine direct labor cost is:

Production units required × Direct labor hours per unit × Rate per hour

EXAMPLE 5

Coates Corporation
Direct Labor Budget
First Quarter, 19XX

	Jan.	Feb.	Mar.	Total
Production units required	880	1,580	790	3,250
	× 3	× 3	× 3	× 3
Direct Labor hours (3 per unit)	2,640	4,740	2,370	9,750
Rate per hour	× $12.25	× $12.25	× $12.25	× $12.25
Direct labor cost	$ 32,340	$ 58,065	$29,032.50	$119,437.50

7.8 FACTORY OVERHEAD BUDGET

Factory overhead costs are budgeted for various levels of production. Total costs are separated into fixed components (assigned by dollar values) and variable components (assigned by rates and based on direct labor hours). The formula used to determine total factory overhead is:

Fixed overhead per item + (total budgeted direct labor hours × variable expense rate per hour)

EXAMPLE 6

Coates Corporation
Factory Overhead Budget
January, 19XX

Direct Labor Hours: 2,640

Type of Expense	Fixed	Variable	Total
Indirect materials	$2,000		$ 2,000
Indirect labor	900	$3,168 (*a*)	4,068
Maintenance	1,200	3,432 (*b*)	4,632
Heat and light	300		300
Power	200	4,092 (*c*)	4,292
Insurance	270		270
Depreciation	1,350		1,350
Taxes	600		600
Payroll taxes		2,904 (*d*)	2,904
Total	$6,820	$13,596	$20,416

(a) 2,640 × $1.20 = $3,168.
(b) 2,640 × $1.30 = $3,432.
(c) 2,640 × $1.55 = $4,092.
(d) 2,640 × $1.10 = $2,904.

Coates Corporation
Factory Overhead Budget
February, 19XX

Direct Labor Hours: 4,740

Type of Expense	Fixed	Variable	Total
Indirect materials	$2,000		$ 2,000
Indirect labor	900	$5,688 (*a*)	6,588
Maintenance	1,200	6,162 (*b*)	7,362
Heat and light	300		300
Power	200	7,347 (*c*)	7,547
Insurance	270		270
Depreciation	1,350		1,350
Taxes	600		600
Payroll taxes		5,214 (*d*)	5,214
Total	$6,820	$24,411	$31,231

(a) 4,740 × $1.20 = $5,688.
(b) 4,740 × $1.30 = $6,162.
(c) 4,740 × $1.55 = $7,347.
(d) 4,740 × $1.10 = $5,214.

Coates Corporation
Factory Overhead Budget
March, 19XX

Direct Labor Hours: 2,370

Type of Expense	Fixed	Variable	Total
Indirect materials	$2,000		$ 2,000.00
Indirect labor	900	$2,844.00 (*a*)	3,744.00
Maintenance	1,200	3,081.00 (*b*)	4,281.00
Heat and light	300		300.00
Power	200	3,673.50 (*c*)	3,873.50
Insurance	270		270.00
Depreciation	1,350		1,350.00
Taxes	600		600.00
Payroll taxes		2,607.00 (*d*)	2,607.00
Total	$6,820	$12,205.50	$19,025.50

(a) 2,370 × $1.20 = $2,844.00.
(b) 2,370 × $1.30 = $3,081.00.
(c) 2,370 × $1.55 = $3,673.50.
(d) 2,370 × $1.10 = $2,607.00.

Coates Corporation
Factory Overhead Budget
First Quarter, 19XX

Month	Amount
January	$20,416.00
February	31,231.00
March	19,025.50
Total	$70,672.50

7.9 ENDING INVENTORIES BUDGET

Budgeted inventory amounts of direct materials and finished goods at month's end are needed for the financial statements. Ending inventory cost is computed as follows:

Ending inventory (units) × Standard cost per unit

EXAMPLE 7

Coates Corporation
Ending Inventories Budget
First Quarter, 19XX

	Ending Inventory (Units)	Standard Cost per Unit	Total Cost
January	900	$84	$ 75,600
February	980	$84	$ 82,320
March	1,100	$84	$ 92,400
			$250,320

Note: The approximate standard unit cost for finished goods is the average of the total manufacturing costs for one unit, calculated as follows:

$$\frac{\text{Direct materials usage budget} + \text{Direct labor budget} + \text{Factory overhead budget}}{\text{Production budget}}$$

For the Coates Corp. this translates into:

$$\frac{\$81{,}250 \text{ (Example 4)} + \$119{,}437.50 \text{ (Example 5)} + \$70{,}672.50 \text{ (Example 6)}}{880 + 1{,}580 + 790} = \frac{\$271{,}360}{3{,}250} = \$83.495$$

which equals approximately $84.

7.10 COST OF GOODS SOLD BUDGET

The component parts of this budget are found in previous budgets.

EXAMPLE 8

Coates Corporation
Cost of Goods Sold Budget
First Quarter, 19XX

	Jan.	Feb.	Mar.	Total
Direct materials (Example 4)	$22,000	$ 39,500	$ 19,750.00	$ 81,250.00
Direct labor (Example 5)	32,340	58,065	29,032.50	119,437.50
Factory overhead (Example 6)	20,416	31,231	19,025.50	70,672.50
Total manufacturing costs	$74,756	$128,796	$67,808.00	$271,360.00
Add: Finished goods, beginning*	(950 × $84) 79,800	(900 × $84) 75,600	(980 × $84) 82,320.00	79,800.00
Subtotal	$154,556	$204,396	$150,128.00	$351,160.00
Less: Finished goods, ending (Example 7)	75,600	82,320	92,400.00	92,400.00
Cost of goods sold	$78,956	$122,076	$57,728.00	$258,760.00

* *Calculation*: Beginning inventory (Example 2) × Standard cost per unit of finished goods (Example 7).

7.11 SELLING EXPENSE BUDGET

This budget is usually divided into its variable and fixed components; the variable costs fluctuate with sales, and the fixed costs remain constant per month. The formula used is

Fixed expenses per item + [Sales dollars × Variable expense rate (%)]

EXAMPLE 9

Coates Corporation
Selling Expense Budget
January, 19XX

Type of Expense	Fixed	Variable	Total
Salaries	$1,400		$ 1,400
Commissions		$ 6,975 (*a*)	6,975
Travel		4,185 (*b*)	4,185
Advertising		9,765 (*c*)	9,765
Selling	1,300		1,300
Total	$2,700	$20,925	$23,625

(a) 5% × $139,500 = $6,975.
(b) 3% × $139,500 = $4,185.
(c) 7% × $139,500 = $9,765.

Coates Corporation
Selling Expense Budget
February, 19XX

Type of Expense	Fixed	Variable	Total
Salaries	$1,400		$ 1,400
Commissions		$11,250 (*a*)	11,250
Travel		6,750 (*b*)	6,750
Advertising		15,750 (*c*)	15,750
Selling	1,300		1,300
Total	$2,700	$33,750	$36,450

(a) 5% × $225,000 = $11,250.
(b) 3% × $225,000 = $ 6,750.
(c) 7% × $225,000 = $15,750.

Coates Corporation
Selling Expense Budget
March, 19XX

Type of Expense	Fixed	Variable	Total
Salaries	$1,400		$ 1,400
Commissions		$ 5,025 (*a*)	5,025
Travel		3,015 (*b*)	3,015
Advertising		7,035 (*c*)	7,035
Selling	1,300		1,300
Total	$2,700	$15,075	$17,775

(a) 5% × $100,500 = $5,025.
(b) 3% × $100,500 = $3,015.
(c) 7% × $100,500 = $7,035.

7.12 ADMINISTRATIVE EXPENSE BUDGET

Administrative expenses are generally fixed in nature; therefore, the budget prepared for one month can be used for every month.

EXAMPLE 10

Coates Corporation
Administrative Expense Budget
Per Month, 19XX

Type of Expense	
Executive salaries	$2,000
Other administrative expense	1,500
Total	$3,500

7.13 BUDGETED INCOME STATEMENT

The final result of all the operations budgets, such as those for sales, cost of goods sold, selling expenses, and administrative expenses, is summarized in the budgeted income statement.

EXAMPLE 11

Coates Corporation
Budgeted Income Statement
First Quarter, 19XX

Supporting Budgets	Jan.	Feb.	Mar.	Total
Sales (Example 1)	$139,500.00	$225,000.00	$100,500.00	$465,000.00
Cost of goods sold (Example 8)	78,956.00	122,076.00	57,728.00	258,760.00
Gross profit (loss)	$ 60,544.00	$102,924.00	$ 42,772.00	$206,240.00
Operating Expenses				
Selling expenses (Example 9)	$ 23,625.00	$ 36,450.00	$ 17,775.00	$ 77,850.00
Administrative (Example 10)	3,500.00	3,500.00	3,500.00	10,500.00
Total operating expenses	$ 27,125.00	$ 39,950.00	$ 21,275.00	$ 88,350.00
Net income before taxes	$ 33,419.00	$ 62,974.00	$ 21,497.00	$117,890.00
Less: Income taxes (50%)	16,709.50	31,487.00	10,748.50	58,945.00
Net income	$ 16,709.50	$ 31,487.00	$ 10,748.50	$ 58,945.00

7.14 CASH BUDGET

Cash budgets are useful for stabilizing a company's cash balances and for keeping these balances reasonably close to continuing cash requirements. To prepare a cash budget, the following information is needed: the beginning cash balance, cash receipts for that period, and cash disbursements for that period.

The estimated amount of cash collections from accounts receivable is based on the cash collection experience of the company. For Coates Corporation a study shows that 10% of the company's current month's credit sales are collected during the same month, as well as 85% of the credit sales made the previous month and 5% of the credit sales made 2 months earlier.

EXAMPLE 12

For this example, assume that all monies due from November sales have been collected by January 1, 19XX. Sales figures are as follows:

	Dec.	Jan.	Feb.	Mar.
Total sales	$153,000	$139,500	$225,000	$100,500
Cash sales	5,300	4,500	8,000	3,500
Credit sales	$147,700	$135,000	$217,000	$ 97,000

Coates Corporation
Cash Receipts Forecast
First Quarter, 19XX

Month of Sale	Credit Sales	Collections Jan.	Feb.	Mar.
December	$147,700			
85%		$125,545		
5%			$ 7,385	
January	135,000			
10%		13,500		
85%			114,750	
5%				$ 6,750
February	217,000			
10%			21,700	
85%				184,450
March	97,000			
10%				9,700
Total		$139,045	$143,835	$200,900

Cash disbursements are based on payments for purchases of direct materials. Payments are 60% in the month of purchase and 40% in the next month.

EXAMPLE 13

Coates Corporation
Cash Disbursements Forecast—Direct Materials
First Quarter, 19XX

	Purchases	Accounts Payable Jan.	Feb.	Mar.
December	$25,750			
40%		$10,300		
January	27,250			
60%		16,350		
40%			$10,900	
February	33,575			
60%			20,145	
40%				$13,430
March	18,325			
60%				10,995
Total		$26,650	$31,045	$24,425

To prepare the cash budget, the following information is needed:

(1) Cash balance, beginning (CBB)
(2) Cash receipts for the period (CR)
(3) Cash disbursements for the period (CD)

The formula then is

$$\text{Cash balance, ending (CBE)} = \text{CBB} + \text{CR} - \text{CD}$$

EXAMPLE 14

Assume that a minimum balance of $3,000 cash is to be maintained by the company during 19XX.

Coates Corporation
Cash Budget
First Quarter, 19XX

	Jan.	Feb.	Mar.	Quarter
Cash balance, beginning	$ 20,700.00	$ 42,354.50	$ 3,761.50	$ 20,700.00
Cash Receipts				
Collections on account	$139,045.00	$143,835.00	$200,900.00	$483,780.00
Cash sales	4,500.00	8,000.00	3,500.00	16,000.00
Total cash receipts	$143,545.00	$151,835.00	$204,400.00	$499,780.00
Total cash available	$164,245.00	$194,189.50	$208,161.50	$520,480.00
Cash Disbursements				
Direct materials	$ 26,650.00	$ 31,045.00	$ 24,425.00	$ 82,120.00
Direct labor	32,340.00	58,065.00	29,032.50	119,437.50
Factory overhead	19,066.00 (*a*)	29,881.00 (*b*)	17,675.50 (*c*)	66,622.50
Selling expenses	23,625.00	36,450.00	17,775.00	77,850.00
Administrative expenses	3,500.00	3,500.00	3,500.00	10,500.00
Income taxes	16,709.50	31,487.00	10,748.50	58,945.00
Total cash disbursements	$121,890.50	$190,428.00	$103,156.50	$415,475.00
Ending balance	$ 42,354.50	$ 3,761.50	$105,005.00	$105,005.00

(a) $20,416 − $1,350 depreciation = $19,066.00.
(b) $31,231 − $1,350 depreciation = $29,881.00.
(c) $19,025.50 − $1,350 depreciation = $17,675.50.

7.15 BUDGETED BALANCE SHEET

Useful for showing a company's financial position, the balance sheet is derived by the formula

$$\text{Assets} = \text{Liabilities} + \text{Equity}$$

EXAMPLE 15

Coates Corporation
Budgeted Balance Sheet
March 31, 19XX

Assets

Current			
Cash		$105,005	
Accounts receivable (*a*)		98,150	
Materials (*b*)		4,500	
Finished goods (*c*)		92,400	
Total			$ 300,055
Plant			
Equipment	$ 75,000		
Less: Accumulated depreciation (*d*)	9,570	$ 65,430	
Building	$800,000		
Less: Accumulated depreciation (*e*)	50,080	749,920	
Total			815,350
Total assets			$1,115,405

Liabilities and Stockholders' Equity

Liabilities		
Accounts payable (*f*)		$ 7,330
Stockholders' Equity		
Common stock, $10 par; 90,000 shares issued and outstanding	$900,000	
Retained earnings (*g*)	208,075	
Total		$1,108,075
Total liabilities and stockholders' equity		$1,115,405

(a) Outstanding accounts = 5% of February sales ($217,000)	$10,850
+ 90% of March sales ($97,000) (see Example 12)	87,300
	$98,150
(b) Materials beginning inventory (Jan. 1 units from Example 3)	264
Add: Purchases for the quarter (units)	3,166
Materials available for use	3,430
Less: Production for the quarter (units from Example 2)	3,250
Total materials ending inventory (Mar. 31 units from Example 3)	180
Units cost	× $25
Cost of materials inventory	$4,500
(c) Finished goods inventory (Mar. 31 units from Example 2)	1,100
Standard cost per unit (Example 7)	× $84
Cost of finished goods inventory	$92,400
(d) Accumulated depreciation of equipment, Jan. 1	$7,140
Add: Depreciation for the quarter ($1,350 × 3 months × 60%)	2,430
Accumulated depreciation of equipment, Mar. 31	$9,570

(e) Accumulated depreciation of buildings, Jan. 1	$48,460
Add: Depreciation for the quarter ($1,350 × 3 months × 40%)	1,620
Accumulated depreciation of buildings, Mar. 31	$50,080
(f) 40% of March purchases ($18,325 from Example 13)	$7,330
(g) Retained earnings, Jan. 1	$149,130
Add: Net income for the quarter (Example 11)	58,945
Retained earnings, Mar. 31	$208,075

Solved Problems

7.1 Production Budget. The Tarver Manufacturing Company has estimated its sales budget at 500,000 units for the quarter ending March 31, 19X1. Anticipated sales for January, February, and March are 37.5%, 25%, and 37.5% of the total, respectively. The desired finished goods inventories are as follows:

	Units
January 1	90,000
January 31	87,500
February 28	93,000
March 31	95,000

Prepare a production budget for the first quarter of 19X1.

SOLUTION

Tarver Manufacturing Company
Production Budget
First Quarter, 19X1

	Units			
	January	**February**	**March**	**Total**
Sales budget	187,500	125,000	187,500	500,000
Add: Desired ending inventory	87,500	93,000	95,000	95,000
Subtotal	275,000	218,000	282,500	595,000
Less: Beginning inventory	90,000	87,500	93,000	90,000
Production units required	185,000	130,500	189,500	505,000

7.2 Direct Materials Purchase Budget. Jimmy Manufacturing Company has estimated its 19X0 production requirements to be as follows:

April	1,500
May	2,000
June	2,500
July	2,800

The company wants a direct materials ending inventory of 35% of the next month's production. The price per unit is $20, and it takes one unit of direct materials to produce one of finished goods. Prepare a direct materials purchase budget for the second quarter of 19X0.

SOLUTION

Jimmy Manufacturing Company
Direct Materials Purchase Budget
Second Quarter, 19X0

	April	May	June	Total
Production units required	1,500	2,000	2,500	6,000
Add: Desired ending	(35% × 2,000)	(35% × 2,500)	(35% × 2,800)	
inventory	700	875	980	980
Subtotal	2,200	2,875	3,480	6,980
Less: Beginning	(35% × 1,500)	(35% × 2,000)	(35% × 2,500)	
inventory	525	700	875	525
Purchases required	1,675	2,175	2,605	6,455
Cost per unit	× $20	× $20	× $20	× $20
Purchases cost	$33,500	$43,500	$52,100	$129,100

7.3 Direct Materials Usage Budget. Using the data for the Jimmy Manufacturing Company in the preceding problem, prepare a direct materials usage budget.

SOLUTION

Jimmy Manufacturing Company
Direct Materials Usage Budget
Second Quarter, 19X0

	April	May	June	Total
Direct materials required (units)	1,500	2,000	2,500	6,000
Materials unit cost	× $20	× $20	× $20	× $20
Direct materials usage cost	$30,000	$40,000	$50,000	$120,000

7.4 Direct Labor Budget. The Carter Manufacturing Company estimates its production requirement to be 30,000 units for October; 38,000 for November; and 41,000 for December. It takes 3 direct labor hours, at a rate of $15 per hour, to complete one unit. Prepare a direct labor budget.

SOLUTION

Carter Manufacturing Company
Direct Labor Budget
Third Quarter

	Oct.	Nov.	Dec.	Total
Production units required	30,000	38,000	41,000	109,000
Direct labor hours (3 per unit)	90,000	114,000	123,000	327,000
Rate per hour	× $15	× $15	× $15	× $15
Direct labor cost	$1,350,000	$1,710,000	$1,845,000	$4,905,000

7.5 Factory Overhead Budget. The Rogers Manufacturing Company estimates its factory overhead to be as follows:

Fixed Expenses per Month

Indirect materials	$2,000
Indirect labor	900
Maintenance	200
Heat and light	500
Power	350
Insurance	540
Taxes	700
Depreciation	1,200

Variable Factory Overhead Rates per Direct Labor Hour

Indirect labor	$0.25
Payroll taxes	0.10
Maintenance	0.30
Power	0.50
Heat and light	0.30

Assuming that the direct labor hours for January, February, and March are 2,500, 4,000, and 3,500 hours, respectively, prepare a factory overhead budget for the first quarter, 19X1.

SOLUTION

Rogers Manufacturing Company
Factory Overhead Budget

January 19X1
Direct Labor Hours: 2,500

Type of Expense	Fixed	Variable	Total
Indirect materials	$2,000		$ 2,000
Indirect labor	900	$ 625	1,525
Maintenance	200	750	950
Heat and light	500	750	1,250
Power	350	1,250	1,600
Insurance	540		540
Taxes	700		700
Payroll taxes		250	250
Depreciation	1,200		1,200
Total	$6,390	$3,625	$10,015

February, 19X1
Direct Labor Hours: 4,000

Indirect materials	$2,000		$ 2,000
Indirect labor	900	$1,000	1,900
Maintenance	200	1,200	1,400
Heat and light	500	1,200	1,700
Power	350	2,000	2,350
Insurance	540		540
Taxes	700		700
Payroll taxes		400	400
Depreciation	1,200		1,200
Total	$6,390	$5,800	$12,190

March, 19X1
Direct Labor Hours: 3,500

Indirect materials	$2,000		$ 2,000
Indirect labor	900	$ 875	1,775
Maintenance	200	1,050	1,250
Heat and light	500	1,050	1,550
Power	350	1,750	2,100
Insurance	540		540
Taxes	700		700
Payroll taxes		350	350
Depreciation	1,200		1,200
Total	$6,390	$5,075	$11,465

7.6 **Cost of Goods Sold Budget.** The Reagan Company has estimated the percentage of total manufacturing cost for each month in relation to the total for the second quarter to be as follows:

April	30%
May	34%
June	36%

The estimated costs for the second quarter are

Direct materials	$100,000
Direct labor	120,000
Factory overhead	90,000

Estimated ending inventories of finished goods are as follows:

March 31	$50,000
April 30	48,000
May 31	56,000
June 30	59,000

Prepare a quarterly cost of goods sold budget.

SOLUTION

Reagan Company
Cost of Goods Sold Budget
Second Quarter

	April	May	June	Total
Direct materials	$ 30,000 (a)	$ 34,000 (b)	$ 36,000 (c)	$100,000
Direct labor	36,000	40,800	43,200	120,000
Factory overhead	27,000	30,600	32,400	90,000
Total manufacturing cost	$ 93,000	$105,400	$111,600	$310,000
Add: Finished goods, beginning	50,000	48,000	56,000	90,000
Subtotal	$143,000	$153,400	$167,600	$360,000
Less: Finished goods, ending	48,000	56,000	59,000	59,000
Cost of goods sold	$ 95,000	$ 97,400	$108,600	$301,000

(a) $100,000 × 30%. (b) $100,000 × 34%. (c) $100,000 × 36%.

7.7 Budgeted Income Statement. The T&M Wild Corporation anticipates sales of $900,000 for the current year. The percentage of gross profit from sales has been 40% in past years. Operating expenses are expected to be $200,000, of which 45% is administrative expenses and 55% is selling expenses. Assuming a 40% tax rate, prepare a budgeted income statement for the T&M Wild Corporation for 19X2.

SOLUTION

T&M Wild Corporation
Budgeted Income Statement
Year Ended, December, 19X2

Sales	$900,000	100%
Cost of goods sold	540,000	60%
Gross profit	$360,000	40%
Operating expenses		
Selling expenses (55%)	$110,000	12%
Administrative expenses (45%)	90,000	10%
Total (100%)	$200,000	22%
Net income before taxes	$160,000	18%
Income tax (40%)	64,000	7%
Net Income	$96,000	11%

7.8 Cash Budget. The Martha Corporation's budget department gathered the following data for the third quarter, 19X9:

	July	August	September
Projected sales (units)	1,000	1,500	1,450
Selling price per unit	$40	$40	$40
Direct materials purchase requirements (units)	1,300	2,000	1,800
Purchase cost per unit	$20	$20	$20
Production requirement (units)	800	1,300	1,100

Direct labor hours	2 per complete unit	
Direct labor rate	$12 per direct labor hour	
Fixed factory overhead	$500 per month (including $200 depreciation)	
Variable factory overhead	$1.50 per direct labor hour	
Selling and administrative expenses	5% of sales	
Net income before taxes	July	$ 6,000
	August	10,000
	September	8,000

All sales and purchases are for cash, and all expenses are paid in the month incurred. Assuming that the beginning cash balance on July 1, 19X9, is $65,000 and the tax rate is 40%, prepare a cash budget for the third quarter, 19X9.

SOLUTION

Martha Corporation
Cash Budget
Third Quarter, 19X9

	July	Aug.	Sept.	Total
Cash balance, beginning	$ 65,000	$ 52,700	$30,300	$ 65,000
Cash Receipts				
Cash sales	40,000 (a)	60,000	58,000	158,000
Total cash available	$105,000	$112,700	$88,300	$223,000
Cash Disbursements				
Direct materials	$ 26,000 (b)	$ 40,000	$36,000	$102,000
Direct labor	19,200 (c)	31,200	26,400	76,800
Factory overhead	2,700 (d)	4,200	3,600	10,500
Selling and administrative expenses	2,000 (e)	3,000	2,900	7,900
Income taxes	2,400 (f)	4,000	3,200	9,600
Total	$ 52,300	$ 82,400	$72,100	$206,800
Ending balance	$ 52,700	$ 30,300	$16,200	$ 16,200

(a) 1,000 units × $40 = $40,000.

(b) 1,300 units × $20 = $26,000.

(c) 800 units × 2 hours per unit = 1,600 hours × $12 per hour = $19,200.

(d) $500 − $200 depreciation	$ 300	fixed (depreciation removed because it is not an outflow of cash.)
1,600 hours × $1.50	2,400	variable
	$2,700	

(e) $40,000 × 5% = $2,000.

(f) $6,000 net income before taxes × 40% = $2,400.

Chapter 8

Standard Costs and Gross Profit Analysis

Standard Costs

8.1 STANDARD COSTS DEFINED

A carefully prepared predetermined or normal standard cost is expressed in terms of a single unit. It represents a product's planned cost and is generally established well before production begins, thus providing a goal to aim for. Standard cost is concerned with unit cost and serves basically the same purpose as a budget, but on a smaller scale, since the latter is concerned with total rather than unit costs.

8.2 TYPES OF STANDARDS

(1) ***Fixed or Basic Standards.*** These are rarely used because once established, these standards are never changed.

(2) ***Ideal Standards.*** Usually these standards cannot be attained and lead to unfavorable variances because they assume:

(A) Minimum prices for all costs (direct materials, direct labor, and factory overhead)

(B) Optimal usage of direct materials, direct labor, and factory overhead

(C) 100% manufacturing capacity

(3) ***Attainable Standards.*** These are standards that can be met even though based on a high degree of efficiency because they recognize:

(A) Good overall prices can be obtained but not necessarily the lowest prices for all costs (direct materials, direct labor, and factory overhead).

(B) Direct labor is not 100% efficient.

(C) Normal spoilage will occur.

(D) Manufacturers do not operate at 100% capacity.

8.3 ESTABLISHMENT OF STANDARDS

(1) ***Direct Materials Standards***

(A) *Direct Materials Price (Rate) Standard.* This standard, which is the unit price for direct materials, must be set for each type of direct material used in production. The determination of this standard includes knowledge of expected production as well as the price/quality relationship of various suppliers.

Since prices are subject to change, a weighted average standard price per unit must be used or, preferably, the standard price per unit should be adjusted as needed.

(B) *Direct Materials Efficiency (Usage) Standard.* This standard is determined as the quantity of direct materials that should be used in each unit produced. Each direct material requires its own standard. This standard is usually based on prior experience and/or engineering studies.

(2) ***Direct Labor Standards***

(A) *Direct Labor Price Standard.* This standard is based upon the predetermined direct labor rates for the period. Changes in labor rates are handled in the same way as changes in direct material rates.

(B) *Direct Labor Efficiency Standard.* This standard is the number of direct labor hours needed to complete one unit. Time and motion studies, taking into consideration the experience of workers, are often used to set this standard.

(3) ***Factory Overhead Standards*** Before this standard can be determined, factory overhead costs must be separated into their fixed and variable components. Separate fixed and variable factory overhead standards are then established based upon past costs and expected economic conditions.

The factory overhead standard is normally expressed in terms of the allocation base used, such as direct labor hours or cost or machine hours.

8.4 ESTABLISHING STANDARDS IN PROCESS AND JOB ORDER COST SYSTEMS

Standards for direct materials, direct labor, and factory overhead are determined by department in a process cost system and by job in a job order cost system.

EXAMPLE 1

Next year the Broadway Company expects to manufacture 2,000 pairs of theater curtains which will sell for $400 per pair. The total amount of direct materials required is 48,000 yards of fabric which can be purchased from a wholesaler for $2 per yard.

Two workers are involved in production—one to cut the fabric and the other to sew the curtains. It takes one hour to cut each pair of curtains, and that worker is paid $10 per hour. It then takes one hour to sew the curtains, and that worker is paid $8 per hour.

The factory overhead to produce 2,000 pairs of curtains is budgeted at $6,000 for variable costs and $8,000 for fixed costs.

All processing is accomplished in one department. The factory closes for two weeks at Christmas.

Direct materials price standard	$2/yard
Direct materials efficiency standard	24 yards/pair
Direct labor price standard ($36,000/4,000)*	$9/direct labor hour

* Computation of total annual direct labor hours and cost:

	Direct Labor Hours/ Week	×	Weeks/ Year	=	Total Annual Direct Labor Hours	×	Hourly Rate/ Direct Labor Hour	=	Total Annual Direct Labor Cost
Worker 1	40		50		2,000		$10.00		$20,000
Worker 2	40		50		2,000		8.00		16,000
					4,000				$36,000

Direct labor efficiency standard:

Worker 1: 1 hour; Worker 2: 1 hour = 2 direct labor hours/pair of curtains

Variable factory overhead application rate:

$$\frac{\$6{,}000}{4{,}000 \text{ direct labor hours}} = \$1.50/\text{direct labor hour}$$

Fixed factory overhead application rate:

$$\frac{\$8{,}000}{4{,}000 \text{ direct labor hours}} = \$2.00/\text{direct labor hour}$$

Total factory overhead application rate:

$$\frac{\$14{,}000}{4{,}000 \text{ direct labor hours}} = \$3.50/\text{direct labor hour}$$

8.5 QUALITY CONTROL

When standard costs are established, the company must consider its policy regarding quality control. If products are defective, rework costs and potential liability claims will increase the costs of the company.

A company should consider such quality items as quality specification (design quality); workmanship (production quality); and product reliability (expectation of satisfactory operation for a specific time under normal usage conditions).

An important element of quality control known as a *zero defect program* is aimed at eliminating defects and therefore improving quality in the product line. It assumes that defects are caused by lack of knowledge, lack of proper facilities, and lack of attention.

A zero defect program conditions employees to realize that defects need not happen. It challenges the individual to establish goals for superior performance and to strive for personal excellence. As an employee achieves this, defects are reduced, and the quality of the product improves. Such a program also provides recognition of individual achievement.

8.6 JUST-IN-TIME PHILOSOPHY

The greater use of automated equipment in the production process has substantially reduced the direct labor content of products while increasing fixed factory overhead costs. The effect is twofold. First, direct labor used to apply factory overhead costs is probably no longer an appropriate base. Second, as increased factory overhead costs are spread over products, inventories build up for finished goods not sold.

An alternative is to reduce costs using a just-in-time (JIT) philosophy. JIT analyzes manufacturing time as:

(1) ***Processing Time.*** Actual time a product is worked on.

(2) ***Inspection Time.*** Inspection of raw materials and of the product at different manufacturing stages to determine if it conforms to standards. Also includes any necessary rework costs.

(3) ***Moving Time.*** The time it takes to move a product from one department to the next.

(4) ***Queue or Waiting Time.*** The time the product remains in a production department before it is worked on.

(5) ***Storage Time.*** The time raw materials, work-in-process, and finished products remain in storage before they are used by a production department or sold.

The sum of these five times is called *throughput time*. It can be seen that only one of these times is actually processing time, i.e., time worked on the product. This processing time is sometimes called *value-added time*. The remaining four times are called *nonvalue-added time* or *waste time*. This can be summarized in the following equation:

$$\text{Throughput time} = \begin{matrix}\text{Value-added time}\\ \text{or}\\ \text{Processing time}\end{matrix} + \begin{matrix}\text{Nonvalue-added time}\\ \text{or}\\ \text{Waste time}\end{matrix}$$

The philosophy of JIT is to identify the *causes* of waste time and implement strategies that will minimize throughput time. Some strategies include:

(1) *Reduce inspection time* by improving quality.

(2) *Reduce moving time* by better plant design.

(3) *Reduce queue (waiting) time* by better coordination among production departments. Better quality will move a product more smoothly and more efficiently. Better design of products and equipment will reduce *set-up time*. Set-up time is the time it takes to reorganize the equipment to produce different product.

(4) *Reduce storage time* by working with suppliers for better delivery and better conformance to specifications to eliminate purchases of excess inventory. Better coordination among departments will reduce the need to store more finished goods.

The elimination of waste time in inspecting and storing raw materials is called *JIT purchasing*. The elimination of waste time in manufacturing the product is called *JIT manufacturing*. Elimination of waste time, that is, to have materials and finished products available *just in time*, will reduce costs.

8.7 VARIANCE ANALYSIS

The use of a standard cost system aids management in controlling costs. Once actual costs are incurred, the differences between the expected and the actual, called variances, are computed and analyzed.

Variances are used to evaluate performance and correct inefficiencies. Following is a list of the variances used in a standard cost system:

(1) ***Direct materials variances***

(A) *Direct materials price variance*

$$\text{Direct materials price variance} = \left(\text{Actual unit price} - \text{Standard unit price}\right) \times \text{Actual quantity purchased}$$

(B) *Direct materials efficiency (quantity or usage) variance*

$$\text{Direct materials efficiency variance} = \left(\text{Actual quantity used} - \text{Standard quantity allowed (a)}\right) \times \text{Standard unit price}$$

(a) $\text{Standard quantity allowed} = \text{Standard quantity per unit} \times \text{Equivalent production}$

(2) ***Direct labor variances***

(A) *Direct labor price (rate) variance*

$$\text{Direct labor price variance} = \left(\text{Actual hourly wage rate} - \text{Standard hourly wage rate}\right) \times \text{Actual number of direct labor hours worked}$$

(B) *Direct labor efficiency variance*

$$\text{Direct labor efficiency variance} = \left(\text{Actual direct labor hours worked} - \text{Standard direct labor hours allowed (b)}\right) \times \text{Standard direct labor hourly wage rate}$$

(b) $$\text{Standard direct labor hours allowed} = \text{Standard number of direct labor hours per unit} \times \text{Equivalent production}$$

(3) ***Factory Overhead Variances***

(A) *One-factor analysis of factory overhead variance*

$$\text{Overall factory overhead variance} = \text{Actual factory overhead} - \text{Applied factory overhead (c)}$$

(c) $$\text{Applied factory overhead} = \text{Standard direct labor hours allowed } (b) \times \text{Standard factory overhead application rate}$$

(B) *Two-factor analysis of factory overhead variances*. With this method, the factory overhead variance has two components: budget (controllable) variance and production volume (denominator or idle capacity) variance. The sum of these two components equals the one-factor variance.

(1) *Budget (controllable) variance*

$$\text{Budget (controllable) variance} = \text{Actual factory overhead} - \text{Budgeted factory overhead at standard direct labor hours allowed (d)}$$

(d) $$\text{Budgeted factory overhead at standard direct labor hours allowed} = \text{Variable factory overhead (standard direct labor hours allowed} \times \text{standard variable factory overhead application rate)} + \text{Fixed (budgeted) factory overhead}$$

(2) *Production volume (denominator or idle capacity) variance*

$$\text{Production volume (denominator or idle capacity) variance} = \left(\text{Denominator direct labor hours (e)} - \text{Standard direct labor hours allowed (f)}\right) \times \text{Standard fixed factory overhead application rate}$$

(e) The denominator direct labor hours are the original expected or normal capacity hours used to determine the factory overhead application rate.

(f) Standard direct labor hours allowed. See (*b*) above.

(C) *Three-factor analysis of factory overhead variances.* With this method, the factory overhead variance has three components: price (spending) variance, efficiency variance, and production volume variance.

The sum of the price (spending) variance and the efficiency variance equals the budget variance in the two-factor analysis. The production volume variance is computed the same way as in the two-factor analysis.

The sum of the three components equals the same total variance as resulted from the one- and two-factor analyses of factory overhead variances.

(1) *Price (spending) variance*

$$\text{Price (spending) variance} = \text{Actual factory ovehead} - \text{Budgeted factory overhead at actual direct labor hours worked (f)}$$

(f) $$\text{Budgeted factory overhead at actual direct labor hours worked} = \text{Variable factory overhead (actual direct labor hrs. worked} \times \text{standard variable factory overhead application rate)} + \text{Fixed (budgeted) factory overhead}$$

(2) *Efficiency variance*

$$\text{Efficiency variance} = \left(\text{Actual direct labor hours worked} - \text{Standard direct labor hours allowed}\right) \times \text{Standard variable factory overhead application rate}$$

This variance will indicate if the workers were efficient (favorable variance) or inefficient (unfavorable variance).

(3) *Production volume variance.* Same as for two-factor analysis method.

EXAMPLE 2

Continuing with the illustration of the Broadway Company, summarized below are the standard and actual amounts:

	Standard	**Actual**
Direct materials purchased	48,000 yds @ \$2/yd	50,000 yds @ \$2.25
Direct materials used		44,000 yds
Direct materials efficiency standard	24 yds/pair	
Direct labor price standard	\$9/dlh	
Direct labor efficiency standard	2 dlh/pair	
Direct labor costs	\$36,000	\$40,000
Direct labor hours	4,000	3,900

	Standard	Actual
Factory overhead:		
Variable	$6,000 or $1.50/dlh*	$6,200
Fixed	$8,000 or $2/dlh	$7,500
Total	$14,000 or $3.50/dlh	$13,700
Production:		
Units started and completed	2,000	1,800
Work-in-process inventory—ending (100% direct materials, 50% conversion costs)	-0-	200

* dlh = direct labor hours

8.8 COMPUTATION OF VARIANCES

(1) *Direct Materials Price Variance*

$$\text{Direct materials price variance} = \left(\text{Actual unit price} - \text{Standard unit price}\right) \times \text{Actual quantity purchased}$$

$$= (\$2.25 - \$2.00) \times 50{,}000 \text{ yds}$$

$$\$12{,}500 \text{ Unfav.} = \$0.25 \times 50{,}000 \text{ yds}$$

(2) *Direct Materials Efficiency Variance*

$$\text{Direct materials efficiency variance} = \left(\text{Actual quantity used} - \text{Standard quantity allowed}\right) \times \text{Standard unit price}$$

$$= [44{,}000 - 48{,}000 \text{ (a)}] \times \$2.00$$

$$(\$8{,}000) \text{ Fav.} = -4{,}000 \times \$2.00$$

(a) $\text{Standard quantity allowed} = \text{Standard quantity per unit} \times \text{Equivalent production}$

$$48{,}000 = 24 \times \left(\begin{array}{l}1{,}800 \text{ units started and completed} \\ + 200 \text{ work-in-process inventory,} \\ \text{ending} \times 100\% \text{ direct materials}\end{array}\right)$$

(3) ***Direct Labor Price Variance***

$$\text{Direct labor price variance} = \left(\begin{array}{c}\text{Actual}\\ \text{hourly}\\ \text{wage rate}\end{array} - \begin{array}{c}\text{Standard}\\ \text{hourly}\\ \text{wage rate}\end{array}\right) \times \begin{array}{c}\text{Actual number}\\ \text{of direct labor}\\ \text{hours worked}\end{array}$$

$$= [(\$40{,}000/3{,}900 \text{ dlh}) - (\$36{,}000/4{,}000 \text{ dlh})] \times 3{,}900 \text{ dlh}$$

$$= (\$10.26 - \$9.00) \times 3{,}900 \text{ dlh}$$

$$\begin{array}{c}\$4{,}914\\ \text{Unfav.}\end{array} = \$1.26 \times 3{,}900 \text{ dlh}$$

(4) ***Direct Labor Efficiency Variance***

$$\text{Direct labor efficiency variance} = \left(\begin{array}{c}\text{Actual direct}\\ \text{labor hours}\\ \text{worked}\end{array} - \begin{array}{c}\text{Standard direct}\\ \text{labor hours}\\ \text{allowed}\end{array}\right) \times \begin{array}{c}\text{Standard direct}\\ \text{labor hourly}\\ \text{wage rate}\end{array}$$

$$= [3{,}900 - 3{,}800 \text{ (b)}] \times \$9.00/\text{dlh}$$

$$\begin{array}{c}\$900\\ \text{Unfav.}\end{array} = 100 \times \$9.00/\text{dlh}$$

$$\text{(b) } \begin{array}{c}\text{Standard direct}\\ \text{labor hours}\\ \text{allowed}\end{array} = \begin{array}{c}\text{Standard number of}\\ \text{direct labor}\\ \text{hours per unit}\end{array} \times \begin{array}{c}\text{Equivalent}\\ \text{production}\end{array}$$

$$3{,}800 = 2 \text{ dlh/pair} \times \left(\begin{array}{l}\text{1,800 units started \&}\\ \text{completed + 100 work-}\\ \text{in-process inventory,}\\ \text{50\% conversion costs}\\ (200 \text{ pair} \times .50)\end{array}\right)$$

(5) ***Factory Overhead Variance***

(A) *One-factor analysis*

$$\begin{array}{c}\text{Overall factory}\\ \text{overhead variance}\end{array} = \begin{array}{c}\text{Actual factory}\\ \text{overhead}\end{array} - \begin{array}{c}\text{Applied factory}\\ \text{overhead}\end{array}$$

$$\begin{array}{c}\$400\\ \text{Unfav.}\end{array} = \$13{,}700 - \$13{,}300 \text{ (c)}$$

$$\text{(c) } \begin{array}{c}\text{Applied}\\ \text{factory}\\ \text{overhead}\end{array} = \begin{array}{c}\text{Standard direct}\\ \text{labor hours allowed}\\ \text{[see (}b\text{) above]}\end{array} \times \begin{array}{c}\text{Standard factory}\\ \text{overhead}\\ \text{application rate}\end{array}$$

$$\$13{,}300 = 3{,}800 \times \$3.50$$

(B) *Two-factor analysis*

(1) Budget (controllable) variance

$$\text{Budget (controllable) variance} = \text{Actual factory overhead} - \text{Budgeted factory overhead at standard direct labor hours allowed}$$

$$\$\text{-0-} = \$13{,}700 - \$13{,}700\ (d)$$

(d) Budgeted factory overhead at standard direct labor hours allowed = Variable factory overhead (standard direct labor hours allowed × standard variable factory overhead application rate) + Fixed (budgeted) factory overhead

= [3,800 (see (*b*) above) × $1.50] + $8,000

$13,700 = $5,700 + $8,000

(2) *Production volume (denominator or idle capacity) variance*

$$\text{Production volume (denominator or idle capacity) variance} = \left(\text{Denominator direct labor hours} - \text{Standard direct labor hours allowed}\right) \times \text{Standard fixed factory overhead application rate}$$

$$= [4{,}000\ \text{dlh (e)} - 3{,}800\ \text{dlh}] \times \$2.00$$

$$\$400\ \text{Unfav.} = 200\ \text{dlh} \times 2.00$$

(e) The 4,000 dlh denominator is the original standard direct labor hours.

Budget variance + Production volume variance = Overall factory overhead variance (as in the one-factor analysis method)

-0- + $400 Unfav. = $400 Unfav.

(C) *Three-factor analysis*

(1) *Price (spending) variance*

$$\text{Price (spending) variance} = \text{Actual factory overhead} - \text{Budgeted factory overhead at actual direct labor hours worked}$$

$$(\$150)\ \text{Fav.} = \$13{,}700 - \$13{,}850\ (f)$$

(f) Budgeted factory overhead at actual direct labor hours worked = Variable factory overhead (actual direct labor hours worked × standard variable factory overhead application rate) + Fixed (budgeted) factory overhead

= (3,900 × $1.50) + $8,000

$13,850 = 5,850 + $8,000

(2) *Efficiency variance*

$$\text{Efficiency variance} = \left(\begin{array}{c}\text{Actual}\\\text{direct}\\\text{labor hours}\\\text{worked}\end{array} - \begin{array}{c}\text{Standard}\\\text{direct}\\\text{labor hours}\\\text{allowed}\end{array}\right) \times \begin{array}{c}\text{Standard variable}\\\text{factory overhead}\\\text{application rate}\end{array}$$

$$= (3{,}900 \text{ dlh} - 3{,}800 \text{ dlh}) \times \$1.50$$

$$\begin{array}{c}(\$150)\\\text{Unfav.}\end{array} = 100 \text{ dlh} \times \$1.50$$

$$\text{Price variance} + \text{Efficiency variance} = \begin{array}{c}\text{Budget variance (as in the}\\\text{two-factor analysis method)}\end{array}$$

$$\begin{array}{c}(\$150)\\\text{Fav.}\end{array} + \begin{array}{c}\$150\\\text{Unfav.}\end{array} = \$\text{-0-}$$

(3) *Production volume variance:* Same as calculated in the two-factor analysis method. $400 Unfav.

$$\begin{array}{c}\text{Price}\\\text{variance}\end{array} + \begin{array}{c}\text{Efficiency}\\\text{variance}\end{array} + \begin{array}{c}\text{Production}\\\text{variance}\end{array} = \begin{array}{c}\text{Overall factory overhead}\\\text{variance (as in the one-}\\\text{factor analysis method)}\end{array}$$

$$\begin{array}{c}(\$150)\\\text{Fav.}\end{array} + \begin{array}{c}\$150\\\text{Unfav.}\end{array} + \begin{array}{c}\$400\\\text{Unfav.}\end{array} = \begin{array}{c}\$400\\\text{Unfav.}\end{array}$$

8.9 JOURNAL ENTRIES IN A STANDARD COST SYSTEM

Standard costs are recorded as journal entries in addition to actual costs recorded for either job order or process cost systems.

In a standard cost system, work-in-process inventory, finished goods inventory, and cost of goods sold are maintained at standard cost. Separate variance accounts are established to record differences from the standard costs. Unfavorable variances are debit entries, and favorable variances are credit entries.

EXAMPLE 3

Continuing the example of the Broadway Company, the journal entries will be illustrated. The standard, actual, and variance data are summarized below:

	Standard	Actual	Variance
Direct materials purchased	48,000 yds @ $2/yd	50,000 yds @ $2.25	
Direct materials used		44,000 yds	
Direct materials efficiency standard	24 yds/ pair		
Direct labor price standard	$9/dlh		
Direct labor efficiency standard	2 dlh/pair		
Direct labor costs	$36,000	$40,000	
Direct labor hours	4,000	3,900	
Factory overhead:			
Variable	$6,000 or $1.50/dlh	$6,200	
Fixed	$8,000 or $2/dlh	$7,500	
Total	$14,000 or $3.50/dlh	13,700	

(Example 3 cont.)

	Standard	Actual	Variance
Production:			
Units started and completed	2,000	1,800	
Work-in-process inventory—ending (100% direct materials, 50% conversion costs)	-0-	200	
Units sold		1,600	
Variances:			
Direct materials price			$12,500 Unfav.
Direct materials efficiency			($ 8,000) Fav.
Direct labor price			$ 4,914 Unfav.
Direct labor efficiency			$ 900 Unfav.
Factory overhead:			
One-factor analysis			$ 400 Unfav.
Two-factor analysis:			
Budget			-0-
Production volume			$ 400 Unfav.
Three-factor analysis:			
Price			($ 150) Fav.
Efficiency			$ 150 Unfav.
Production volume			$ 400 Unfav.

	Direct Materials	**Conversion Costs**
Equivalent production:		
Started and completed	1,800	1,800
Work-in-process inventory	200 (100%)	100 (50%)
Total	2,000	1,900

To record the purchase of direct materials:

Materials inventory (50,000 yds × $2.00)	100,000	
Direct Materials price variance	12,500*	
Accounts payable (50,000 yds. × $2.25)		112,500

* ($2.25 − $2.00 = $.25 × 50,000 yds)

To record the use of direct materials:

Work-in-process inventory (2,000 equivalent production × 24 yds = 48,000 yds × $2)	96,000	
Direct materials efficiency variance (44,000 yds − 48,000 yds = 4,000 × $2)		8,000
Materials Inventory (44,000 yds × $2.00)		88,000

To record direct labor costs:

Work-in-Process Inventory (1,900 equivalent production × 2 dlh/pair = 3,800 × $9.00)	34,200	
Direct Labor Price Variance ($10.26 − $9.00 = $1.26 × 3,900)	4,914	
Direct Labor Efficiency Variance (3,900 − 3,800 = 100 × $9.00)	900	
Payroll Payable (3,900 dlh × $10.26)		40,014

To record actual factory overhead costs:

Factory Overhead Control	13,700	
Various Credits ($6,200 + $7,500)		13,700

To record applied factory overhead costs:

Work-in-Process Inventory (3,800 dlh × $3.50/dlh)	13,300	
Factory Overhead Applied		13,300

To record factory overhead variances:

One-variance method:

Factory Overhead Applied	13,300	
Total Factory Overhead Variance	400	
Factory Overhead Control		13,700

Two-variance method:

Factory Overhead Applied	13,300	
Factory Overhead Budget Variance	0	
Factory Overhead Production Volume Variance	400	
Factory Overhead Control		13,700

Three-variance method:

Factory Overhead Applied	13,300	
Factory Overhead Efficiency Variance	150	
Factory Overhead Production Volume Variance	400	
Factory Overhead Price Variance		150
Factory Overhead Control		13,700

8.10 DISPOSITION OF ALL VARIANCES

Variances will either be charged off as a period cost (if inventories are reported on financial statements at standard costs) or prorated among work-in-process inventory, finished goods inventory, and cost of goods sold (if inventories are reported on financial statements at actual costs). If the variances are prorated, then they are considered product costs.

Proration of Variances. If the variances are large (the actual costs depart significantly from standard costs), the variances should be prorated to the inventory accounts (if any) and cost of goods sold.

The proration is based on a ratio (fraction) of the quantities or dollar amounts of each account to the total quantity or dollar amounts of all accounts.

Direct materials and conversion costs are allocated separately when they are at different stages of completion.

Gross Profit Analysis

8.11 GROSS PROFIT ANALYSIS DEFINED

Another area of cost accounting that utilizes variances is known as gross profit analysis. Deviations from the amount of gross profit that is expected must be evaluated carefully.

Gross profit or gross margin is the excess of sales over cost of goods sold. Gross profit analysis is the determination of the causes for the increase or decrease in gross profit. Any variances that affect gross profit are reported to management so that corrective steps can be taken.

8.12 CHANGE IN GROSS PROFIT

The principal causes of a difference between budgeted and actual gross profit are changes in sales price, sales volume, cost of goods sold, and product mix. Analysis of the changes provides the data needed to bring actual operations in line with budgeted expectations. Comparisons can be made between budgeted and actual operations for the current year or between actual operations for the prior year and those for the current year. It is preferable to compare actual with budget when a realistic budget has been prepared.

In addition to computing the gross profit ratio (gross profit ÷ sales), the changes in gross profit can also be analyzed by the following three variances:

(1) ***Volume Variance.*** Due to a change in quantity. It is computed as follows:

$$\text{Volume variance} = \left(\text{Budgeted volume} - \text{Actual volume}\right) \times \text{Budgeted gross profit per unit}$$

(2) ***Sales Price Variance.*** Due to change in selling price.

$$\text{Sales price variance} = \left(\text{Budgeted unit sales price} - \text{Actual unit sales price}\right) \times \text{Actual volume}$$

(3) ***Cost Variance.*** Due to change in costs.

$$\text{Cost variance} = \left(\text{Budgeted cost per unit} - \text{Actual cost per unit}\right) \times \text{Actual volume}$$

EXAMPLE 4

The following is an illustration of a company's budgeted and actual gross profit for a single product:

	Budget	**Actual**	**Change**	**Percent**
Sales	$50,000	$53,000	$ + 3,000	6.0%
Cost of goods sold	25,000	27,500	− 2,500	10.0%
Gross profit	$25,000	$25,500	$ 500	2.0%
Gross profit ratio (GPR = gross profit ÷ sales)	50.0%	48.1%		
Cost-of-goods-sold ratio (CSR = cost of goods sold ÷ sales)	50.0%	51.9%		
Total	100.0%	100.0%		

Cost Data per Unit

	Budget (5,000 Units)		Actual (4,000 Units)		Change (−1,000 Units)
Sales price	$ 10.00	100%	$ 13.25	100%	$+3.25
Cost of sales	5.00	50%	6.875	51.9%	+1.875
Gross profit	$ 5.00	50%	$ 6.375	48.1%	$+1.375

$$\text{Volume variance} = \left(\text{Budgeted volume} - \text{Actual volume}\right) \times \text{Budgeted gross profit per unit}$$
$$= (5{,}000 - 4{,}000) \times \$5$$
$$= 1{,}000 \times \$5$$
$$= \$5{,}000 \text{ Unfav.}$$

$$\text{Sales price variance} = \left(\text{Budgeted sales price per unit} - \text{Actual sales price per unit}\right) \times \text{Actual volume}$$
$$= (\$10.00 - \$13.25) \times 4{,}000$$
$$- \$3.25 \times 4{,}000$$
$$= \$13{,}000 \text{ Fav.}$$

$$\text{Cost variance} = \left(\text{Budgeted cost per unit} - \text{Actual cost per unit}\right) \times \text{Actual volume}$$
$$= (\$5.00 - \$6.875) \times 4{,}000$$
$$= -\$1.875 \times 4{,}000$$
$$= \$7{,}500 \text{ Unfav.}$$

The gross profit variance is summarized as follows:

Volume variance	$ 5,000	Unfavorable
Sales price variance	(13,000)	Favorable
Cost variance	7,500	Unfavorable
Total	($ 500)	Favorable

8.13 MULTIPRODUCTS

Most manufacturing companies produce more than one product. Sales, cost of goods sold, and gross profit are usually different for each product. Analysis of cost data is handled in the same way as standard cost variance computations if the products cannot be substituted for each other. If substitutions can be made, the sales price and cost variances are computed as shown above, but the volume variance is separated into a pure volume and a mix variance.

(1) ***Pure Volume Variance.*** Indicates the effect of changes in the physical volume of the product sold. The formula is:

$$\text{Pure volume variance} = \left(\text{Budgeted volume} - \text{Actual volume}\right) \times \text{Budgeted average gross profit*}$$

$$\text{* Budgeted average gross profit} = \frac{\text{Total budgeted gross profit}}{\text{Total budgeted units}}$$

(2) *Mix Variance.* Indicates the effect of changes in the physical volume of.the more profitable or less profitable product. The determination of more profitable or less profitable is made by comparing the gross profit per unit with the average gross profit per unit for all units. A mix variance is unfavorable if a company sold more units of the less profitable product or sold fewer units of the more profitable product. The formula is:

$$\text{Mix variance} = \left(\begin{array}{c}\text{Budgeted}\\ \text{volume}\end{array} - \begin{array}{c}\text{Actual}\\ \text{volume}\end{array}\right) \times \left(\begin{array}{c}\text{Budgeted average}\\ \text{gross profit}\end{array} - \begin{array}{c}\text{Budgeted}\\ \text{gross profit}\end{array}\right)$$

EXAMPLE 5

Consider the following gross profit analysis for a multiproduct company:

J. C. Manufacturing Co.
Budgeted Gross Profit Statement
Year 19XX

		Sales		Cost		Gross Profit		
Product	**Units Sold**	**Price**	**Amount**	**Unit**	**Amount**	**Unit**	**Amount**	**Percen**
A	50,000	$6.25	$312,500	$5.10	$255,000	$1.15	$ 57,500	18.4 %
B	38,000	5.50	209,000	4.20	159,600	1.30	49,400	23.64%
C	18,000	4.00	72,000	3.00	54,000	1.00	18,000	25.00%
Total	106,000	$5.60 (a)	$593,500	$4.42 (b)	$468,600	$1.18 (c)	$124,900	21.04%

(a) $593,500 ÷ 106,000.
(b) $468,600 ÷ $106,000.
(c) $124,900 ÷ 106,000.
(d) $124,900 ÷ $593,500.

J. C. Manufacturing Co.
Actual Gross Profit Statement
Year 19XX

		Sales		Cost		Gross Profit		
Product	**Units Sold**	**Price**	**Amount**	**Unit**	**Amount**	**Unit**	**Amount**	**Percen**
A	53,000	$6.50	$344,500	$5.78	$306,340	$0.72	$ 38,160	11.08%
B	35,300	$5.20	183,560	4.30	151,790	0.90	31,770	17.31%
C	18,200	$4.15	75,530	3.60	65,520	0.55	10,010	13.25%
Total	106,500	$5.67 (a)	$603,590	$4.92 (b)	$523,650	$0.75 (c)	$ 79,940	13.24%

(a) $603,590 ÷ 106,500.
(b) $523,650 ÷ 106,500.
(c) $79,940 ÷ 106,500.
(d) $79,940 ÷ $603,590.

Budgeted gross profit	$124,900	
Actual gross profit	79,940	
Variance—to be analyzed	$ 44,960	Unfav.

(1) No Substitutes

$$\text{Volume variance} = \left(\text{Budgeted volume} - \text{Actual volume}\right) \times \text{Budgeted gross profit}$$

Product A	Product B	Product C
(50,000 − 53,000)	(38,000 − 35,300)	(18,000 − 18,200)
× 1.15	× \$1.30	× \$1.00
−3,000 × \$1.15	2,700 × \$1.30	−200 × \$1.00
(\$3,450) Fav.	\$3,510 Unfav.	(\$200) Fav.

$$\text{Sales price variance} = \left(\text{Budgeted sales price per unit} - \text{Actual sales price per unit}\right) \times \text{Actual volume}$$

Product A	Product B	Product C
(\$6.25 − \$6.50)	(\$5.50 − \$5.20)	(\$4.00 − \$4.15)
× 53,000	× 35,300	× 18,200
−\$0.25 × 53,000	\$0.30 × 35,300	−\$0.15 × 18,200
(\$13,250) Fav.	\$10,590 Unfav.	(\$2,730) Fav.

$$\text{Cost variance} = \left(\text{Budgeted cost per unit} - \text{Actual cost per unit}\right) \times \text{Actual volume}$$

Product A	Product B	Product C
(\$5.10 − \$5.78)	(\$4.20 − \$4.30)	(\$3.00 − \$3.60)
× 53,000	× 35,300	× 18,200
−\$0.68 × 53,000	−\$0.10 × 35,300	−\$0.60 × 18,200
\$36,040 Unfav.	\$3,530 Unfav.	\$10,920 Unfav.

Summary of Variances
Multiproducts—No Substitutes

	Product A		Product B		Product C		Total	
Volume variance	\$ (3,450)	Fav.	\$ 3,510	Unfav.	\$ (200)	Fav.	\$ (140)	Fav.
Sales price variance	(13,250)	Fav.	10,590	Unfav.	(2,730)	Fav.	(5,390)	Fav.
Cost variance	36,040	Unfav.	3,530	Unfav.	10,920	Unfav.	50,490	Unfav.
Total	\$ 19,340	Unfav.	\$17,630	Unfav.	\$ 7,990	Unfav.	\$ 44,960	Unfav.

(2) Substitutes

$$\text{Pure volume variance} = \left(\text{Budgeted volume} - \text{Actual volume}\right) \times \text{Budgeted average gross profit*}$$

Product A	Product B	Product C
(50,000 − 53,000)	(38,000 − 35,300)	(18,000 − 18,200)
× \$1.18	× \$1.18	× \$1.18
−3,000 × \$1.18	2,700 × \$1.18	−200 \$× \$1.18
(\$3,540) Fav.	\$3,186 Unfav.	(\$236) Fav.

* \$124,900 ÷ 106,000 = \$1.18

$$\text{Mix variance} = \left(\text{Budgeted volume} - \text{Actual volume}\right) \times \left(\text{Budgeted average gross profit*} - \text{Budgeted gross profit}\right)$$

Product A	Product B	Product C
(50,000 − 53,000) × ($1.18 − $1.15)	(38,000 − 35,300) × ($1.18 − $1.30)	(18,000 − 18,200) × ($1.18 − $1.00)
−3,000 × $0.03	2,700 × −$.12	−200 × $0.18
$90 Unfav.	$324 Unfav.	$36 Unfav.

* $124,900 ÷ 106,000 = $1.18

Sales price variance. Same as calculated for no substitutes.

Cost variance. Same as calculated for no substitutes.

Summary of Variances
Multiproducts—Substitutes

	Product A		Product B		Product C		Total	
Pure volume variance	$ (3,540)	Fav.	$ 3,186	Unfav.	$ (236)	Fav.	$ (590)	Fav.
Mix variance	90	Unfav.	324	Unfav.	36	Unfav.	450	Unfav.
Sales price variance	(13,250)	Fav.	10,590	Unfav.	(2,730)	Fav.	(5,390)	Fav.
Cost variance	36,040	Unfav.	3,530	Unfav.	10,920	Unfav.	50,490	Unfav.
Total	$ 19,340	Unfav.	$17,630	Unfav.	$ 7,990	Unfav.	$ 44,960	Unfav.

Solved Problems

8.1 Variance Analysis, Journal Entries. Operations of the Ralph Corporation are based on the following data: direct labor hours, 12,500; estimated overhead: fixed, $5,000; variable, $9,000.

Actual results were as follows: Direct labor hours, 9,300; overhead: fixed, $5,075; variable, $8,900.

There are 10,300 standard hours allowed for actual production.

Compute (*a*) the variable, fixed and total overhead rates, and (*b*) overhead variances using the three-variance method. Prepare (*c*) all necessary journal entries for the three-variance method.

SOLUTION

(*a*)

Variable rate:	$9,000 ÷ 12,500 =	$ .72
Fixed rate:	$5,000 ÷ 12,500 =	.40
Total rate:	$14,000 ÷ 12,500 =	$1.12

(*b*) **Variances**

(1) *Price (spending) variance:*

$$\text{Price (spending) variance} = \text{Actual factory overhead} - \text{Budgeted factory overhead at actual direct labor hours worked}$$

= \$13,975 − [(9,300 × \$0.72) + \$5,000]

= \$13,975 − \$11,696

= \$ 2,279 Unfav.

(2) *Efficiency variance:*

$$\text{Efficiency variance} = \left(\begin{array}{c}\text{Actual direct labor hours worked}\end{array} - \begin{array}{c}\text{Standard direct labor hours allowed}\end{array}\right) \times \text{Standard variable factory overhead application rate}$$

= (9,300 − 10,300) × \$0.72

= 1,000 × \$0.72

= (\$720) Fav.

(3) *Production volume (denominator or idle capacity) variance:*

$$\text{Production volume (denominator or idle capacity) variance} = \left(\text{Denominator direct labor hours} - \text{Standard direct labor hours allowed}\right) \times \text{Standard fixed factory overhead application rate}$$

= (12,500 − 10,300) × \$0.40

= 2,200 × \$0.40

= \$880 Unfav.

(*c*)

Factory Overhead Applied (10,300 hours × \$1.12)	11,536	
Factory Overhead Price Variance	2,279	
Factory Overhead Production Volume Variance	880	
Factory Overhead Efficiency Variance		720
Factory Overhead Control		13,975

8.2 Variance Analysis. Hardwood Furniture, Incorporated manufactures all types of office furniture. The company has one giant plant and office complex in California, and employs a full-time cost accounting department to control and analyze production costs. At the end of the year, the cost accounting department showed the following data:

The factory overhead rate is based on a normal capacity of 8,000 hours. Total budgeted factory overhead expenses were \$11,560, consisting of variable expenses, \$4,960, and fixed expenses, \$6,600.

The standard cost card showed:

Direct materials	\$5.00 per unit
Direct labor	4.00 per hour

Actual Data

Materials:	Purchased	10,000 units @ $4.94
	Requisitioned	7,100 units
	Standard quantity allowed	7,000 units
Direct labor:	Actual hours worked	3,760 hours
	Standard hours allowed	3,180 hours
	Actual rate paid	$4.20 per hour
Factory overhead (actual):		$10,994

Compute the variances for (*a*) direct materials, (*b*) direct labor, and (*c*) factory overhead, showing (1) computation of overhead rates and (2) variances using the three-factor analysis.

SOLUTION

(*a*) (1) **Direct Materials Price Variance**

$$\text{Direct materials price variance} = \left(\text{Actual unit price} - \text{Standard unit price}\right) \times \text{Actual quantity purchased}$$

$$= (\$4.94 - \$5.00) \times 10{,}000$$
$$= \$0.06 \times 10{,}000$$
$$= (\$600)\text{ Fav.}$$

(2) **Direct Materials Efficiency Variance**

$$\text{Direct materials efficiency variance} = \left(\text{Actual quantity used} - \text{Standard quantity allowed}\right) \times \text{Standard unit price}$$

$$= (7{,}100 - 7{,}000) \times \$5.00$$
$$= 100 \times \$5.00$$
$$= \$500\text{ Unfav.}$$

(*b*) (1) **Direct Labor Price Variance**

$$\text{Direct labor price variance} = \left(\text{Actual hourly wage rate} - \text{Standard hourly wage rate}\right) \times \text{Actual number of direct labor hours worked}$$

$$= (\$4.20 - \$4.00) \times 3{,}760$$
$$= \$1.20 \times 3{,}760$$
$$= \$752\text{ Unfav.}$$

(2) **Direct Labor Efficiency Variance**

$$\text{Direct labor efficiency variance} = \left(\text{Actual direct labor hours worked} - \text{Standard direct labor hours allowed}\right) \times \text{Standard direct labor hourly wage rate}$$

$$= (\$3{,}760 - 3{,}180) \times \$4.00$$
$$= 580 \times \$4.00$$
$$= \$2{,}320\text{ Unfav.}$$

(*c*) (1) **Overhead Rates**

Fixed rate: $6,600 ÷ 8,000 =	$ .825
Variable rate: $4,960 ÷ 8,000 =	.620
Total overhead rate:	$1.445

(2) **Three-factor Analyses**

Price (spending) variance

$$\text{Price (spending) variance} = \text{Actual factory overhead} - \text{Budgeted factory overhead at actual direct labor hours worked}$$

$$= \$10{,}994 - [(3{,}760 \times \$0.62) + \$6{,}600]$$

$$= \$10{,}994 - \$8{,}931.20$$

$$= \$2{,}062.80 \text{ Unfav.}$$

Efficiency variance

$$\text{Efficiency variance} = \left(\text{Actual direct labor hours worked} - \text{Standard direct labor hours allowed}\right) \times \text{Standard variable factory overhead application rate}$$

$$= (3{,}760 - 3{,}180) \times \$0.62$$

$$= 580 \times \$0.62$$

$$= \$359.60 \text{ Unfav.}$$

Production volume (denominator or idle capacity) variance

$$\text{Production volume (denominator or idle capacity) variance} = \left(\text{Denominator direct labor hours} - \text{Standard direct labor hours allowed}\right) \times \text{Standard fixed factory overhead application rate}$$

$$= (8{,}000 - 3{,}180) \times \$0.825$$

$$= 4{,}820 \times \$0.825$$

$$= \$3{,}976.50 \text{ Unfav.}$$

8.3 Factory Overhead Variances; Journal Entries. From the data below prepare (*a*) an analysis of factory overhead variances using (1) the two-variance method and (2) the three-variance method, and (*b*) journal entries for the three-variance analysis.

	Budgeted (normal capacity)	**Actual**
Direct labor hours	20,000	25,600
Factory overhead:		
Fixed	$14,000	$17,000
Variable	16,000	19,000

Standard allowed for actual production: 24,000 hours

SOLUTION

(*a*) (1) **Factory Overhead Variance—Two-factor Analysis**

$$\text{Budget (controllable) variance} = \text{Actual factory overhead} - \text{Budgeted factory overhead at standard direct labor hours allowed}$$

$$= \$36{,}000 - \left[\left(\frac{16{,}000}{20{,}000} \times 24{,}000\right) + \$14{,}000\right]$$

$$= \$36{,}000 - \$33{,}200$$

$$= \$2{,}800 \text{ Unfav.}$$

Production volume (denominator or idle capacity) variance

$$\text{Production volume (denominator or idle capacity) variance} = \left(\begin{array}{c}\text{Denominator}\\\text{direct labor}\\\text{hours}\end{array} - \begin{array}{c}\text{Standard}\\\text{direct labor}\\\text{hours allowed}\end{array}\right) \times \begin{array}{c}\text{Standard fixed}\\\text{factory overhead}\\\text{application rate}\end{array}$$

$$= (20{,}000 - 24{,}000) \times \$0.70^*$$
$$= -4{,}000 \times \$.070$$
$$= (\$2{,}800)\text{ Fav.}$$

* ($14,000 ÷ 20,000 hours)

(2) **Factory Overhead Variance—Three-factor Analysis**

$$\begin{array}{c}\text{Price}\\\text{(spending)}\\\text{variance}\end{array} = \begin{array}{c}\text{Actual}\\\text{factory}\\\text{overhead}\end{array} - \begin{array}{c}\text{Budgeted factory overhead}\\\text{at actual direct}\\\text{labor hours worked}\end{array}$$

$$= \$36{,}000 - [(\$.80^* \times 25{,}600) + \$14{,}000]$$
$$= \$36{,}000 - \$34{,}480$$
$$= \$1{,}520\text{ Unfav.}$$

* $16,000 ÷ 20,000 dlh

Efficiency variance

$$\begin{array}{c}\text{Efficiency}\\\text{variance}\end{array} = \left(\begin{array}{c}\text{Actual}\\\text{direct}\\\text{labor hours}\\\text{worked}\end{array} - \begin{array}{c}\text{Standard}\\\text{direct}\\\text{labor hours}\\\text{allowed}\end{array}\right) \times \begin{array}{c}\text{Standard variable}\\\text{factory overhead}\\\text{application rate}\end{array}$$

$$= (25{,}600 - 24{,}000) \times \$0.80$$
$$= 1{,}600 \times \$0.80$$
$$= \$1{,}280\text{ Unfav.}$$

Production volume (denominator or idle capacity) variance

$$\text{Production volume (denominator or idle capacity) variance} = \left(\begin{array}{c}\text{Denominator}\\\text{direct labor}\\\text{hours}\end{array} - \begin{array}{c}\text{Standard}\\\text{direct labor}\\\text{hours allowed}\end{array}\right) \times \begin{array}{c}\text{Standard fixed}\\\text{factory overhead}\\\text{application rate}\end{array}$$

$$= (20{,}000 - 24{,}000) \times \$0.70$$
$$= -4{,}000 \times \$0.70$$
$$= (\$2{,}800)\text{ Fav.}$$

(*b*) **Journal Entries**

Factory Overhead Applied	36,000*	
Factory Overhead Price Variance	1,520	
Factory Overhead Efficiency Variance	1,280	
Factory Overhead Production Volume Variance		2,800
Factory Overhead Control		36,000

* (24,000 standard hours allowed × $1.50 factory overhead application rate)

8.4 Gross Profit Analysis. The following data pertain to the R. W. Mauro Company:

R. W. Mauro Company

	Budget	Actual	Change	Percent
Sales	$65,000	$69,000	$+4,000	6.2%
Cost of goods sold	50,000	53,000	+3,000	6.0%
Gross profit	$15,000	$16,000	$ 1,000	6.7%
Gross profit ratio	23.1%	23.2%		

Cost Data per Unit

	Budget (5,000 Units)	Actual (5,520 Units)	Change (+520 Units)
Sales price	$13.00	$12.50	$−0.50
Cost	10.00	9.60	−0.40
Gross profit	$ 3.00	$ 2.90	$−0.10

Compute (*a*) the volume variance, the sales variance, and the cost variance; and (*b*) their combined effect on gross profit.

SOLUTION

(*a*)

$$\text{Volume variance} = \left(\begin{array}{c}\text{Budgeted}\\\text{volume}\end{array} - \begin{array}{c}\text{Actual}\\\text{volume}\end{array}\right) \times \begin{array}{c}\text{Budgeted gross}\\\text{profit per unit}\end{array}$$
$$= (5{,}000 - 5{,}520) \times \$3$$
$$= -520 \times \$3$$
$$= (\$1{,}560)\ \text{Fav.}$$

$$\begin{array}{c}\text{Sales price}\\\text{variance}\end{array} = \left(\begin{array}{c}\text{Budgeted}\\\text{sales price}\\\text{per unit}\end{array} - \begin{array}{c}\text{Actual sales}\\\text{price per unit}\end{array}\right) \times \begin{array}{c}\text{Actual}\\\text{volume}\end{array}$$
$$= (\$13.00 - \$12.50) \times 5{,}520$$
$$= \$0.50 \times 5{,}520$$
$$= \$2{,}760\ \text{Unfav.}$$

$$\text{Cost variance} = \left(\begin{array}{c}\text{Budgeted cost}\\\text{per unit}\end{array} - \begin{array}{c}\text{Actual cost}\\\text{per unit}\end{array}\right) \times \begin{array}{c}\text{Actual}\\\text{volume}\end{array}$$
$$= (\$10.00 - \$9.60) \times 5{,}520$$
$$= \$0.40 \times 5{,}520$$
$$= (\$2{,}208)\ \text{Fav.}$$

(*b*) Summary

Volume variance	($1,560) Fav.
Sales price variance	2,760 Unfav.
Cost variance	(2,208) Fav.
Total	($1,008) Fav.

8.5 Multiproduct Gross Profit Analysis. Following are the budgeted and actual gross profit data for McHandy Company. Prepare a gross profit analysis assuming that products S, K, and L can be substituted for each other.

McHandy Company
Budgeted Gross Profit Statement
Year 19XX

		Sales		Cost		Gross Profit		
Product	Units Sold	Price	Amount	Unit	Amount	Unit	Amount	Percent
S	5,500	$4.75	$26,125	$3.50	$19,250	$1.25	$ 6,875	26.3%
K	4,500	3.00	13,500	2.50	11,250	0.50	2,250	16.7%
L	2,200	4.75	10,450	4.00	8,800	0.75	1,650	15.8%
Total	12,200	$4.10	$50,075	$3.22	$39,300	$0.88	$10,775	21.5%

McHandy Company
Actual Gross Profit Statement
Year 19XX

		Sales		Cost		Gross Profit		
Product	Units Sold	Price	Amount	Unit	Amount	Unit	Amount	Percent
S	6,000	$5.00	$30,000	$3.25	$19,500	$1.75	$10,500	35.0%
K	4,000	3.25	13,000	2.75	11,000	.50	2,000	15.4%
L	2,000	4.50	9,000	3.75	7,500	0.75	1,500	16.6%
Total	12,000	$4.34	$52,000	$3.17	$38,000	$1.17	$14,000	26.9%

SOLUTION

Pure Volume Variance

Product S	Product K	Product L
(5,500 − 6,000)	(4,500 − 4,000)	(2,200 − 2,000)
× $0.88	× $0.88	× $0.88
−500 × $0.88	500 × $0.88	200 × $0.88
($440) Fav.	$440 Unfav.	$176 Unfav.

Mix Variance

Product S	Product K	Product L
(5,500 − 6,000)	(4,500 − 4,000)	(2,200 − 2,000)
× ($0.88 − $1.25)	× ($0.88 − $0.50)	× ($0.88 − $0.75)
−500 × $0.37	500 × $0.38	200 × $0.13
($185) Fav.	($190) Fav.	($26) Fav.

Sales Price Variance

Product S	Product K	Product L
($4.75 − $5.00)	($3.00 − $3.25)	($4.75 − $4.50)
× 6,000	× 4,000	× 2,000
−$0.25 × 6,000	−$0.25 × 4,000	$0.25 × 2,000
($1,500) Fav.	($1,000) Fav.	$500 Unfav.

Cost Variance

Product S	Product K	Product L
(\$3.50 − \$3.25)	(\$2.50 − \$2.75)	(\$4.00 − \$3.75)
× 6,000	× 4,000	× 2,000
\$0.25 × 6,000	−\$0.25 × 4,000	\$0.25 × 2,000
(\$1,500) Fav.	\$1,000 Unfav.	(\$500) Fav.

Summary of Variances

	Product S		Product K		Product L		Total	
Pure volume variance	\$ (440)	Fav.	\$ 440	Unfav.	\$ 176	Unfav.	\$ 176	Unfav.
Mix variance	(185)	Fav.	(190)	Fav.	(26)	Fav.	(401)	Fav.
Sales price variance	(1,500)	Fav.	(1,000)	Fav.	500	Unfav.	(2,000)	Fav.
Cost variance	(1,500)	Fav.	1,000	Unfav.	(500)	Fav.	(1,000)	Fav.
Total	\$(3,625)	Fav.	\$ 250	Unfav.	\$ 150	Unfav.	\$(3,225)	Fav.

Chapter 9

Direct Costing, Break-Even Analysis, and Cost-Volume-Profit Planning

Direct Costing

9.1 MEANING OF DIRECT COSTING

Under absorption costing, all production costs (direct materials, direct labor, and factory overhead—both variable and fixed) are treated as product costs.

Under direct costing, only the production costs that vary with volume (direct materials, direct labor, and variable factory overhead) are treated as product costs. Fixed factory overhead is treated as a period cost.

9.2 DIRECT COSTING: PRODUCT AND PERIOD COSTS

Direct costing makes a distinction between *product costs* and *period costs*. Product costs consist only of prime costs for direct materials and direct labor plus variable factory overhead. These are the costs assigned to inventories (work in process and finished goods) and cost of goods sold. Fixed factory overhead is included with other period expenses, such as selling and administrative expenses.

Thus, the primary difference between direct costing and absorption costing is the treatment of fixed factory overhead. Direct costing excludes it as a product cost; absorption costing includes it as a product cost in inventories and cost of goods sold.

9.3 DIRECT COSTING VS. ABSORPTION COSTING: INCOME STATEMENTS

The conceptual differences between income statements prepared under direct costing and absorption costing procedures are as follows:

(1) ***Gross marginal income vs. gross profit.*** Under direct costing, the gross marginal income figure represents the difference between sales and variable manufacturing costs. It is the equivalent of the gross profit figure under absorption costing, and reflects the exclusion of fixed costs from inventory valuation and cost of goods sold. Thus, gross marginal income will always be greater than gross profit. It is also important to note that this method allows the cost of goods sold to vary directly with sales.

(2) ***Contribution margin.*** Also known as marginal income, the contribution margin is the excess of sales over total variable costs (i.e., manufacturing, selling, administrative). Its usefulness as a profit planning device makes this a significant feature of the direct costing income statement (see Section 9.4).

(3) ***Inventory costs.*** Under direct costing, fixed overhead is eliminated from inventories. This is contrary to the AICPA's view; *ARB No. 43* specifically states that ". . . exclusion of all overheads from inventory costs does not constitute an accepted accounting procedure." Neither the IRS nor the SEC will accept direct costing until the Financial Accounting

Standards Board approves its use. As a result, many firms use direct costing for internal reports but adjust inventories to conform with absorption costing procedures for external reports.

(4) ***Net operating profit*** **(NOP).** The difference in net operating profit under the two methods is due to the amount of fixed costs charged to inventories. If there are no beginning or ending inventories, the NOP under both methods will be the same.

EXAMPLE 1

The standard and actual data for the Broadway Company used in Chapter 8 are summarized below. These data are used to illustrate the cost of goods manufactured statement and the income statement, using both absorption costing and direct costing.

Standard unit cost:			
Direct materials	$48.00		
Direct labor	18.00		
Factory overhead:			
Variable	3.00		
Fixed	4.00	$ 73.00	
Budgeted fixed factory overhead		$ 8,000	
Standard costs put into production:			
Direct materials (2,000 × $48)	$96,000		
Direct labor (1,900 × $18)	34,200		
Factory overhead:			
Variable (1,900 × $3)	5,700		
Fixed (1,900 × $4)	7,600		
Ending work-in-process inventory (100 units):			
Direct materials (100 × $48)	4,800		
Direct labor (100 × $18 × 50%)	900		
Factory overhead:			
Variable (100 × $3 × 50%)	150		
Fixed (100 × $4 × 50%)	200		
Units in ending finished goods inventory:			
Units started and completed	1,900		
Units sold	1,500	400	
Variances:			
Direct materials price		$12,500 Unfav.	
Direct materials efficiency		8,000 Fav.	
Direct labor price		4,914 Unfav.	
Direct labor efficiency		900 Unfav.	
Factory overhead:			
Budget	-0-		
Production volume	$ 400 Unfav.	400 Unfav.	$ 10,714 Unfav.
Marketing and administrative expense (assume $500 are fixed costs)			$ 1,500
Sales (1,500 × $400)			$600,000

Assume there are no opening inventories; variances are not prorated but charged to cost of goods sold; ignore income taxes.

Broadway Company
Cost of Goods Manufactured

Absorption Costing

Costs put into production during the period at standard:		
Direct materials		$ 96,000
Direct labor		34,200
Factory overhead:		
Variable	$5,700	
Fixed	7,600	13,300
Total costs put into production at standard		143,500
Plus: Work-in-process inventory at beginning of the period		-0-
Cost of goods in process during the period at standard		$143,500
Less: Work-in-process inventory at the end of the period at standard		6,050 (*a*)
Cost of goods manufactured at standard		$137,450

Direct Costing

Variable costs put into production during the period at standard:	
Direct materials	$ 96,000
Direct labor	34,200
Variable factory overhead	5,700
Total variable costs put into production at standard	$135,900
Plus: Variable work-in-process inventory at beginning of the period	-0-
Variable cost of goods in process during the period at standard	$135,900
Less: Variable work-in-process inventory at the end of the period at standard	5,850 (*b*)
Variable cost of goods manufactured at standard	$130,050

(a) Work-in-process inventory at the end of the period:

Direct materials		$4,800
Direct labor		900
Factory overhead:		
Variable	$150	
Fixed	200	350
Total		$6,050

(b) Work-in-process inventory at the end of the period:

Direct materials	$4,800
Direct labor	900
Factory overhead:	
Variable	150
Total	$5,850

Note the difference in the cost of goods manufactured between the two methods:

Amount: Absorption costing	$137,450
Direct costing	130,050
Difference	$ 7,400

Analysis: The difference is due to fixed costs included in absorption costing but not included in direct costing as follows:

Fixed costs put into production	$7,600
Less: Fixed costs in ending work-in-process inventory	200
Net fixed costs included in production (absorption costing only)	$7,400

Broadway Company
Income Statement

Absorption Costing

Sales		$600,000
Cost of goods sold:		
Opening finished goods inventory	-0-	
Plus: Cost of goods manufactured at standard	$137,450	
Net total unfavorable variances	10,714	
Goods available for sale	$148,164	
Less: Closing finished goods inventory at standard (400 × $73)	29,200	
Cost of goods sold		118,964
Gross profit		$481,036
Less: Marketing and administrative expenses		1,500
Operating income		$479,536

Direct Costing

Sales		$600,000
Variable cost of goods sold:		
Opening finished goods inventory	$-0-	
Plus: Variable cost of goods manufactured at standard	130,050	
Net unfavorable variances	10,314 (*c*)	
Goods available for sale	$140,364	
Less: Closing finished goods inventory at standard [400 × $69 (*d*)]	27,600	
Variable cost of goods sold	$112,764	
Plus: Variable marketing and administrative expenses	1,000	
Total variable costs		113,764
Contribution margin		$486,236
Less: Budgeted fixed factory overhead	8,000	
Fixed marketing and administrative expenses	500	8,500
Operating income		$477,736

(c) $10,714 total variance − $400 production volume variance = $10,314

(d) $73 standard unit cost − $4 fixed factory overhead application rate = $69

Note the difference between the two methods:

Amount:	Absorption costing	$479,536
	Direct costing	477,736
	Difference	$ 1,800

Analysis: The difference is due to the amount of fixed factory overhead included in inventories under absorption costing but not under direct costing:

	Work-in-Process	Finished Goods	Totals
Absorption costing	$6,050	$29,200	$35,250
Direct costing	5,850	27,600	33,450
Difference	$ 200	$ 1,600	$ 1,800

9.4 USES OF DIRECT COSTING

By distinguishing between product and period costs, direct costing offers a variety of uses for both internal and external purposes. Some of the benefits accruing from this costing method are described below.

Direct costing is a useful analytic device in budget preparation, since such *profit planning* involves both short- and long-run operations. The isolation of product costs emphasizes the cost-volume-profit relationship, providing data for such planning problems as breakeven analysis, return on investment, etc.

The simplified techniques associated with the contribution margin also make direct costing a useful tool for product pricing; managerial decisions related to production levels, new products and markets, special activities, etc. Finally, as a control tool, direct costing facilitates the preparation of responsibility-based income statements for managers, enabling them to recognize and act upon discrepancies and variances occurring in their areas.

The separation of accounts into fixed and variable components under direct costing simplifies the processes of assigning costs to inventory and determining income. It allows net income to vary more directly with sales since no fixed costs are deferred in inventories. It also results in clear, easily understood financial reports. Finally, direct costing guards against profit manipulation. It reduces the possibility of having increased sales with decreased earnings because fixed expenses are considered period, not product, costs. With fixed overhead costs remaining constant, an increase in sales will increase profits.

9.5 ADVANTAGES AND DISADVANTAGES OF DIRECT COSTING

Advantages of Direct Costing

(1) Establishes cost-volume-profit relationships.

(2) Excludes fixed overhead from inventories, which both simplifies the report and leaves it less open to misinterpretation by management.

(3) Makes the impact of fixed overhead on management more effective because fixed overhead is shown as a separate charge.

(4) Provides a basis for comparison of the profitability of different products.

(5) Conforms to the concept of assigning current out-of-pocket expenditures to the cost of manufacturing a product.

Disadvantages of Direct Costing

(1) Makes no clear-cut distinction between fixed and variable overhead costs—many are hybrid.

(2) Violates the principle that manufacturing cost should include all manufacturing charges, including fixed overhead.

(3) Allows an item to be fixed or variable, depending on the (depreciation) method used.

(4) Is not in accordance with the tax laws and generally accepted accounting principles.

(5) Cannot be used for long-range pricing policies, which must include fixed overhead as part of cost.

Break-Even Analysis

9.6 USE OF BREAK-EVEN ANALYSIS

Break-even analysis provides a concise presentation of the relationship between cost and volume changes and the effect of such changes on profit. The *break-even point* is the sales volume or other appropriate base at which *total revenue equals total costs, resulting in neither a profit nor a loss.*

Although the break-even point is important, its usefulness is limited by the assumptions on which it is based and the short time during which the data used may be valid. Although management is interested primarily in the profit at various levels of operation, management must also know the effect on profit of changes in sales price or volume and variable or fixed costs.

The principal break-even analysis methods are the (1) equation method, (2) contribution-margin method, and (3) graphic method. Their results are generally expressed in dollars or units.

Basic Data Used. To make comparisons possible, the various methods will be illustrated by using the same basic data. Company A manufactures an electronic device and sells it for $5 a unit, with a variable cost of $3 per unit. Sales volume and any other variables will be given in each example.

9.7 EQUATION METHOD

The method in general use is the equation or algebraic method. It is based on the income statement equation:

$$\text{Sales} - \text{Variable costs} - \text{Fixed costs} = \text{Profit}$$

For calculating the break-even point the equation is restated as:

$$\text{Sales} = \text{Variable costs} + \text{Fixed costs} + \text{Profit}$$

Note that the profit at the break-even point will be zero.

EXAMPLE 2

Find the number of units that must be sold to break even with fixed costs of $800. Substituting the basic data in the equation and solving for x, the number of units needed, we have:

$$\begin{aligned} \$5x &= \$3x + \$800 + 0 \\ \$2x &= \$800 \\ x &= 400 \text{ units} \end{aligned}$$

Replacing x with 400 units gives:

$$\begin{aligned} \text{Sales} &= \text{Variable costs} + \text{Fixed costs} + \text{Profit} \\ \$2{,}000 &= \$1{,}200 + \$800 + 0 \end{aligned}$$

Thus it takes sales of 400 units, or $2,000, to break even.

9.8 CONTRIBUTION MARGIN METHOD

The *contribution margin* is the excess of sales over variable costs. The contribution is applied first to fixed costs, and any excess is considered profit. The break-even point under this method is stated as:

$$\text{Break-even point} = \frac{\text{Fixed costs}}{\text{Contribution margin}}$$

When the contribution margin per unit is used, the break-even point in units results. For a break-even point in dollars the contribution margin as a percentage of sales (contribution margin per unit divided by the selling price per unit) must be used.

EXAMPLE 3

Assuming a fixed cost of \$800, the break-even point in (*a*) units and (*b*) dollars is calculated as follows:

(*a*)

$$\frac{\$800}{\$5 - \$3} = 400 \text{ units}$$

(*b*) The contribution margin as percentage of sales is:

$$\frac{\$2}{\$5} = 40\%$$

The break-even point in dollars then is:

$$\frac{\$800}{40\%} = \$2{,}000$$

9.9 GRAPHIC METHOD

The graphic method affords a concise, easy-to-understand picture of the cost-volume-profit relationship of the firm. Information about sales, total costs, variable and fixed costs, and profit at any given volume can be easily read from the chart. Therefore, break-even charts are an especially effective means of presenting data when management lacks familiarity with interpreting detailed statistical or financial reports.

Many pages of detailed data can be presented in a single break-even chart. Although the focus often is on the break-even point, where the total sales revenue line and the total cost line intersect, this is not the most important information on the break-even chart. Management is usually more interested in seeing the relationship of costs and revenue to profit at various volume levels.

In constructing the chart, certain factors and their behavior must be considered. For example, total sales and total variable costs change in direct proportion to changes in volume. However, such cost-volume-profit relationships are valid only within the prescribed limits, defined as the *relevant range*. The chart may not be valid for volumes outside the limits.

The break-even charts in Examples 4 and 5 are the two principal types generally in use. Although more sophisticated charts are sometimes presented, their interpretation often requires previous experience with break-even charts. Example 4 shows a break-even chart in which fixed costs are parallel to the horizontal line and *below variable costs*. Example 5 shows the type of chart in which fixed costs are shown *above variable costs*.

EXAMPLE 4 FIXED COSTS SHOWN BELOW VARIABLE COSTS (Fig. 9.1)

The basic data (\$5 sales price per unit and \$3 variable cost per unit) still apply. The relevant range is from 1 to 600,000 units. Fixed costs are assumed to be \$500,000. The following steps are used to construct a break-even chart.

Step 1: Total Sales Revenue Line. Choose any number of units greater than zero on the horizontal line and multiply by the selling price per unit (\$5). The result will equal total sales revenue (TSR) for that number of units. For example, choosing 300,000 units will result in \$1,500,000 TSR. Because the chart is in thousands, this point is plotted at the coordinate (\$1,500;300). Other points are plotted similarly. A straight line representing TSR is then drawn through the points.

Step 2: Total Costs Line. The total costs (TC) line represents the sum of fixed costs and variable costs at any particular point on the chart. Fixed costs are \$500,000 in this example and are assumed to remain unchanged from 1 to 600,000 units (the relevant range). Variable costs are \$3 per unit. At 300,000 units the calculations are:

$$\text{Total variable costs} = 300{,}000 \text{ units} \times \$3 \text{ per unit} = \$900{,}000$$
$$\text{Total costs} = \$500{,}000 \text{ fixed} + \$900{,}000 \text{ variable} = \$1{,}400{,}000$$

A point is then plotted at (\$1,400;300). Total costs at other volumes are plotted similarly. A straight line representing TC is then drawn from \$500 (=\$500,000) on the vertical axis (fixed-cost portion) through the points.

Step 3: Break-Even Point. The total costs line (TC) intercepts the total sales revenue line (TSR) at the breakeven point.

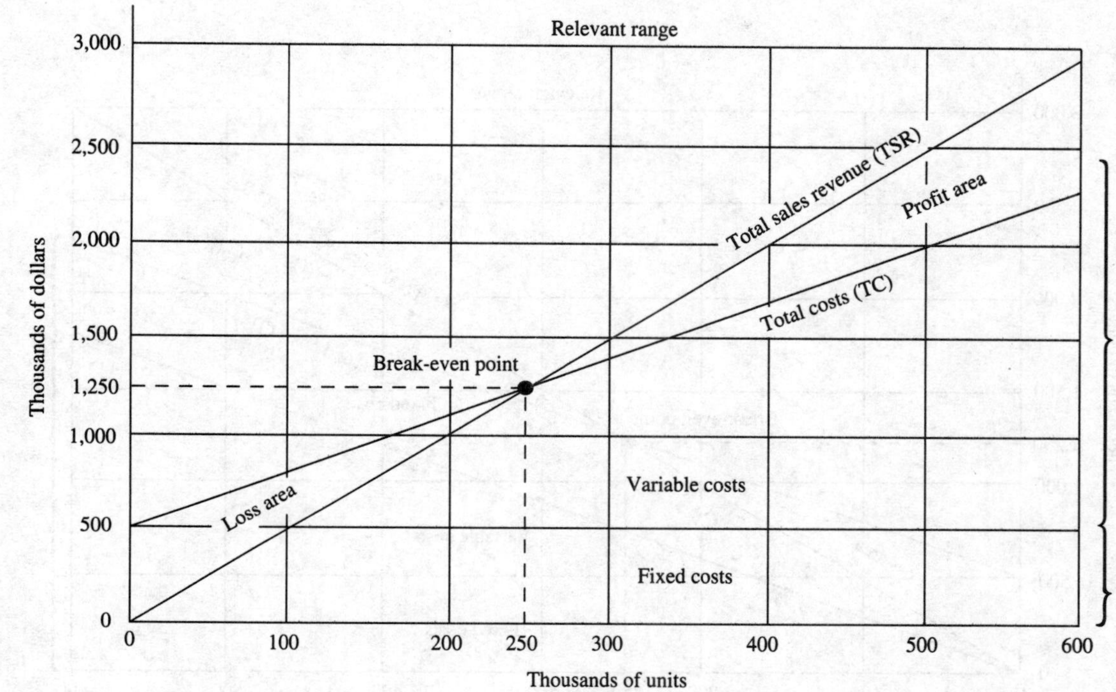

Fig. 9-1

As Fig. 9-1 shows, the break-even point is at a volume of 250,000 units. Here the sales are $1,250,000, total costs are $1,250,000, variable costs are $750,000 ($1,250,000 − $500,000), fixed costs are $500,000, and the profit, of course, is zero. Any level of activity below 250,000 units will fall in the loss area shown in the chart, and any level of activity above 250,000 units will fall in the profit area.

Initially, the various relationships depicted on the chart may be more easily understood if the data are shown in tabulated form as follows:

Tabulation of Fig. 9-1 Data

	Thousands					Per Unit		
Units	**Sales at $5**	**Variable Costs at $3**	**Fixed Costs**	**Total Costs**	**Profit (Loss)**	**Total Costs**	**Profit (Loss)**	**Profit (Loss), %***
100	$ 500	$ 300	$500	$ 800	$(300)	$8.00	$ (3.00)	(60)
200	1,000	600	500	1,100	(100)	5.50	(0.50)	(10)
250†	1,250	750	500	1,250	0	5.00	0	
300	1,500	900	500	1,400	100	4.67	0.33	6.7
400	2,000	1,200	500	1,700	300	4.25	0.75	15
500	2,500	1,500	500	2,000	500	4.00	1.00	20
600	3,000	1,800	500	2,300	700	3.83	1.17	23.3

* Calculated as $\frac{\text{profit (loss)}}{\text{sales}}$ = profit (loss), %. For example, for 100,000 units, loss, % = $\frac{\$300,000}{\$500,000}$ = 60%.

† Break-even point.

EXAMPLE 5 FIXED COSTS SHOWN ABOVE VARIABLE COST (Fig. 9.2)

In Fig. 9-1 the emphasis was on fixed costs remaining the same for all levels of activity. Many accountants prefer the approach in Fig. 9-2, which emphasizes the contribution margin (CM) for the various levels. The data are the same as in the previous tabulation except that the contribution margin is now shown.

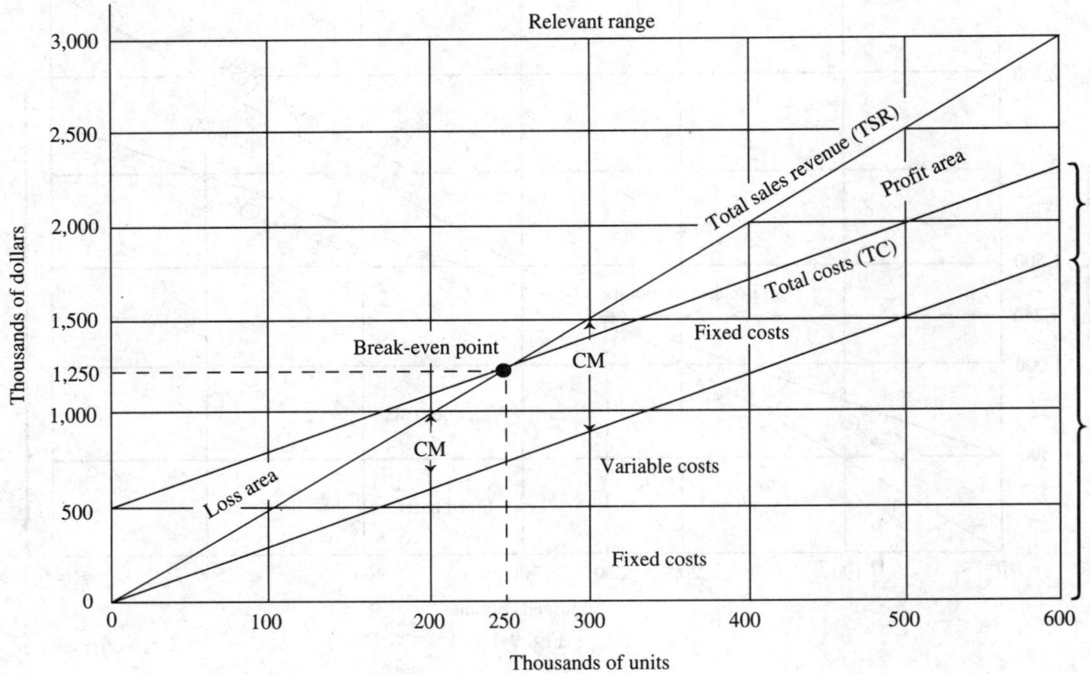

Fig. 9-2

Tabulation of Fig. 9-2 Data (Thousands)

Units	Sales at $5	Variable Costs at $3	Contribution Margin
100	$ 500	$ 300	$ 200
200	1,000	600	400
250*	1,250	750	500
300	1,500	900	600
400	2,000	1,200	800
500	2,500	1,500	1,000
600	3,000	1,800	1,200

* Break-even point.

Note that the total sales revenue line and the total cost line are the same for both charts. The contribution margin shown by the tabulation can easily be read on the chart. For example, at 200,000 units the sales are $1,000,000 and the variable costs $600,000. The difference between the two, $400,000, is the contribution margin at this level of activity. The area between the total sales revenue line and total costs line to the left of the break-even point is that portion of fixed costs which is not covered by the contribution margin. The area between the total sales revenue line and the total costs line to the right of the break-even point shows the amount of profit realized after fixed costs have been fully covered.

Cost-Volume-Profit Planning

9.10 USE OF COST-VOLUME-PROFIT PLANNING

Cost-volume-profit planning can be used by management in the following ways:

(1) To determine the level of profit for a given level of sales.
The formula to determine profit for any level of sales is:

$$\text{Profit} = \text{Total revenue} - \text{Total variable cost} - \text{Total fixed cost}$$

or

$$\text{Profit} = PQ - VQ - F$$

where:

P = Unit selling price
Q = Quantity
V = Variable cost
F = Fixed cost

For example, assuming the same data from Example 5, if the level of sales is 8,000 units, the profit is:

$$\begin{aligned}\text{Profit} &= \$5\ (8{,}000) - \$3\ (8{,}000) - \$800 \\ &= \$15{,}200\end{aligned}$$

(2) To determine the level of sales necessary to achieve a target profit.
The formula to determine the level of sales needed to achieve a target profit is:

$$\text{Sales to realize target profit (in units)} = \frac{\text{Target profit} + \text{Total fixed costs}}{\text{Selling price per unit} - \text{Variable costs per unit}}$$

$$\text{Sales to realize target profit (in dollars)} = \frac{\text{Target profit} + \text{Total fixed costs}}{1 - \text{Variable costs as a \% of dollar sales}}$$

EXAMPLE 6

Using data from Example 2, and assuming that the target profit is $25,000, then:

$$\begin{aligned}\text{Sales to realize target profit (in units)} &= \frac{\$25{,}000 + \$800}{\$5 - \$3} \\ &= 12{,}900 \text{ units}\end{aligned}$$

$$\begin{aligned}\text{Sales to realize target profit (in dollars)} &= \frac{\$25{,}000 + \$800}{1 - \$0.60\ (a)} \\ &= \$64{,}500\end{aligned}$$

(*a*) $3 (variable cost) ÷ $5 (selling price)

Adjustment for income taxes. To incorporate income taxes into the analysis, the formulas given above must be modified. Letting T denote the income tax rate, then:

$$\text{After-tax profit} = (1 - T) \cdot (PQ - VQ - F)$$

$$\text{Sales to realize target after-tax profit (in units)} = \frac{\dfrac{\text{Target after-tax profit}}{(1 - T)} + \text{Total fixed costs}}{\text{Selling price per unit} - \text{Variable costs per unit}}$$

$$\text{Sales to realize target after-tax profit (in dollars)} = \frac{\dfrac{\text{Target after-tax profit}}{(1 - T)} + \text{Total fixed costs}}{1 - \text{Variable costs as a \% of dollar sales}}$$

9.11 RISK AND PROFIT ANALYSIS

The margin of safety is a measure of the risk of not breaking even. It indicates by what percentage expected sales can decline and still allow the firm to break even. The higher the percentage, the smaller the risk of not realizing the break-even point.

The formula for the margin of safety is

$$\text{Margin of safety} = \frac{\text{Expected sales} - \text{Break-even sales}}{\text{Expected sales}}$$

The formula is used for both the break-even point in units, and dollars.

Suppose, for example, that the expected sales are 550 units. Recall that the break-even point in units is 400. The margin of safety is:

$$\text{Margin of safety} = \frac{550 - 400}{550}$$
$$= 27\%$$

This means that if sales are 27% less than expected, the company will still break even.

To see that the formula is the same with dollars, recall that the selling price per unit is $5. Since unit sales are expected to be 550, dollar sales are expected to be $2,750 ($5 × 550). The break-even point in dollars is $2,000.

$$\text{Margin of safety} = \frac{\$2{,}750 - \$2{,}000}{\$2{,}750}$$
$$= 27\%$$

Solved Problems

9.1 Direct vs. Absorption Costing. The financial data for Meghan Company follows:

Production (in units)	10,000
Selling price (per unit)	$40
Beginning inventory (units)	0
Ending inventory (units)	3,000
Costs per unit:	
Direct materials	$5
Direct labor	$10
Variable factory overhead	$3
Fixed factory overhead	$4
Selling and administrative expenses	
($2,000 fixed)	$5,000

Prepare cost of goods manufactured statements under direct and absorption costing.

SOLUTION

Meghan Company
Cost of Goods Manufactured

Absorption Costing

Costs put into production during the period at standard:		
Direct materials		$ 50,000
Direct labor		100,000
Factory overhead:		
Variable	$30,000	
Fixed	40,000	70,000
Total costs put into production at standard		$220,000
Plus: Work-in-process inventory at beginning of the period		-0-
Cost of goods in process during the period at standard		$220,000
Less: Work-in-process inventory at the end of the period at standard ($22 × 3,000)		66,000
Cost of goods manufactured at standard		$154,000

Direct Costing

Variable costs put into production during the period at standard:	
Direct materials	$ 50,000
Direct labor	100,000
Variable factory overhead	30,000
Total variable costs put into production at standard	$180,000
Plus: Variable work-in-process inventory at beginning of the period	-0-
Variable cost of goods in process during the period at standard	$180,000
Less: Variable work-in-process inventory at the end of the period at standard	54,000 (*a*)
Variable cost of goods manufactured at standard	$126,000

(*a*) $22 (Total cost per unit) − $4 (fixed factory overhead) = $18

$18 × 3,000 = $54,000

9.2 Break-Even Analysis—Contribution-Margin Method. Using the following data, determine the break-even point (BEP) in (*a*) units and (*b*) dollars for the K & B Corporation:

Sales price (SP) per unit	\$10
Fixed costs (FC)	\$200,000
Contribution margin (CM)	50% of sales

SOLUTION

(*a*)

$$\text{BEP (units)} = \frac{\text{FC}}{\text{CM per unit*}} = \frac{\$200{,}000}{\$5 \text{ per unit}} = 40{,}000 \text{ units}$$

$$* \text{ CM per unit} = \text{SP per unit} \times \text{CM\%} = \$10 \times 50\% = \$5.$$

(*b*)

$$\text{BEP (dollars)} = \text{SP per unit} \times \text{BEP (units)} = \$10 \times 40{,}000 \text{ units} = \$400{,}000$$

or

$$\text{BEP (dollars)} = \frac{\text{FC}}{\text{CM\%}} = \frac{\$200{,}000}{50\%} = \$400{,}000$$

9.3 Break-Even Analysis—Graphic Method. Using the data given for the K&B Corporation in Prob. 9.2, illustrate the break-even point on a graph with fixed costs below variable costs.

SOLUTION

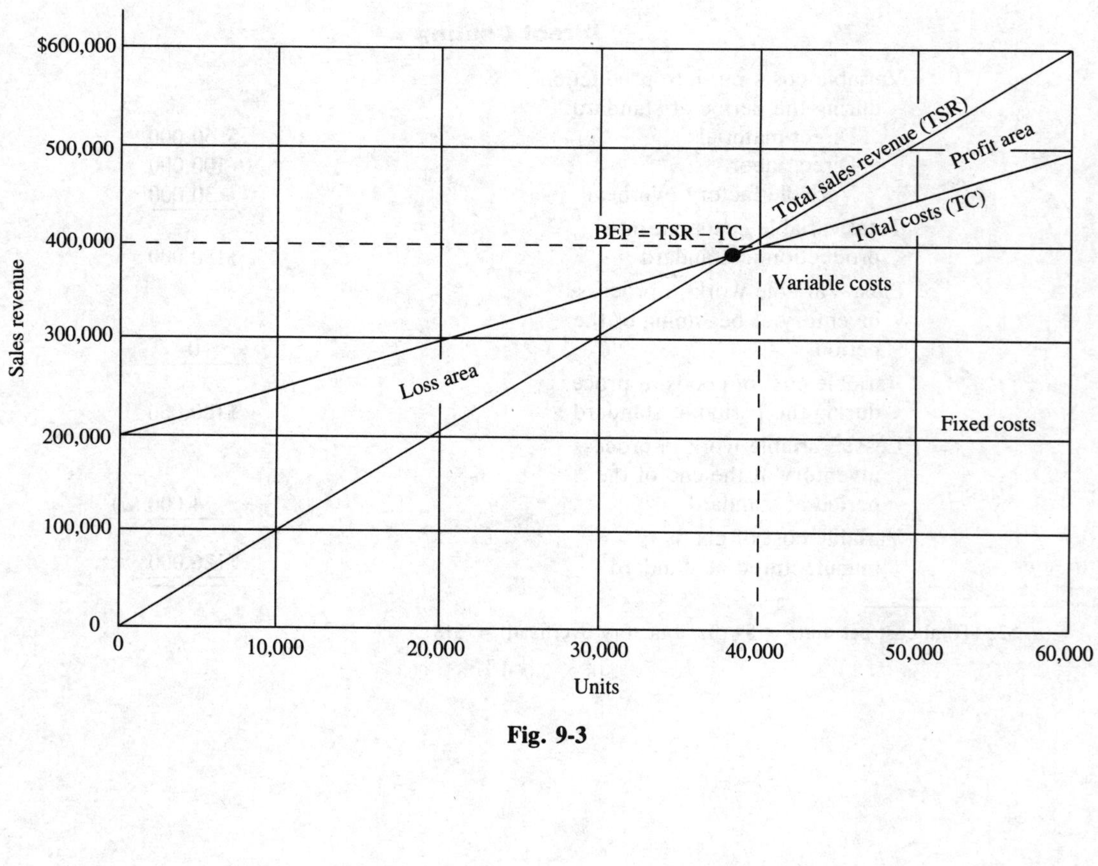

Fig. 9-3

9.4 Break-Even Point in Units. Given the following data:

	Per Unit	Percent
Price of product	$6	100%
Variable costs	4	67%
Contribution margin	$2	33%
Total fixed costs	$500	

determine the break-even point in *units* by (*a*) the contribution-margin method and (*b*) the equation method.

SOLUTION

(*a*)

$$\frac{\text{FC}}{\text{CM per unit}} = \frac{\$500}{\$2} = 250 \text{ units}$$

(*b*)

$$\begin{aligned} \text{Sales} &= \text{VC} + \text{FC} + \text{Profit} \\ \$6x &= \$4x + \$500 + 0 \\ \$2x &= \$500 \\ x &= 250 \text{ units} \end{aligned}$$

9.5 Cost-Volume-Profit Analysis. Assume the following data for the Forster Corporation:

		Per Unit
Sale price		$25.00
Variable cost		18.75
Total fixed costs	$1,250	
Tax rate	40%	

How many units must be sold to (*a*) break even, (*b*) attain a profit before taxes of $1,000, (*c*) attain a profit after taxes of $12,000?

SOLUTION

(*a*)

$$\begin{aligned} \text{Sales} &= \text{Variable costs} + \text{Fixed costs} + \text{Profit} \\ \$25x &= \$18.75x + \$1{,}250 + 0 \\ x &= 200 \text{ units} \end{aligned}$$

(*b*)

$$\frac{\text{Target profit} + \text{Total fixed costs}}{\text{Selling price per unit} - \text{Variable costs per unit}} = \text{Sales}$$

$$\frac{\$1{,}000 + \$1{,}250}{\$25 - \$18.75} = 360 \text{ units}$$

(*c*)

$$\frac{\dfrac{\text{Target after-tax profit}}{(1 - \text{T})} + \text{Total fixed cost}}{\text{Selling price per unit} - \text{Variable costs per unit}} = \text{Sales}$$

$$\frac{\dfrac{\$12{,}000}{(1 - 40\%)} + \$1{,}250}{\$25 - \$18.75} = 3{,}400 \text{ units}$$

Chapter 10

Capital Budgeting

10.1 CAPITAL BUDGETS

Capital expenditures involve the long-term commitments of a firm's resources.

The capital budget, which is generally prepared for a 1-year period, is the key to controlling capital expenditures. Long-range capital budgets can also be prepared for periods of 5 to 10 years and are used to plan for future expenditures. The capital budget is an efficient means of consolidating requests for funds, comparing the consolidated budget with funds made available by management, and ranking projects in order of priority.

10.2 METHODS OF EVALUATION

Quantitative methods have been developed to evaluate proposed projects. The six principal methods of evaluation are (1) payback, (2) accounting rate of return, (3) internal rate of return, (4) net present value, (5) index of profitability, and (6) discounted payback.

10.3 PAYBACK METHOD

The payback method determines the length of time it takes a project to recover its initial investment. If the annual cash flows are constant,

$$\text{Payback period } (P) = \frac{\text{Investment } (I)}{\text{Annual cash flow from operations } (C)}$$

or

$$P = \frac{I}{C}$$

Cash flow from operations is equal to net income after taxes plus depreciation.

The project with the shortest payback period would be favored. This method has several advantages: (1) it is simple to compute, (2) it is easy to understand, and (3) it is superior to the rule-of-thumb method. Among its disadvantages are that it ignores the time value of money and profitability beyond the payback period.

EXAMPLE 1

A firm is considering purchasing a machine costing \$50,000. Its useful life is estimated to be 10 years. Straight-line depreciation will be taken assuming no salvage value. The expected income is \$10,000 per year before depreciation and taxes. Assuming a 40% tax rate, the payback period is computed as follows:

$$P = \frac{I}{C}$$

Income before depreciation and taxes	\$10,000
Less: Depreciation (\$50,000 ÷ 10 years)	5,000
Income before taxes	\$ 5,000
Less: Income taxes (40%)	2,000
Net income	3,000
Plus: Depreciation	5,000
Annual cash flow from operations	\$ 8,000

$$\text{Payback period} = \frac{\$50,000}{\$8,000} = 6.25 \text{ years}$$

10.4 ACCOUNTING RATE OF RETURN

The accounting rate of return is computed by dividing net income by the original investment. The project with the highest rate of return would be favored. Among the advantages of this method are that it considers income over the life of the project and is simple to compute. Among its disadvantages are that it ignores the time value of money and is not applicable if any investment is made after the project begins.

EXAMPLE 2

A $50,000 project is expected to result in net income of $10,000 per year for 10 years. The accounting rate of return is computed as follows:

$$\text{Accounting rate of return} = \frac{\text{Net income}}{\text{Original investment}} = \frac{\$10{,}000}{\$50{,}000} = 20\%$$

10.5 INTERNAL-RATE-OF-RETURN METHOD (IRR)

The IRR for an investment is the discount (interest) rate that will make the present (or discounted) value of the cash flow from operations equal to the initial outlay for an investment.

An IRR above the minimum rate of return specified by management (called the *hurdle rate*) is considered acceptable. When mutually exclusive projects are being compared, the project with the highest IRR will be preferred.

Among the advantages of the IRR are (1) that it recognizes the time value of money, (2) that it recognizes income over the whole life of the project, and (3) that it is expressed as a percentage return, thereby allowing a sound basis for ranking. Its major disadvantage is that it implies that earnings are reinvested at the internal rate of return, which may not be the prevailing interest rate for that type of investment.

To find the IRR of a project, one of two tables is used, depending on whether the yearly cash flows from a project are equal or not. The tables appear at the end of this chapter. Table 10-1, Present Value of $1, is used when the cash flow varies from year to year; Table 10-2, Present Value of $1 Received Annually for *N* Years, is used when yearly cash flows are equal.

Case 1. If cash flows are conventional (equal cash flows for each year of the project), the IRR can be computed by using the following technique:

$$\text{IRR annuity factor} = \frac{\text{Initial investment}}{\text{Annual cash flow}}$$

The resulting annuity factor is converted into the IRR by looking up the annuity factor on a table showing the present value (PV) of $1 received annually over a period of years (Table 10-2). Limit your search for the IRR annuity factor to the row of the table that represents the number of years the project is expected to last. Move along that row until the IRR annuity factor (or the amount closest to it) is found. The interest rate appearing at the top of that column is the IRR for the project.

EXAMPLE 3

A project under consideration requires an initial investment of $54,000 and is expected to result in a cash flow from operations equal to $15,000 per year for 7 years.

The IRR is computed as follows:

$$\text{IRR annuity factor} = \frac{\text{Initial investment}}{\text{Annual cash flow}} = \frac{\$54{,}000}{\$15{,}000} = 3.6$$

To convert the annuity factor into the IRR, Table 10-2 is used. Since the duration of the project is 7 years, the row designated as year 7 is searched for the nearest value to 3.6. An annuity factor of 3.605 is listed in this row under the 20% column. The IRR is therefore 20%.

Case 2. When the cash flow from operations is not equal each year, the computation to determine the IRR is more complex and involves trial-and-error procedures. Table 10-1, Present Value of $1, is used instead of Table 10-2 because the cash flow varies from year to year and therefore the present value of each year's cash flow must be independently computed.

EXAMPLE 4

Assume an initial outlay of $32,318 and that the cash flow from operations is as follows:

Year	Cash Flow from Operations
1	$ 8,000
2	8,000
3	10,000
4	16,000

The objective is to find the discount rate that will make the present value of the cash flow from operations equal to the initial outlay.

If we start with 12%, the results are as follows:

Year	Cash Flow from Operations	×	12% Discount Rate PV of $1 (Table 10-1)	=	Present Value
1	$ 8,000		0.893		$ 7,144
2	8,000		0.797		6,376
3	10,000		0.712		7,120
4	16,000		0.636		10,176
					$30,816

The total present value is $30,816, but since this is not equal to the $32,318 initial outlay, 12% is not the IRR. The lower the discount rate used, the higher the present value; therefore, in our next attempt to find IRR, we will use a lower discount rate in order to get a higher present value.

At 10% the following results:

Year	Cash Flow from Operations	×	10% Discount Rate PV of $1 (Table 10-1)	=	Present Value
1	$ 8,000		0.909		$ 7,272
2	8,000		0.826		6,608
3	10,000		0.751		7,510
4	16,000		0.683		10,928
					$32,318

The IRR is 10% because at this discount rate, the cash flow from operations is equal to the initial outlay.

Sometimes an IRR falls between two values of a given table (for example, suppose the IRR calculated above was somewhere between 10 and 12 percent). In that case either a more detailed present value table is consulted or an approximation method based on interpolation is used to arrive at the IRR.

10.6 NET-PRESENT-VALUE METHOD (NPV)

To calculate the NPV, the cash flow from operations is discounted at the required minimum rate of return (hurdle rate) and the initial outlay is then deducted. If the discounted cash flow is greater than the initial outlay (i.e., the NPV is positive), the project is profitable and therefore acceptable.

The primary advantages of the NPV are (1) that the NPV can always be calculated (unlike the IRR), (2) that it considers the time value of money, and (3) that it recognizes income over the whole life of the project.

EXAMPLE 5

The initial outlay for a project is $40,000. It is expected to generate $10,000 per year as cash flow from operations for the next 10 years. Assuming a hurdle rate of 16%, the NPV is computed as follows.

From Table 10-2 the present value of $1 received annually for 10 years at 16% is found to be 4.833. So the cash flow discounted at the hurdle rate is

$$4.833 \times \$10{,}000 = \$48{,}330$$

Then the net present value is

$$\begin{aligned} \text{NPV} &= \text{Cash flow discounted at hurdle rate} - \text{Initial investment} \\ &= \$48{,}330 - \$40{,}000 = \$8{,}330 \end{aligned}$$

Since the NPV is positive, the project is profitable and therefore acceptable.

10.7 INDEX OF PROFITABILITY METHOD (IP)

The IP, also called the profitability index or the benefit-cost ratio, is found by dividing the present value of the cash flow from operations by the initial outlay. The IP must be greater than 1 for a project to be considered attractive.

EXAMPLE 6

From the information given in Example 5 the IP is computed as follows:

$$\frac{\text{PV of cash flow } (4.833 \times \$10{,}000)}{\text{Initial outlay}} = \frac{\$48{,}330}{\$40{,}000} = 1.20825$$

This project is acceptable.

10.8 DISCOUNTED-PAYBACK METHOD

The discounted-payback method restates the payback method by taking the time value of money into consideration. The annual cash flow from operations is discounted at the required rate of return before the payback period is computed.

EXAMPLE 7

Assume that a project costing $20,000 is expected to return $7,000 per year for the next 10 years and that the firm's required rate of return is 14%. The discounted payback period is computed as follows:

Year	Cash Flow from Operations	Present Value of $1 at 14% (Table 10.1)	Present Value	Discounted Payback Period (Years)
1	$7,000.00	0.877	$ 6,139	1.00
2	7,000.00	0.769	5,383	1.00
3	7,000.00	0.675	4,725	1.00
4	6,339.53*	0.592	3,753†	0.91‡
			$20,000	3.91

* $3,753 ÷ 0.592 = $6,339.53.

† $20,000 − ($6,139 + $5,383 + $4,725) = $3,753.

‡ $6,339.53 ÷ $7,000 = 0.906 ≈ 0.91.

10.9 REPLACEMENT CHAINS

Replacement chains are established only for mutually exclusive projects (competing projects that do the same job) with different lives. By definition, the adoption of one mutually exclusive project results in the immediate rejection of the others. However, when project lives differ, conflicts may arise over which project to adopt because the IRR and NPV have different implicit assumptions for the reinvestment of the cash flow from operations. The replacement chain is simply a technique that repeats the cash flows of one project until both projects have equal lives. Once the replacement chains have been developed, the adjusted cash flows are used for computing the IRR and NPV of each project. This is done only to make a comparison possible; a more precise determination of profitability would require an investigation of how each project would actually be continued beyond its projected life.

EXAMPLE 8

Assume two mutually exclusive projects have cash flows from operations as follows:

End of Year	Project A	Project B
0 (initial outlay)	$ − 5,000	$ − 5,000
1	+3,000	+2,000
2	+5,500	+2,500
3		+3,000
4		+2,500

A replacement chain for project A is set up that simply repeats the initial outlay and cash flow from operations, starting at the end of year 2.

End of Year	Project A (Original)	Replacement Chain	Project A (Assuming Replacement)
0	$ − 5,000	—	$ − 5,000
1	+3,000	—	+3,000
2	+5,500	$ − 5,000	+500
3	—	+3,000	+3,000
4	—	+5,500	+5,500

Had project B lasted 3 years instead of 4, a common-denominator year would be chosen (in this example, 6 years), and a replacement chain would be constructed for both projects based on 6 years.

10.10 COMPUTATION OF CASH FLOW FROM OPERATIONS

Cash flow from operations is the net income after taxes expected to be generated from a project plus depreciation.

For purposes of analysis the following adjustments to cash flow from operations may be necessary:

(1) When mutually exclusive projects with different lives are analyzed, the cash flows must be adjusted by using replacement chains.

(2) If an investment is expected to have a salvage value, the salvage value is considered a lump-sum payment to be received at the end of the investment. The estimated salvage value must therefore be discounted to its present value and treated as an addition to cash flow from operations.

(3) If additional working capital is needed for a project and is expected to be recouped at the end of the project, the working capital is considered as an initial outlay. The working capital which is expected to be recouped is considered a lump-sum payment to be received at the end of the investment. The estimated working capital expected at the end of the investment must therefore be discounted to its present value and treated as an addition to cash flow from operations.

Solved Problems

10.1 Payback and Accounting Rate of Return. The Arnold Manufacturing Company is considering the purchase of a new machine. Its cost is $30,000; its expected useful life is 10 years (assume no salvage value); and it will be depreciated on a straight-line basis. Income before depreciation and taxes is expected to be $15,000. Assuming a 40% tax rate, compute the (*a*) payback period and (*b*) the accounting rate of return.

SOLUTION

(*a*) **Payback Period** $P = \frac{I}{C}$

Income before depreciation and taxes	$15,000
Less: Depreciation ($30,000 ÷ 10 years)	3,000
Income before taxes	$12,000
Less: Income taxes (40%)	4,800
Net income	7,200
Add: Depreciation	3,000
Annual cash flow from operations	$10,200

$$\text{Payback period} = \frac{\$30{,}000}{\$10{,}200} = 2.94 \text{ years}$$

(*b*) **Accounting Rate of Return**

$$\frac{\text{Net income}}{\text{Original investment}} = \frac{\$7{,}200}{\$30{,}000} = 24\%$$

10.2 The Internal Rate of Return. S. Vollmer Co. is considering a project that requires an initial investment of $79,800. It is expected to result in a cash flow from operations of $35,000 per year for 3 years. Compute the internal rate of return.

SOLUTION

$$\frac{\$79{,}800}{\$35{,}000} = 2.28 \text{ IRR annuity factor} \approx 16\% \text{ IRR}$$

Because the cash flow is conventional, Table 10.2 is used to convert the annuity factor into the IRR as follows. The value closest to 2.28 in the row for 3 years (the life of the project) is 2.246, which is in the 16% column. Hence the IRR is approximately 16%.

10.3 Net Present Value. A. Gee is thinking about a project that needs an initial outlay of $54,000. It is expected to return $12,000 per year as cash flow from operations for the next 9 years. The company's hurdle rate is 16%. Using the NPV method, determine whether the project should be accepted or rejected.

SOLUTION

4.607 [PV of $1 received annually (Table 10.2) at 16% for 9 years] × $12,000	$55,284
Less: Initial outlay	54,000
Net present value	$ 1,284

Since the NPV is positive, the project should be accepted.

10.4 Index of Profitability. The JGH Manufacturing Company is considering the purchase of a new machine. The present value of the cash flow from operations is $37,650. The machine requires an initial outlay of $32,000.

(*a*) Compute the index of profitability and (*b*) determine whether you would invest in the new machine.

SOLUTION

(*a*)
$$\text{Index of profitability} = \frac{\text{Present value of cash flows}}{\text{Initial outlay}} = \frac{\$37{,}650}{\$32{,}000} = 1.177$$

(*b*) Yes, the investment should be considered because the IP is greater than 1.

10.5 Discounted Payback Method. The Hoffman Corporation bought a new machine costing $25,000 and which is expected to generate cash flows from operations of $10,000 per year for the next 5 years. The firm's required rate of return is 12%. Compute the discounted payback period.

SOLUTION

Year	Cash Flow from Operations	Present Value of $1 at 12% (Table 10-1)	Present Value	Discounted Payback Period (Years)
1	$10,000.00	0.893	$ 8,930	1.00
2	10,000.00	0.797	7,970	1.00
3	10,000.00	0.712	7,120	1.00
4	1,540.88*	0.636	980†	0.15†
			$25,000	3.15

* $980 ÷ 0.636 = $1,540.88.

† $25,000 − ($8,930 + $7,970 + $7,120) = $980.

‡ $1,540.88 ÷ $10,000 = 0.15.

Table 10-1 Present Value of $1

Years *N*	5%	6%	8%	10%	12%	14%	16%	18%	20%	22%	24%	25%
1	0.952	0.943	0.926	0.909	0.893	0.877	0.862	0.847	0.833	0.820	0.806	0.800
2	0.907	0.890	0.857	0.826	0.797	0.769	0.743	0.718	0.694	0.672	0.650	0.640
3	0.864	0.840	0.794	0.751	0.712	0.675	0.641	0.609	0.579	0.551	0.524	0.512
4	0.823	0.792	0.735	0.683	0.636	0.592	0.552	0.516	0.482	0.451	0.423	0.410
5	0.784	0.747	0.681	0.621	0.567	0.519	0.476	0.437	0.402	0.370	0.341	0.328
6	0.746	0.705	0.630	0.564	0.507	0.456	0.410	0.370	0.335	0.303	0.275	0.262
7	0.711	0.665	0.583	0.513	0.452	0.400	0.354	0.314	0.279	0.249	0.222	0.210
8	0.677	0.627	0.540	0.467	0.404	0.351	0.305	0.266	0.233	0.204	0.179	0.168
9	0.645	0.592	0.500	0.424	0.361	0.308	0.263	0.225	0.194	0.167	0.144	0.134
10	0.614	0.558	0.463	0.386	0.322	0.270	0.227	0.191	0.162	0.137	0.116	0.107
11	0.585	0.527	0.429	0.350	0.287	0.237	0.195	0.162	0.135	0.112	0.094	0.086
12	0.557	0.497	0.397	0.319	0.257	0.208	0.168	0.137	0.112	0.092	0.076	0.069
13	0.530	0.469	0.368	0.290	0.229	0.182	0.145	0.116	0.093	0.075	0.061	0.055
14	0.505	0.442	0.340	0.263	0.205	0.160	0.125	0.099	0.078	0.062	0.049	0.044
15	0.481	0.417	0.315	0.239	0.183	0.140	0.108	0.084	0.065	0.051	0.040	0.035
16	0.458	0.394	0.292	0.218	0.163	0.123	0.093	0.071	0.054	0.042	0.032	0.028
17	0.436	0.371	0.270	0.198	0.146	0.108	0.080	0.060	0.045	0.034	0.026	0.023
18	0.416	0.350	0.250	0.180	0.130	0.095	0.069	0.051	0.038	0.028	0.021	0.018
19	0.396	0.331	0.232	0.164	0.116	0.083	0.060	0.043	0.031	0.023	0.017	0.014
20	0.377	0.312	0.215	0.149	0.104	0.073	0.051	0.037	0.026	0.019	0.014	0.012

Table 10-2 Present Value of $1 Received Annually for *N* Years

Years *N*	5%	6%	8%	10%	12%	14%	16%	18%	20%	22%	24%	25%
1	0.952	0.943	0.926	0.909	0.893	0.877	0.862	0.847	0.833	0.820	0.806	0.800
2	1.859	1.833	1.783	1.736	1.690	1.647	1.605	1.566	1.528	1.492	1.457	1.440
3	2.723	2.673	2.577	2.487	2.402	2.322	2.246	2.174	2.106	2.042	1.981	1.952
4	3.546	3.465	3.312	3.169	3.037	2.914	2.798	2.690	2.589	2.494	2.404	2.362
5	4.330	4.212	3.993	3.791	3.605	3.433	3.274	3.127	2.991	2.864	2.745	2.689
6	5.076	4.917	4.623	4.355	4.111	3.889	3.685	3.498	3.326	3.167	3.020	2.951
7	5.786	5.582	5.206	4.868	4.564	4.288	4.039	3.812	3.605	3.416	3.242	3.161
8	6.463	6.210	5.747	5.335	4.968	4.639	4.344	4.078	3.837	3.619	3.421	3.329
9	7.108	6.802	6.247	5.759	5.328	4.946	4.607	4.303	4.031	3.786	3.566	3.463
10	7.722	7.360	6.710	6.145	5.650	5.216	4.833	4.494	4.192	3.923	3.682	3.571
11	8.306	7.887	7.139	6.495	5.937	5.453	5.029	4.656	4.327	4.035	3.776	3.656
12	8.863	8.384	7.536	6.814	6.194	5.660	5.197	4.793	4.439	4.127	3.851	3.725
13	9.394	8.853	7.904	7.103	6.424	5.842	5.342	4.910	4.533	4.203	3.912	3.780
14	9.899	9.295	8.244	7.367	6.628	6.002	5.468	5.008	4.611	4.265	3.962	3.824
15	10.380	9.712	8.559	7.606	6.811	6.142	5.575	5.092	4.675	4.315	4.001	3.859
16	10.838	10.106	8.851	7.824	6.974	6.265	5.669	5.162	4.730	4.357	4.033	3.887
17	11.274	10.477	9.122	8.022	7.120	6.373	5.749	5.222	4.775	4.391	4.059	3.910
18	11.690	10.828	9.372	8.201	7.250	6.467	5.818	5.273	4.812	4.419	4.080	3.928
19	12.085	11.158	9.604	8.365	7.366	6.550	5.877	5.316	4.844	4.442	4.097	3.942
20	12.462	11.470	9.818	8.514	7.469	6.623	5.929	5.353	4.870	4.460	4.110	3.954

Chapter 11

Relevant Costing in Decision Making and Performance Measurement

Relevant Costing in Decision Making

11.1 INTRODUCTION

Management is often required to make critical decisions. Should a new product line be added or an old product line deleted? Should a special order be accepted or rejected? Should component parts or raw materials be produced or purchased? Should old machinery be kept or replaced? It is the cost accountant's responsibility to summarize all relevant data that will serve as the basis for making the decision. This section of the chapter concerns itself with costs relevant to decision analyses.

11.2 RELEVANT VS. IRRELEVANT COSTS

Relevant costs are expected future costs that differ among alternatives. They are directly affected by management's actions. Irrelevant costs, on the other hand, are unaffected by the decision. Relevancy is not an attribute of a particular cost; the identical cost may be relevant in one circumstance and irrelevant in another.

EXAMPLE 1

A college student graduating this year is deciding whether to take a job immediately or enter graduate school. The costs relevant to continuing her education are tuition, fees, books, and supplies. Room, board, and clothing costs are irrelevant since they will be incurred regardless of her decision. Also important to her decision is the potential salary she would forego while attending school. If she decides to attend graduate school, this particular relevant cost would be considered an opportunity cost. (See Section 11.5 for a more detailed discussion of opportunity costs.)

11.3 DIFFERENTIAL OR INCREMENTAL COSTS

Differential, or incremental, costs are those costs which differ from the base cost incurred by all alternatives. As such, differential costs are composed of only that portion of the total cost which is specifically incurred by an alternative. Such costs are relevant when they differ from the alternatives being considered.

When analyzing a special decision, the key is the differential effects of each option on the company's profits. Frequently, variable costs and incremental costs are the same. However, should an additional batch or special order extend production beyond the relevant range, both variable and total fixed costs would increase. In that event, the differential fixed costs should be included in the analysis.

EXAMPLE 2

Stephen is driving from New York City to Houston, Texas and would like some companionship on the trip. He asks his friend Sarah to accompany him. Stephen asks Sarah to pay for only the incremental costs of the trip. The trip expenses are as follows:

Gasoline	$ 80.00
Tolls	10.00
Motel rooms ($30 for each single room)	60.00
Sarah's meals	28.00
Stephen's meals	23.00
Total trip expenses	$201.00

Sarah's incremental costs for the trip would be $58.00. This includes the $30 charge for her motel room and the $28 for her meals. Stephen will incur all the other expenses even if he travels alone.

The adjective ''relevant'' denotes the pertinence of a cost to the evaluation process, whereas ''differential'' denotes how that relevance is determined. Furthermore, not all differential costs need be relevant, since the latter depend on the situation. So, if Stephen were trying to determine whether to ask Laura or Sarah to accompany him on the trip, the incremental costs would be irrelevant since they would be the same for both.

11.4 SUNK COSTS

In managerial accounting, historical costs are frequently referred to as *sunk costs*. Sunk costs are past committed costs that are now irrevocable. They are not relevant to future decisions and should not be considered in an analysis, except for possible tax effects upon their disposition and lessons to be learned from the past decisions.

EXAMPLE 3

Ellis Industries, a computer manufacturer, has in its inventory $80,000 worth of disk-drive housings for a computer line that is now obsolete. The housings can be remachined to fit a newer line at a cost of $15,000 and then sold for $33,000. Ellis Industries' other alternative is to sell the housings as scrap for $12,000.

	Decision		
	(1) Remachine	**(2) Scrap**	**(1) − (2) Incremental Effect**
Revenues	$33,000	$12,000	$21,000
Additional costs	15,000	-0-	15,000
Net profit	$18,000	$12,000	$ 6,000

The $80,000 inventory cost is an irrelevant sunk cost and is therefore not considered in that analysis. The only relevant factors are the future revenues and the future costs. By choosing to remachine the housings instead of scrapping them, Ellis Industries can increase its profits—or decrease its losses—by $6,000.

11.5 OPPORTUNITY COSTS

When a decision to pursue one alternative is made, the benefits of the other options are foregone. Benefits lost from rejecting the second-best option are the *opportunity costs* of the chosen action.

Since opportunity costs are not actually incurred, they are not recorded in the accounting records. They are, however, relevant costs for decision making and should be considered in evaluating a proposed alternative.

The real value of opportunity costs is often difficult to determine since other factors impinge. For example, a decision by management to minimize carrying costs by keeping inventory levels low may result in stock shortages. The sales lost become the opportunity cost of this decision. The level of inventory that will profitably minimize *both* carrying costs and possibility of stock shortages would then have to be determined.

In determining opportunity costs, one should be certain that the costs are derived from viable alternatives. For example, lost rent is an opportunity cost only if there are potential tenants willing to rent the facilities at a determined price.

EXAMPLE 4

Jim Martin owns a men's clothing store in Philadelphia. He was recently offered the position of store manager at Anthony's, a large retail chain store in the area. Working at Anthony's, Jim would earn an annual salary of $50,000. Jim knows that he could sell the net assets of his business for $115,000 but is uncertain whether to sell the business and manage Anthony's or continue operating his own store. Jim begins his analysis of the two alternatives by examining his store's income statement from last year:

Revenue from sales		$225,000
Cost of goods sold		135,000
Gross profit		$ 90,000
Operating expenses		
Rent	$ 7,200	
Employee wages	17,000	
Utilities	3,640	
Supplies	560	
Advertising	1,450	
Professional fees	1,150	
Insurance	820	
Miscellaneous	630	
Total operating expenses		32,450
Net income		$ 57,550

Jim's analysis should not stop here. He must now subtract from his net income the two opportunity costs involved in the decision:

(1) The salary he would forego if he continues to operate his own clothing store.
(2) The interest income he would receive from investing the proceeds from the sale of his business.

Further analysis considering opportunity costs is as follows:

Net income (from income statement)		$ 57,550
Less: Opportunity costs		
Foregone salary	$50,000	
Foregone interest income at assumed 17% interest rate ($115,000 × 17%)	19,550	
Total opportunity costs		69,550
Loss of income from failure to accept the offer		$(12,000)

Had he ignored the opportunity costs, Jim Martin might have erroneously concluded that it would be more profitable to stay with his store, since his present income is $7,550 above the salary offered by Anthony's. However, after studying the opportunity costs involved, Jim knows that he would be losing $12,000 in the first year by keeping his business.

This analysis is purely quantitative, and Jim Martin must also measure the qualitative factors, such as loss of independence in being self-employed compared with the $12,000 loss in income.

11.6 SEGMENTAL ANALYSIS

In the process of segmenting a company by departments, product lines, divisions, types of customers, etc., management can analyze specific areas of the firm to determine whether they should be continued, expanded, or dropped.

In the event that a segment is dropped, the impact on that segment's total costs depends on the nature of the costs involved. The segment's variable costs will disappear if the segment is dropped, but the total fixed costs may or may not be affected. Fixed costs can be classified as *separable costs* and *joint costs*. A separable fixed cost exists only because the segment exists; it will be eliminated if the segment is discontinued. Joint costs, however, remain after the disposal and must be absorbed by the remaining segments. Variable costs are always separable and are eliminated when the segment is eliminated.

11.7 DISCONTINUING A SEGMENT

Quantitatively, a segment should be dropped if by doing so the reduction in costs exceeds the revenue lost. The qualitative factors include the impact of discontinuing the segment on the rest of the business and management's ability to use resources in an alternative manner. Often the elimination of a product line causes the sales of other lines to decrease. Both the qualitative and quantitative elements must be measured before arriving at a decision to drop a segment.

The following example pertains to segmenting by product line. The same format could be followed for evaluating other types of segmenting, such as by divisions or services provided. Generally, the incremental approach (Sec. 11.2) is used to determine whether a segment should be dropped.

EXAMPLE 5

Jennings, Inc., a manufacturer of hair-care products, is considering dropping from its line a finishing rinse, which is presently losing money. The following information concerns Jennings' three products:

	Shampoo	**Finishing Rinse**	**Conditioner**	**Total**
Sales revenue	$500,000	$300,000	$400,000	$1,200,000
Variable costs	270,000	202,000	220,000	692,000
Contribution margin	$230,000	$ 98,000	$180,000	$ 508,000
Fixed Costs				
Separable	$ 56,000	$ 59,000	$ 45,000	$ 160,000
Joint*	100,000	60,000	80,000	240,000
Total	$156,000	$119,000	$125,000	$ 400,000
Profit (loss)	$ 74,000	$(21,000)	$ 55,000	$ 108,000

* Allocated on the basis of total sales dollars.

From the above, it appears that by dropping the finishing rinse line, Jennings, Inc. would save $21,000 a year. However, incremental analysis leads to quite a different conclusion:

Finishing Rinse
Incremental Analysis of Dropping Line

Benefits		
Variable costs avoided	$202,000	
Separable fixed costs avoided	59,000	
Total costs avoided		$261,000

Losses	
Decrease in revenue	(300,000)
Increase (decrease) in net income	$ (39,000)

In actuality, a $39,000 decrease in total company income ($18,000 more than the $21,000 loss from keeping the line) would result if the finishing rinse line were dropped. The revenue of the product covers both the variable costs and the separable fixed costs, therefore helping to cover the joint costs and to provide income. Jennings, Inc. should discontinue the line only if the opportunity cost of using the space and resources in another way exceeds the incremental profit of the present course of action.

Another method of evaluating this problem is by constructing an income statement based on the assumption that the line is dropped:

	Shampoo	Conditioner	Total
Sales revenue	$500,000	$400,000	$900,000
Variable costs	270,000	220,000	490,000
Contribution margin	$230,000	$180,000	$410,000
Fixed costs			
Separable	$ 56,000	$ 45,000	$101,000
Joint*	133,333	106,667	240,000
Total	$189,333	$151,667	$341,000
Profit (loss)	$ 40,667	$ 28,333	$ 69,000

* Allocated on the basis of total sales dollars.

The same result, a decrease of $39,000 ($108,000 − $69,000) in total company net income, is arrived at whichever method is used.

It should also be noted that eliminating the finishing rinse line may have a considerable effect on the sales of the other hair products. A consumer may stop buying the shampoo and conditioner if the rinse is not available and may switch to a competitor's products if the competitor provides the entire product line.

11.8 SELL OR PROCESS FURTHER

Joint products are the result of a single production process that yields two or more products. Joint products are frequently found in industries that process raw materials. Examples include the chemical, petroleum, and wood industries, as well as producers of cattle or dairy products. In the cattle industry, products such as various cuts of meat, leather from hide, and sundries from bones are obtained from the cattle.

If external markets exist for these semifinished products, the manufacturer must decide which products are more profitable to sell at the split-off point and which ones should be processed further before sale. The *split-off point* is that point where the separate products emerge from the joint process. Products emerging from the process that are not salable at any point are simply discarded.

The costs incurred before split-off are irrelevant in determining whether or not the products should be processed further. They need to be considered only in determining whether the entire process should be undertaken at all.

Incremental analysis provides the basis for solving this problem. Generally, if the additional revenue earned by processing further is greater than the additional cost, the product should be processed further; however, if the converse is true, the product should be sold at the split-off point.

Performance Measurement

11.12 APPROACHES TO PERFORMANCE MEASUREMENT

After the company divisions have been established and the related authorities and responsibilities assigned, it is vital that an adequate system be developed for measuring the performance of both the divisions and the division managers.

There are many approaches to an evaluation program. Their selection depends on the needs of the enterprise and the wishes of management. For example, should performance be gauged in terms of net income, net sales, or net income in relation to investment? Should income after income taxes or income before income taxes be used? Should the basis of measurement for the divisions be the same as that for the company as a whole? No one answer will suit the needs of all companies. However, one of the most common methods of performance measurement in use is the *return on investment* (ROI).

11.13 RETURN ON INVESTMENT (ROI)

The return-on-investment or return-on-capital method has been used for many years by banks to measure the performance of borrowers. The rate of return on investment for the total company is usually computed by dividing net income by total assets. Total assets may be referred to as investment, invested capital, capital employed, etc. (the terms are often used interchangeably).

The ROI method has many important advantages over most other methods. It is simple to compute and can be used to measure and compare divisional or company performance, returns on competing companies, returns on competing capital projects, and many other factors, thereby permitting management to select the most favorable option from alternatives.

EXAMPLE 10

The ROI method and its advantage over the return-on-sales method are illustrated in the following comparison of companies X and Y:

	Company X	Company Y
Sales	\$2,000,000	\$2,000,000
Net income	300,000	300,000
Return on sales	15%	15%
Investment	\$3,000,000	\$1,500,000
Return on investment	10%	20%

Both companies have the same sales volume, the same net income, and the same return on sales. However, to earn that income, Company X is using \$3,000,000 in assets, twice as much as Company Y. Thus Company X is earning only 10% on assets employed while Company Y is earning 20% on assets employed.

11.14 RETURN-ON-INVESTMENT RATIO

A simple way to express the return on investment is by an equation. The ROI equation is generally shown in two parts, the *investment turnover* and the *earnings ratio*. The investment turnover is stated as:

$$\text{Investment turnover} = \frac{\text{Sales}}{\text{Total assets}}$$

The earnings ratio shows the sales-expense relationship and is stated as:

$$\text{Earnings ratio} = \frac{\text{Net income}}{\text{Sales}}$$

Investment turnover indicates management's efficiency in using available assets to generate sales volume and earnings. The earnings ratio indicates the percentage of profit in each dollar of sales. The ROI equation is made up of both the above components:

$$\text{ROI} = \text{Investment turnover} \times \text{Earnings ratio}$$

Upon superficial examination, it appears that the equation could be simplified by canceling out sales in the two components. If this were done, however, the independence of the two separate variables, investment turnover and earnings ratio, would be lost.

11.15 ADVANTAGES AND DISADVANTAGES OF ROI

The advantages of this method are that ROI can

(1) Act as a comprehensive measure, sensitive to every influence affecting the financial status of a company.

(2) Focus management's attention upon maximizing earnings on invested capital (total assets employed).

(3) Serve as a basis for measuring management's performance in utilizing total assets as well as divisional resources.

(4) Help make the goals of the division manager coincide with those of corporate management.

(5) Provide a means for objective comparison of various internal performance results among divisions and with projected external performance results.

(6) Help division managers evaluate and improve their own performance.

(7) Provide an incentive to use existing assets to their full extent, thereby limiting the acquisition of additional resources to those which will increase the return on investment ratio.

The disadvantages of the ROI method are that

(1) It focuses on maximizing a ratio rather than improving absolute profit amounts.

(2) The established rate of return may be too high and could discourage divisional incentive.

(3) A division manager may be reluctant to acquire additional investments that might lower the ROI.

(4) Division managers may make decisions which help raise the divisional ROI ratio but which are not good for the long-term interest of the company.

11.16 TOTAL COMPANY EVALUATION

Total company evaluation is often used when one company wishes to compare its return on investment with that of another company. This is an *external evaluation* rather than the *internal evaluation* done in measuring divisional performance. Total data for most companies can generally be obtained from such published reports as the annual report to stockholders or to the Securities and Exchange Commission. Generally, only final results such as net sales and net income are needed, and the invested capital is the total assets used in the business. There are differences of opinion over which figures should be included for some of the factors of the equation. For example, should net income be used, or would it be better to use operating income so that nonoperating expense and income are deleted? Care must be exercised in making comparisons between companies when further data are lacking. Such comparisons may be distorted if, for example, entirely different products or divisions are included in the totals.

EXAMPLE 11

Company B is considering the acquisition of Company Y, a small company in the same kind of business. Company B wishes to earn at least 16% on the Company Y investment, the same as it earns on its own invested capital. Given the following data for Company Y,

Sales	$ 60,000
Investment required	$100,000
Earnings ratio	20%

the return on investment is calculated as follows:

$$\text{ROI} = \text{Investment turnover} \times \text{Earnings ratio} = \frac{\text{Sales}}{\text{Total assets}} \times \text{Earnings ratio}$$

$$= \frac{\$60{,}000}{\$100{,}000} \times 20\% = 0.60 \times 20\% = 12\%$$

Because of the low investment turnover of 0.60, or 60%, the resulting ROI is only 12%, well below the required 16%, therefore the investment would not be undertaken.

11.17 DIVISIONAL EVALUATION

The ROI concept has proven to be very effective for internal evaluation in many large industrial companies. In order for a company to obtain maximum results from decentralization, constant monitoring of divisional operations is essential. In the past, central management was mostly concerned with dollar sales, dollar earnings, and profit margins. Generally, the operating income figure is used in comparing divisional results. Nonoperating expense and income would generally be maintained on the headquarters books. The divisional ROI equation is usually stated as:

$$\text{ROI} = \frac{\text{Divisional sales}}{\text{Divisional total assets}} \times \frac{\text{Divisional operating income}}{\text{Divisional sales}}$$

or

$$\text{ROI} = \text{Divisional investment turnover} \times \text{Divisional earnings ratio}$$

EXAMPLE 12

The Adams Company wants to compare the ROIs of two of its divisions, the Venice Division and the Englewood Division. The pertinent information is as follows:

Division	Sales	Operating Income	Total Assets
Venice	$1,200,000	$135,000	$950,000
Englewood	475,000	75,000	550,000

The ROI for each division is calculated as follows:

$$\text{Venice ROI} = \frac{\$1{,}200{,}000}{\$950{,}000} \times \frac{\$135{,}000}{\$1{,}200{,}000} = 1.26 \times 11.3\% = 14.2\%$$

$$\text{Englewood ROI} = \frac{\$475{,}000}{\$550{,}000} \times \frac{\$75{,}000}{\$475{,}000} = 0.86 \times 15.8\% = 13.6\%$$

We can see the significance of individual computations for investment turnover and earnings ratio. The Venice Division turned over its investment 1.26 times, while Englewood turned over its investment only 0.86 time. However, the earnings ratio, or percentage, was just the reverse. Venice earned only 11.3% on sales, while Englewood earned 15.8%. The net result shows that Venice had an ROI of 14.2% and Englewood had an ROI of 13.6%.

11.18 RESIDUAL INCOME

One of the stated shortcomings of ROI is its emphasis on *rate* of return rather than on absolute dollars. To overcome this, some companies use a target rate or *imputed-interest rate*, and the excess of net income above this figure is considered the *residual income*. The formula is

$$\text{Residual income} = \text{Net income} - (\text{Investment} \times \text{Imputed-interest rate})$$

An important advantage of this method is that a particular division may expand as long as it earns a rate in excess of the charge for invested capital (imputed interest). Under this method, managers generally concentrate on increasing dollars rather than improving only the ROI percentage rate.

EXAMPLE 13

The Fred Williams Company used the residual-income method in performance measurement of its divisional operations. The following are the results for the past year for Division A:

Division A		
Invested capital (Total assets)	$100,000	
Net income		$18,000
Return on investment	18%	
Investment charge at 12% imputed-interest rate ($100,000 × 12%)		12,000
Residual income		$ 6,000

Division A earned $18,000, or 18%, on the assets the company had invested in that division. If it had had to borrow those funds outside, the company would have had to pay 12%. Therefore, the division is expected to earn in excess of 12% and can expand as long as it can generate such a residual income.

Solved Problems

11.1 Discontinuing a Segment. The management of Franco Corporation is concerned about Department B, which showed a loss of $1,300 last quarter. You have been asked to prepare an analysis that will help management decide whether to discontinue the department. Below is Franco's income statement for last quarter.

	Department A	**Department B**	**Total**
Sales revenue	$260,000	$130,000	$390,000
Variable costs	156,000	117,000	273,000
Contribution margin	$104,000	$ 13,000	$117,000
Fixed costs			
Separable	$ 11,300	$ 5,700	$ 17,000
Joint	17,400	8,600	26,000
Total	$ 28,700	$ 14,300	$ 43,000
Profit (loss)	$ 75,300	$ (1,300)	$ 74,000

Showing all calculations, determine the effect of closing Department B on Franco Corporation and make a recommendation.

SOLUTION

Incremental Analysis of Discontinuing Department B

Benefits		
Variable costs avoided	$117,000	
Separable fixed costs avoided	5,700	
Total		$ 122,700
Losses		
Decrease in revenues		$(130,000)
Increase (decrease) in net income		$ (7,300)

Franco Corporation should continue operating Department B, because dropping it would decrease the corporation's income by $7,300 (almost 6 times as much as the current operating loss of $1,300).

11.2 Sell or Process Further. Mead Industries produces three products from a joint process. Each product can be sold at the split-off point or processed further. From the data given below, determine for management which products should be sold at split-off and which should be processed further.

Product	Sales Revenue at Split-Off	Additional Processing Costs	Sales Revenue If Processed Further
1	$37,500	$13,500	$63,000
2	61,500	10,500	67,500
3	36,000	12,000	50,000

SOLUTION

Product	Incremental Revenue*	Incremental Contribution of Further Processing**
1	$25,500	$12,000
2	6,000	(4,500)
3	14,000	2,000

* Revenue if processed further − Revenue at split-off.

** Incremental revenue − Additional processing costs.

Mead Industries should sell product 2 at split-off and process products 1 and 3 further.

11.3 Special Orders. Howard Industries produces a single product in large quantities. The company is currently operating at 60% of capacity and wishes to increase its production level. Howard is considering accepting a government contract for next year for 15,000 units at $3.60 per unit. The company's normal selling price is $5.25, and its annual capacity is 60,000 units. The fixed costs are $30,000, and the variable costs are $2.80 per unit. The company does not pay sales commissions.

Assuming that the government contract would not create any market retaliation, should Howard Industries accept it? (Support your answer with computations.)

SOLUTION

	Units
Current production (60% × 60,000 unit capacity)	36,000
Government requirement	15,000
Total	51,000

Incremental Analysis

	Per Unit	Total
Sales (15,000 units)	\$3.60	\$54,000
Variable manufacturing costs	2.80	42,000
Incremental profit	\$0.80	\$12,000

Assuming that sales do not increase by more than 9,000 units (60,000 − 51,000) next year, Howard Industries would have the necessary capacity to produce the units required by the government contract. The company should, therefore, accept the contract, which will increase profit by \$12,000.

11.4 Make-or-Buy Decisions and Opportunity Costs. J. W. Haines Corporation annually produces 10,000 units of assembly part number 206. An outside supplier has offered to manufacture the part for Haines at \$19 per part. If Haines decides to buy the part, they will be able to rent the existing area for \$8,000 a year. Listed below are Haines' total costs to produce part 206.

	Per Unit	Total
Direct materials	\$ 2.50	\$ 25,000
Direct labor	14.00	140,000
Variable overhead	2.25	22,500
Fixed overhead	0.75	7,500
Total costs	\$19.50	\$195,000

Assuming that no additional costs are incurred in purchasing the part, should Haines make or buy? Support your answer with computations.

SOLUTION

	Make	Buy
Purchase price		
(\$19 × 10,000 units)		\$190,000
Incremental cost to make		
[(\$2.50 + \$14 + \$2.25) × 10,000 units]	\$187,500	
Opportunity cost—Rent	8,000	
Net relevant costs	\$195,500	\$190,000

J. W. Haines Corporation would save \$5,500 (\$195,500 − \$190,000) by purchasing assembly part 206 and renting the facilities.

11.5 Performance Measurement. Santoro Corporation has two divisions, A and B. Total sales for the year were \$1,200,000. It is estimated that Division B will account for 60% of the total sales. Santoro wishes to earn 14% on its investment. Compute (*a*) investment turnover, (*b*) earnings ratio, (*c*) return on investment, and (*d*) residual income for each division from the following data:

	Division A	Division B
Cost of goods sold	$300,000	$500,000
Selling and administrative expenses	150,000	150,000
Plant investment	200,000	300,000

SOLUTION

	Division A	Division B
Sales	$480,000 (40%)	$720,000 (60%)
Cost of goods sold	300,000	500,000
Gross profit	$180,000	$220,000
Selling and administrative expenses	150,000	150,000
Net income	$ 30,000	$ 70,000

(*a*)

$$\text{Investment turnover} = \frac{\text{Sales}}{\text{Plant investment}}$$

Division A: $\dfrac{\$480{,}000}{\$200{,}000} = 2.40 \text{ or } 240\%$ Division B: $\dfrac{\$720{,}000}{\$300{,}000} = 2.40 \text{ or } 240\%$

(*b*)

$$\text{Earnings ratio} = \frac{\text{Net income}}{\text{Sales}}$$

Division A: $\dfrac{\$30{,}000}{\$480{,}000} = 6.25\%$ Division B: $\dfrac{\$70{,}000}{\$720{,}000} = 9.72\%$

(*c*)

$$\text{ROI} = \text{Investment turnover} \times \text{Earnings ratio}$$

Division A: $240\% \times 6.25\% = 15\%$ Division B: $240\% \times 9.72\% = 23\%$

(*d*) Residual income = Net income − (Investment × Imputed-interest rate)

	Department A	Department B
Net income	$30,000	$70,000
Investment charge* (14%)	28,000**	42,000***
Residual income	$ 2,000	$28,000

* Investment charge = Investment × Imputed-interest rate.

** $200,000 × 14% = 28,000. *** $300,000 × 14% = $42,000.

11.6 ROI—Divisional Income. Hennessey Corporation must close one of its divisions. From the following data determine which division should be kept open on the basis of ROI and residual income. The company wants to earn 18% on its investment.

	Division A	Division B
Net income	$160,000	$225,000
Investment turnover	80%	90%
Earnings ratio	20%	25%

SOLUTION

$$\text{ROI} = \text{Investment turnover} \times \text{Earnings ratio}$$

Division A: $\text{ROI} = 80\% \times 20\% = 16\%$ Division B: $\text{ROI} = 90\% \times 25\% = 22.5\%$

$$\text{Residual income} = \text{Net Income} - \text{Investment charge}$$

	Division A	Division B
Net income	$160,000	$225,000
Investment charge (18%)*	180,000	180,000
Residual income (loss)	$ (20,000)	$ 45,000

* *Calculation:*

$$\text{ROI} = \frac{\text{Sales}}{\text{Investment}} \times \frac{\text{Net income}}{\text{Sales}}$$

Division A:

$$\text{Investment} = \frac{\text{Net income}}{\text{ROI}} = \frac{\$160{,}000}{16\%} = \$1{,}000{,}000$$

$$\text{Investment charge} = \$1{,}000{,}000 \times 18\% \text{ imputed-interest rate} = \$180{,}000$$

Division B:

$$\text{Investment} = \frac{\$225{,}000}{22.5\%} = \$1{,}000{,}000$$

$$\text{Investment charge} = \$1{,}000{,}000 \times 18\% = \$180{,}000$$

The Hennessey Corporation should keep Division B open.

Chapter 12

Decision Theory and Economic Order Quantity

Decision Theory

12.1 AN OUTLINE OF THE DECISION-THEORY METHOD

Decision theory is an area of statistics used when data are uncertain or incomplete. Decision theory evaluates different courses of action open to a manager when those courses can be measured monetarily.

Usually, the decision-theory method is stated mathematically. The following elements are generally used in developing a decision-theory model.

Quantifiable Objective. A specified goal that can be measured; particularly, that function whose monetary value management wants to maximize or minimize (for example, profit or cost).

Decision Variables or Actions. Alternatives available to the decision maker. They must be defined and mutually exclusive.

Payoff. The monetary reward or consequence for each decision variable or action.

Uncontrollable Variables or Events. States of nature that are uncontrollable in the decision-theory model. They must be completely defined and mutually exclusive.

Probabilities. The likelihood of the occurrence of each event.

12.2 GENERAL APPROACH TO UNCERTAINTY

The general approach to dealing with uncertainty is to (1) delineate possible events (E) and actions (A) for the problem, (2) estimate the probability of occurrence of each event, and (3) determine which event is most likely to yield the greatest profit.

EXAMPLE 1

A small store sells fresh relish at \$2 per jar. It costs the proprietors \$1.25 per jar. If the relish is not sold by the end of the month, it spoils and the proprietors take a loss on the unsold jars. The proprietors believe that they can estimate the demand and make the following predictions:

Demand (Jars)	Probability of Event $P(E)$
E_1 0	0.10
E_2 1	0.60
E_3 2	0.30

Thus, the possible actions of the proprietors are:

A_1 = Order no relish
A_2 = Order 1 jar of relish
A_3 = Order 2 jars of relish

These data can be analyzed by formulating the following payoff table:

Payoff

		A_1: Order 0		A_2: Order 1		A_3: Order 2	
Demand (Events)	$P(E)$	Actual Profit	Expected Profit*	Actual Profit	Expected Profit*	Actual Profit	Expected Profit*
E_1	0.10	0	0	$\$-1.25$	$\$-0.125$	$\$-2.50$	$\$-0.25$
E_2	0.60	0	0	0.75	0.45	-0.50	-0.30
E_3	0.30	0	0	0.75	0.225	1.50	0.45
Expected profit for each action†			0		\$ 0.55		$\$-0.10$

* Expected profit = Actual profit × Probability of events $P(E)$.
† Expected profit for each action = Σ expected profit for E_1, E_2, E_3.

Based on the results of the payoff table, the optimal strategy under uncertainty is to order 1 jar of relish since this yields the highest expected payoff (a profit of \$0.55).

EXAMPLE 2

Suppose the proprietors knew exactly how many jars of relish to order. For example, if they knew the demand for that month would be exactly 1 jar, they would order only one jar. With this idea in mind, the expected value of having such perfect information would be calculated as follows:

Demand (Jars)	$P(E)$	Actual Profit	Expected Profit*
0	0.10	0	0
1	0.60	\$0.75	\$0.45
2	0.30	1.50	0.45
Expected value of profit under perfect information			\$0.90

* Expected profit = Probability × Actual profit.

If we subtract the optimal expected value of profit under uncertainty (\$0.55) from the expected value of the profit under perfect information (\$0.90), we have computed the expected value of perfect information (EVPI).

Expected value of profit under perfect information	\$0.90
Expected value of profit under uncertainty	0.55
EVPI	\$0.35

EVPI is the highest price one should pay for having perfect demand information.

12.3 PROJECT PROPOSALS AND UNCERTAINTY

To evaluate competing projects the process is basically the same, except that cash flows constitute possible events and the following formula is used to compute the expected value of each project:

$$\overline{X} = \sum_{i=1}^{n} X_i P_i$$

where $\overline{X}$ = Expected value of all cash flows
Σ = Sum of
X_i = Individual cash flows
P_i = Probabilities assigned to each cash flow

n and i specify the conditions of the summation, so that for $\sum_{i=1}^{n}$ we proceed from 1 on up to the nth degree:

$$\sum_{i=1}^{n} X_i P_i = X_1 P_1 + X_2 P_2 + X_3 P_3 + \cdots + X_n P_n$$

$$\overline{X} = \sum_{i=1}^{n} X_i P_i$$

EXAMPLE 3

Company D is considering two projects, each having a one-year "use" period.

Project I		Project II	
Probability	Cash Flow	Probability	Cash Flow
0.25	$4,000	0.10	$ 0
0.50	5,000	0.50	3,000
0.25	8,000	0.40	10,000

To determine which project to choose, the manager of the company decided to compute the expected value of each project. The project with the highest expected value would then be chosen.

Project I (X_1): $\overline{X}_1 = [0.25(\$4,000) + 0.50(\$5,000) + 0.25(\$8,000)] = \$5,500$
Project II (X_2): $\overline{X}_2 = [0.10(0) + 0.50(\$3,000) + 0.40(\$10,000)] = \$5,500$

Since each project has the same expected value ($5,500), this computation of the expected value will not help the manager choose one project over the other. In a situation of this sort, the standard deviation of each project is computed to determine the risk involved. The standard deviation describes the dispersion of the probabilities assigned to the events

$$S = \sqrt{\sum_{i=1}^{n} (X_i - \overline{X})^2 P_i}$$

where X_i = Individual cash flows
$\overline{X}$ = Expected value of all cash flows
P_i = Probabilities assigned to each cash flow

EXAMPLE 4

The computation of the standard deviation for each project follows.

Project I (S_1):

$$\begin{aligned} S_1 &= \sqrt{0.25(4,000 - 5,500)^2 + 0.50(5,000 - 5,500)^2 + 0.25(8,000 - 5,500)^2} \\ &= \sqrt{562,500 + 125,000 + 1,562,500} = \sqrt{2,250,000} \\ &= 1,500 \end{aligned}$$

Project II (S_2):

$$\begin{aligned} S_2 &= \sqrt{0.10(0 - 5,500)^2 + 0.50(3,000 - 5,500)^2 + 0.40(10,000 - 5,500)^2} \\ &= \sqrt{3,025,000 + 3,125,000 + 8,100,000} = \sqrt{14,250,000} \\ &= 3,774.92 \end{aligned}$$

The project with the *lowest* standard deviation involves the *least* risk. Project I would be less risky and is therefore preferred.

The standard deviation is a relative measure of uncertainty when expected values are equal. If the expected values are *not* equal, the standard deviation is not an appropriate measure of risk. The appropriate measure of risk or uncertainty in this circumstance would be the *coefficient of variation*:

$$\text{Coefficient of variation} = \frac{\text{Standard deviation of project}}{\text{Expected value of project}}$$

The *higher* the coefficient of variation, the *greater* the risk.

12.4 PROGRAM EVALUATION AND REVIEW TECHNIQUE (PERT) AND UNCERTAINTY

PERT is a tool used for management planning and control and involves the theory of the critical-path method (CPM). PERT can be used to minimize production delays, to schedule research and development, and to help complete projects on time.

The following terms are used with PERT:

Activity. One step in the production process necessary to complete a project.

Event. The incident or accomplishment at a specific location or stage that marks the beginning or end of an activity.

Project. Sequence of interrelated activities, each of which requires resources and a given duration in order to be completed.

The objective is to identify those activities and events which, if delayed, will cause the whole project to be delayed.

EXAMPLE 5

The following schedule depicts the activities and events necessary to produce a product.

Activity	Predecessor Activity	Network Representation for Activity	Beginning Event	Ending Event
A	—	1–2	1	2
B	—	1–3	1	3
C	*A*	2–4	2	4
D	*B*	3–4	3	4
E	*C,D*	4–5	4	5

From the above data, the PERT network in Fig. 12-1 can be developed.

Because the duration of each activity cannot be predicted perfectly, variable time estimates are used. They are determined by beta distribution as follows:

a = Optimistic estimate (shortest time)
m = Most likely estimate
b = Pessimistic estimate (longest time)

The estimated time t_e for each activity is then calculated by using the algebraic formula:

$$t_e = \frac{a + 4m + b}{6}$$

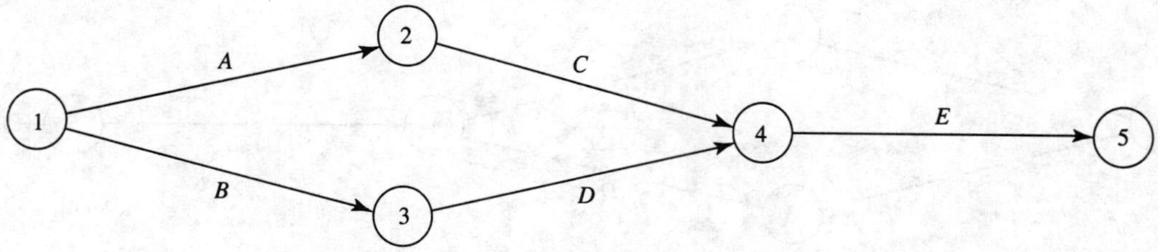

Fig. 12-1. Pert Network.

EXAMPLE 6

Given the following values for a, m, and b, the t_e for each activity depicted in the PERT network (Fig. 12-1) is as follows:

	Time (Calendar Weeks)			
Activity	a	m	b	$t_e = \dfrac{a + 4m + b}{6}$
A	2	3	4	3
B	5	8	11	8
C	2	4	6	4
D	4	6	8	6
E	0.5	2	3.5	2

The critical path, the longest path through the network, can now be determined. Any delay along this path will delay production as a whole. Also, in order to shorten the total time, the critical path must be shortened.

EXAMPLE 7

The time to complete a path is the sum of the activity durations Σt_e along that path.
For the network in Fig. 12-1 the two paths are

Path	Duration Σt_e (weeks)
ACE	$3 + 4 + 2 = 9$
BDE	$8 + 6 + 2 = 16$

The longer path, BDE, determines the overall duration of the production and is called the *critical path*. Another method for determining the critical path uses the following terminology:

T_E = earliest expected time to complete activity
T_L = latest expected time to complete activity before delays occur
S = slack time for activity $= T_L - T_E$

EXAMPLE 8

From the data given in Example 6, the critical path is calculated as follows:

Step 1: Calculate T_E by adding t_e of the predecessor activities to t_e of the current activity.

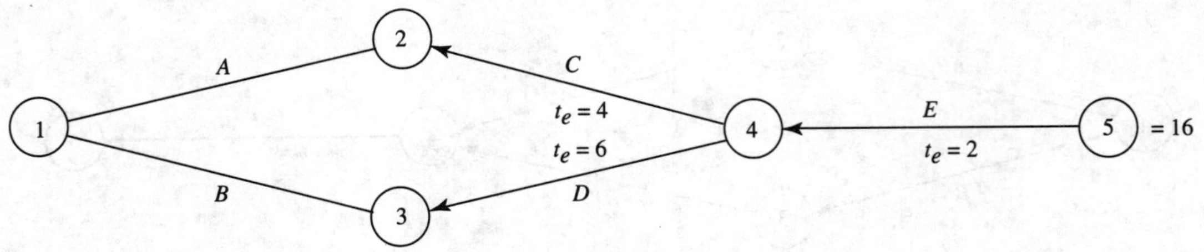

Fig. 12-2. Critical Path.

Current Activity	t_e	t_e (Weeks)
A	$0 + 3A$	3
B	$0 + 8B$	8
C	$0 + 3A + 4C$	7
D	$0 + 8B + 6D$	14
E	$0 + 8B + 6D + 2E$	16*

* The longest path to an activity is chosen.

Step 2: Calculate T_L. This requires working backward along the PERT network (Fig. 12-1) from the longest T_E (critical path) (Fig. 12-2). So the T_L for A would be

$$\text{Longest } T_E - (t_{e,E} + t_{e,C})$$

where $t_{e,E}$ stands for t_e of activity E, or

$$16 - (2 + 4) = 10$$

Activity	T_L	Computation
A	10	$16 - (2t_{e,E} + 4t_{e,C})$
B	8	$16 - (2t_{e,E} + 6t_{e,D})$
C	14	$16 - 2t_{e,E}$
D	14	$16 - 2t_{e,E}$
E	16	$16 - 0$

Step 3: Calculate S by subtracting T_E from T_L.

Activity	T_L	T_E	$S = T_L - T_E$
A	10	3	7
B	8	8	0
C	14	7	7
D	14	14	0
E	16	16	0

The critical path comprises those activities with zero slack.

12.5 INVENTORY COSTS AND CONTROL—ECONOMIC ORDER QUANTITY

The control of inventories is necessary to safeguard against shortages and to provide for a continuous, even flow of production. The three costs included in the *total cost* of any inventory are (1) total ordering costs, (2) total carrying costs, and (3) total acquisition costs.

Total Ordering Costs. Those clerical and processing costs incurred in the purchase of raw materials.

Total Carrying Costs. Those costs incurred to keep an inventory of raw materials in a company's possession; for example, costs stemming from insurance, breakage, and storage space.

Total Acquisition Costs. The actual price paid to suppliers. These costs are often irrelevant when planning inventory policy, except when a discount is offered.

EXAMPLE 9

The annual materials requirement is estimated to be 1,000 units. It costs $10 to place an order. Materials cost per unit is currently $2. The annual carrying cost as a percent of average annual inventory value is 10%. Assuming that one order is placed annually, the total cost of inventory is as follows:

Total Annual Inventory Cost

	Cost
Total ordering cost	$ 10
Total carrying cost*	100
Total acquisition cost	
(1,000 units at $2 cost per unit)	2,000
Total cost of inventory	$2,110

* *Calculation:*

$$\frac{1{,}000 \text{ units}}{2 \text{ units}} = \text{Average annual inventory of 500 units}$$

$$500 \text{ units} \times \$2 \text{ cost per unit} \times 10\% = \$100$$

Note that the *average* annual number of units on hand during the year (computed by dividing the annual materials requirement by 2) is used to calculate the total carrying cost.

12.6 DETERMINATION OF ECONOMIC ORDER QUANTITY

A major aim of an inventory policy is to minimize total inventory costs. The policy must properly balance two costs (total carrying costs and total ordering costs). The order size that results in the minimum total inventory cost is called the *economic order quantity* (EOQ). The EOQ can be determined by using the tabular, graphic, or formula method.

(1) ***Tabular Method.*** Several purchase-order quantity alternatives are listed in separate columns. Both the carrying and ordering costs are calculated for each alternative. The column with the *lowest* cost will give a good approximation of the economic order quantity.

EXAMPLE 10

Assume the following:

Estimated annual required inventory	2,000 units
Materials cost per unit	$2.00
Ordering cost per order	$3.00
Inventory carrying cost	
Per unit per year	$0.20
or as % of unit inventory	10%

The EOQ is computed using the tabular method as follows:

	Order Size (Units)					
Quantity Data	**100**	**200**	**225**	**250**	**275**	**300**
Number of orders (annual required inventory ÷ order size)	20	10	8.9	8	7.3	6.7
Average inventory (order size ÷ 2)	50	100	112.5	125	137.5	150
Cost Data						
Annual carrying cost (average inventory units × \$0.20)	\$10	\$20	\$22.50	\$25	\$27.50	\$30.00
Annual ordering cost (number of orders × \$3)	60	30	26.70	24	21.90	20.10
Total annual inventory cost	\$70	\$50	\$49.20	\$49	\$49.40	\$50.10

The limitations of this method are evident. Since not every possible order quantity was calculated, the EOQ is not precise; it may fall between 225 and 250 units or between 250 and 275 units. Further analysis would be needed to determine the exact EOQ.

(2) ***Graphic Method.*** The EOQ is determined by plotting the annual ordering costs, annual carrying costs, and total inventory costs on a graph. In Fig. 12-3 the horizontal axis represents the order quantity, and the vertical axis represents ordering and carrying costs. The EOQ is the point where total ordering costs equal total carrying costs.

EXAMPLE 11

A graphic presentation of the data tabulated in Example 10 is presented in Fig. 12-3.

The EOQ is between 225 and 250 units since the lines representing annual ordering and carrying costs intersect at a point between these two order quantities. It is possible to determine exact units if the graph is sufficiently detailed.

(3) ***Formula Method.*** The following equations can be used to calculate the EOQ in *units*:

$$\text{EOQ (units)} = \sqrt{\frac{2 \times \text{RU} \times \text{CO}}{\text{CU} \times \text{CC}}} = \sqrt{\frac{2 \times \text{RU} \times \text{CO}}{\text{S}}}$$

where RU = Annual required units
CO = Ordering cost per order
CU = Materials cost per unit
CC = Carrying cost as a percentage of unit inventory value
S = Carrying cost per unit per year

The equation for EOQ in *dollars* is

$$\text{EOQ (dollars)} = \sqrt{\frac{2AB}{I}}$$

where A = Annual required inventory, dollars
B = Ordering cost per order
I = Inventory carrying costs as percentage of unit inventory value

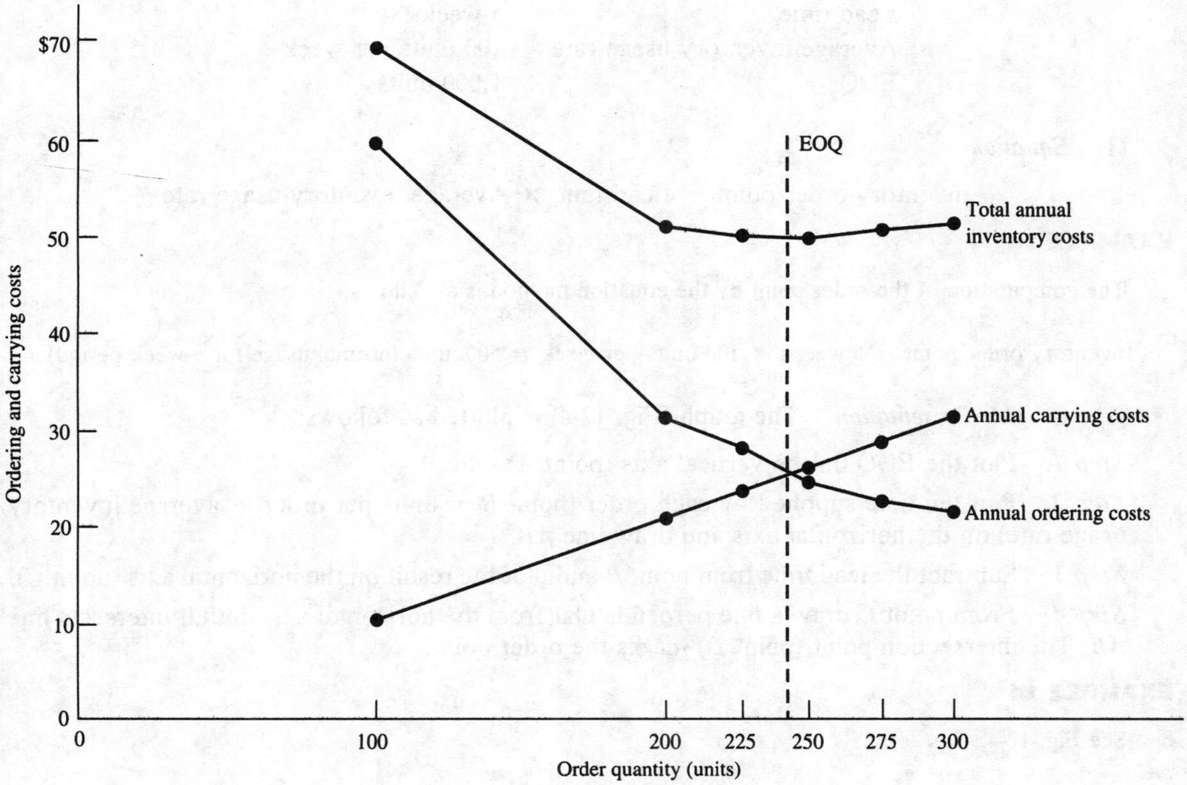

Fig. 12-3.

EXAMPLE 12

The data are the same as those given for Example 10.

RU = 2,000 units CU = \$2 materials cost per unit CO = \$3 per order CC = 10% carrying cost

The EOQ in units is computed as follows:

$$\text{EOQ (units)} = \sqrt{\frac{2 \times 2{,}000 \times \$3}{\$2 \times 10\%}} = \sqrt{\frac{12{,}000}{0.2}} = 244.95 \approx 245$$

The EOQ in dollars is computed as follows:

A = 2,000 units × \$2 materials cost per unit = \$4,000
B = \$3 ordering cost per order
I = 10% inventory carrying cost

$$\text{EOQ (dollars)} = \sqrt{\frac{2 \times \$4{,}000 \times \$3}{10\%}} = \sqrt{\frac{\$24{,}000}{0.10}} = \$489.90$$

12.7 INVENTORY ORDER POINT

The *order point* (when to place an order) should be at the time the inventory level reaches the number of units that would be consumed during the lead time. The *lead time* is the period between placing an order and receiving the materials. The *average inventory usage rate* is the quantity of materials used over a period of time. An equation or a graphic presentation can be used to determine the order point. The following data will be used to illustrate both methods:

Lead time	5 weeks
Average inventory usage rate	100 units per week
EOQ	1,000 units

(1) ***Equation.***

$$\text{Inventory order point} = \text{Lead time} \times \text{Average inventory usage rate}$$

EXAMPLE 13

The computation of the order point by the equation method is as follows:

Inventory order point = 5 weeks × 100 units per week = 500 units (normal usage for 5-week period)

(2) ***Graphic Presentation.*** The graph (Fig. 12-4) is plotted as follows:

Step 1: Plot the EOQ on the vertical axis (point A).

Step 2: Plot the time supplied by each order (point B = units per order ÷ average inventory usage rate) on the horizontal axis and draw line AB.

Step 3: Subtract the lead time from point B and plot the result on the horizontal axis (point C).

Step 4: From point C draw a line perpendicular from the horizontal axis until it intersects line AB. The intersection point (point D) marks the order point.

EXAMPLE 14

See Fig. 12-4.

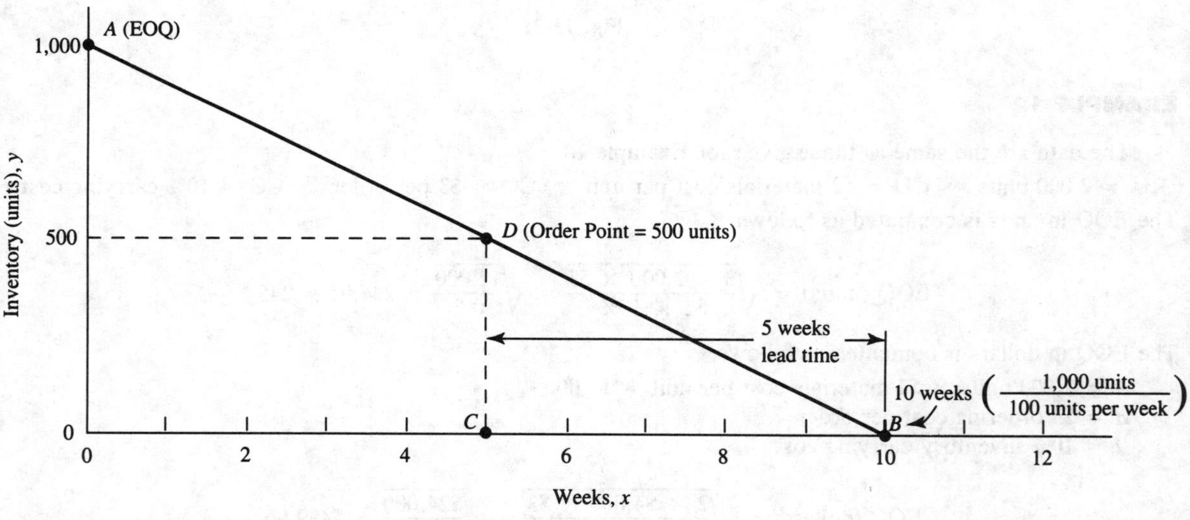

Fig. 12-4. Determining Order Point.

12.8 SAFETY STOCK

Many companies carry a safety stock (additional inventory) as a cushion against possible stockouts. A safety-stock calculation should properly balance the risk of a stockout against the additional carrying costs incurred by the extra inventory.

(1) ***Computation.*** Safety stock is the number of additional units needed above the normal order point to offset possible increases in lead time and usage rate. Its computation is straightforward.

EXAMPLE 15

The normal lead time is 3 weeks, the normal inventory usage rate is 50 units per week, and the EOQ is 250 units. On the assumption that delivery could take as long as 5 weeks and the usage rate could be as much as 75 units a week, the order point for safety stock in units is calculated as follows:

Normal order point (3 weeks × 50 units)		150
Usage for additional 2-week delay (50 units × 2 weeks)	100	
Usage-rate variance*	125	
Safety stock		225
Revised order point		375

* *Calculation:* (75 units maximum usage − 50 units average usage) × 5 weeks lead time.

(2) ***Graphic Method.*** The graphic presentation of safety stock is almost identical to the graphic presentation of the order point. The only difference is that now the safety stock must be added to the EOQ before plotting the EOQ on the vertical axis.

EXAMPLE 16

See Fig. 12-5.

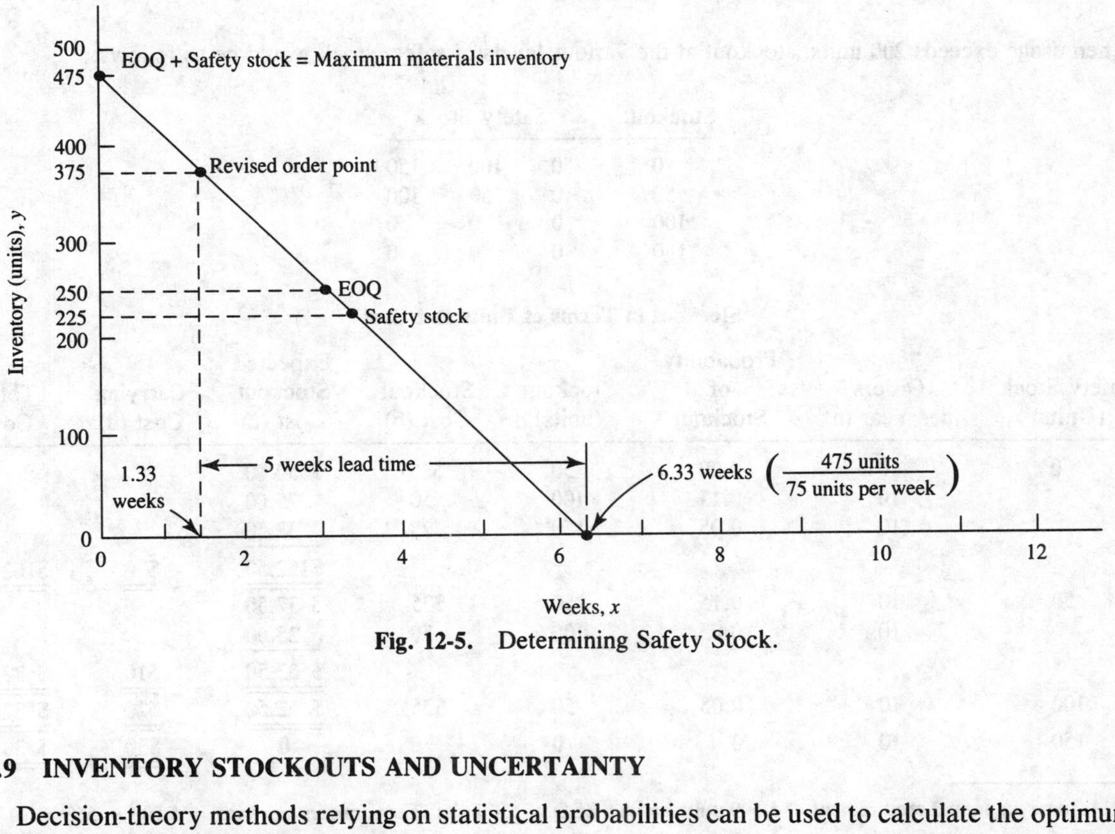

Fig. 12-5. Determining Safety Stock.

12.9 INVENTORY STOCKOUTS AND UNCERTAINTY

Decision-theory methods relying on statistical probabilities can be used to calculate the optimum safety stock for a company's inventory.

A probability distribution for various levels of inventory usage is developed, and these usage levels are compared with normal usage. The optimal safety-stock level is the amount with the least cost involved.

EXAMPLE 17

Assume the following information:

Total Usage and Probability of Stockout (2-Week Period)

Total usage (units)	150	200	250	300	350
Probability of stockout	0.25	0.40	0.20	0.15	0.05

Normal usage for a 2-week period is 200 units. Stockouts will occur whenever total usage exceeds normal usage (usage of 250, 300, and 350 units).

The following can be developed from the above data:

Stockout (Units)

	Probability		
	$P = 0.20$	$P = 0.15$	$P = 0.05$
Total actual usage (units)	250	300	350
Less: Normal usage (units)	200	200	200
Excess usage	50	100	150

When usage exceeds 200 units, stockout at the various levels of safety stock would be as follows:

Stockout	Safety Stock		
0	50	100	150
50	0	50	100
100	0	0	50
150	0	0	0

Stockout in Terms of Units and Cost

Safety Stock (Units)	Orders per Year (a)	Probability of Stockout	Stockout (units)	Stockout Cost (b)	Expected Stockout Cost (c)	Carrying Cost (d)	Total Cost
0	10	0.20	50	$25	$ 50.00		
	10	0.15	100	50	75.00		
	10	0.05	150	75	37.50		
					$162.50	$ 0	$162.50
50	10	0.15	50	$25	$ 37.50		
	10	0.05	100	50	25.00		
					$ 62.50	$10	$ 72.50
100	10	0.05	50	$25	$ 12.50	$20	$ 32.50
150	10	0	0	0	0	$30	$ 30.00

(a) Assume an annual requirement of 5,500 units and an EOQ of 550 units. Then, orders per year = 5,500 ÷ 550 = 10.

(b) Assume stockout cost is $0.50 × Stockout in units.

(c) Expected stockout costs = Number of orders per year × Probability × Stockout cost.

(d) Safety stock × Carrying costs per unit per year; assume a carrying cost of $0.20 per unit.

Safety stock of 150 units should be maintained because it entails the lowest total cost of $30.

Solved Problems

12.1 Expected Value and Standard Deviation. The P.M.E. Co. has a choice between two projects. Using the following information, compute (*a*) the expected value and (*b*) the standard deviation. (*c*) Which project should be chosen?

Project A		Project P	
Probability	Cash Flow	Probability	Cash Flow
0.25	$3,000	0.10	$ -0-
0.50	4,000	0.50	4,000
0.25	5,000	0.40	5,000

SOLUTION

(*a*) Expected Value

$$\overline{X} = \sum_{i=1}^{n} X_i P_i$$

Project A: $\overline{X}_A = 0.25(\$3{,}000) + 0.50(\$4{,}000) + 0.25(\$5{,}000) = \$4{,}000$

Project P: $\overline{X}_P = 0.10(0) + 0.50(\$4{,}000) + 0.40(\$5{,}000) = \$4{,}000$

(*b*) Standard Deviation

$$S = \sqrt{\sum_{i=1}^{n} (X_i - \overline{X})^2 P_i}$$

Project A:

$$S_A = \sqrt{0.25(3{,}000 - 4{,}000)^2 + 0.50(4{,}000 - 4{,}000)^2 + 0.25(5{,}000 - 4{,}000)^2}$$
$$= \sqrt{250{,}000 + 0 + 250{,}000} = \sqrt{500{,}000} = 707.11$$

Project P:

$$S_P = \sqrt{0.10(0 - 4{,}000)^2 + 0.50(4{,}000 - 4{,}000)^2 + 0.40(5{,}000 - 4{,}000)^2}$$
$$= \sqrt{1{,}600{,}000 + 0 + 400{,}000} = \sqrt{2{,}000{,}000} = 1{,}414.21$$

(*c*) Project A is preferable because it has a lower standard deviation, which means that it involves less risk.

12.2 PERT Network—Critical Path. Using the following information, (*a*) prepare a PERT network and (*b*) determine the critical path for the Moran Corporation's production of computers.

Activity	Activity Representation	T_L	T_E
A	1–2	42	42
B	1–3	50	42
C	1–4	38	35
D	2–5	30	30
E	3–5	25	22
F	3–4	28	26
G	4–5	33	27
H	4–6	37	24
I	5–6	22	22

SOLUTION

(*a*) **PERT Network.** See Fig. 12-6.

(*b*) **Critical Path**

$$T_L - T_E = S$$

Activity	T_L	T_E	S
A	42	42	0
B	50	42	8
C	38	35	3
D	30	30	0
E	25	22	3
F	28	26	2
G	33	27	6
H	37	24	13
I	22	22	0

The critical path *ADI* is formed by those activities with zero slack.

12.3 **EOQ.** Kelly O'Donnell Inc. manufactures life jackets. The annual materials requirement is estimated to be 50,000 units, and the ordering cost is $6 per order. The carrying cost is 10% of the unit inventory value. The materials cost per unit is $25.

Compute the EOQ in units using (*a*) the tabular method for order sizes of 400, 450, 500, 550, and 600, (*b*) the formula method, (*c*) the graphic method for order sizes from 200 to 700 units.

SOLUTION

(a) **Tabular Method**

	Order size				
Quantity Data:	**400**	**450**	**500**	**550**	**600**
Number of orders (annual requirement ÷ order size)	125	111.1	100	90.9	83.3
Average inventory (order size ÷ 2)	200	225	250	275	300
Cost Data:					
Annual carrying costs (average inventory units × $2.50)	$ 500	$ 562.50	$ 625	$ 687.50	$ 750.00
Annual ordering costs (number of orders × $6)	750	666.60	600	545.40	499.80
Total annual inventory cost	$1,250	$1,229.10	$1,225	$1,232.90	$1,249.80

The EOQ would either fall between 450 and 500 units or 500 and 550 units. Further analysis would allow a more precise estimate of the EOQ.

(b) **Formula Method**

$$\text{EOQ units} = \sqrt{\frac{2 \times \text{RU} \times \text{CO}}{\text{S}}} = \sqrt{\frac{2 \times 50{,}000 \times \$6}{\$25 \times 0.10}} = \sqrt{\frac{600{,}000}{2.50}} = \sqrt{240{,}000} = 490 \text{ units}$$

(c) **Graphic Method.** See Fig. 12-7.

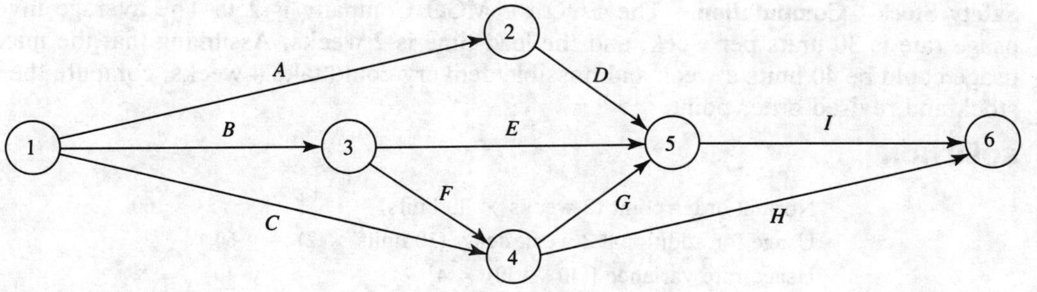

Fig. 12-6

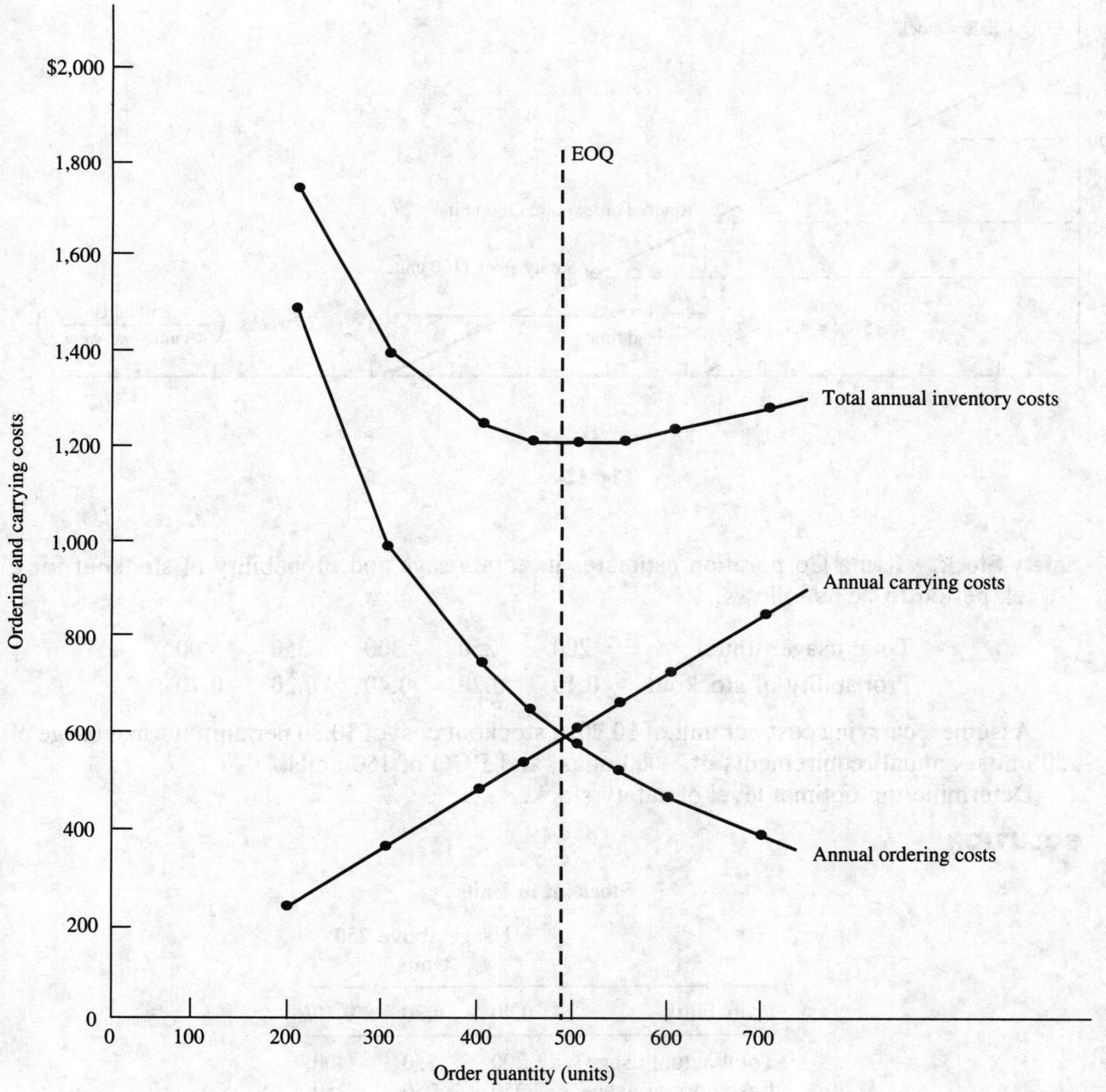

Fig. 12-7

12.4 Safety Stock—Computation. The EOQ for MGO Company is 250. The average inventory usage rate is 30 units per week, and the lead time is 2 weeks. Assuming that the maximum usage could be 40 units a week and possible delivery could take 4 weeks, compute the safety stock and revised order point.

SOLUTION

Normal order point (2 weeks × 30 units)		60
Usage for additional 2-week delay (30 units × 2)	60	
Usage-rate variance [(40 − 30) × 4]	40	
Safety stock		100
Revised order point		160

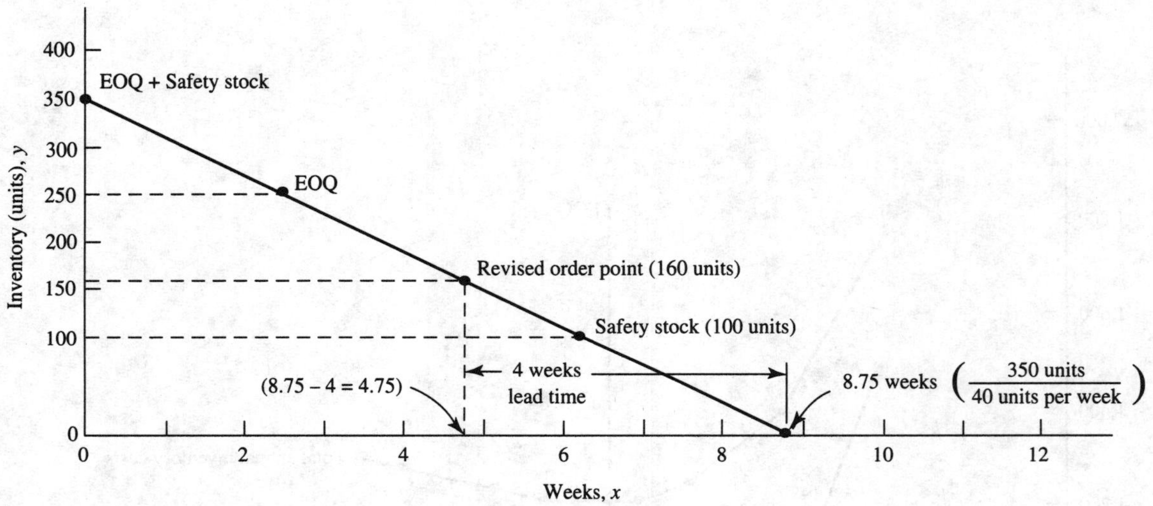

Fig. 12-8

12.5 Safety Stock. Kruta Corporation estimates its total usage and probability of stockout for a 4-week period to be as follows:

Total usage (units)	200	250	300	350	400
Probability of stockout	0.10	0.20	0.40	0.20	0.10

Assume a carrying cost per unit of $0.20, a stockout cost of $0.30 per unit, normal usage of 250 units, annual requirements of 3,000 units, and EOQ of 150 units.

Determine the optimal level of safety stock.

SOLUTION

Stockout in Units

	Usage above 250 Units		
Probability	0.40	0.20	0.10
Total actual usage	300	350	400
Less normal usage	250	250	250
Excess usage	50	100	150

Stockout	Safety Stock		
	50	100	150
0	50	100	150
50	0	50	100
100	0	0	50
150	0	0	0

Stockout in Units and Cost

Safety Stock (Units)	Orders per Year*	Probability of Stockout	Stockout (Units)	Stockout Cost†	Expected Stockout Cost‡	Carrying Cost§	Total Cost
0	20	0.40	50	$15	$120		
	20	0.20	100	30	120		
	20	0.10	150	45	90		
					$330	$ 0	$330
50	20	0.20	50	$15	$ 60		
	20	0.10	100	30	60		
					$120	$10	$130
100	20	0.10	50	$15	$ 30	$20	$ 50
150	20	0	0	0	0	$30	$ 30

* $\frac{3,000 \text{ units annually}}{150 \text{ units EOQ}}$

† $0.30 per unit × Stockout units.

‡ Orders per year × Probability × Stockout cost.

§ $0.20 per unit × Safety-stock units.

The optimal level of safety stock for the Kruta Corporation is 150 units because it entails the lowest cost of $30.

Chapter 13

Decentralized Operations, Responsibility Accounting, and Transfer Pricing

13.1 INTRODUCTION

The degree of decentralization in a company has an important effect on the nature of the cost accounting system used. The question of how much decentralization is desirable remains controversial. In recent years, this question has become even more important, especially with the great expansion of multinational companies and the continuing trend of diversification and growth in conglomerate companies. In addition to the economic factors always present in decentralization, we now have a new factor, the political factor, which may be very significant for multinational companies.

As a company grows, top management must continually rearrange responsibilities among the various executives in order to maximize productivity. When it is desirable or necessary to rearrange physical units or other activities, top management must decide how to (1) divide activities and related responsibilities, (2) coordinate such divisions, and (3) evaluate divisional performance.

In the last few years, greater attention has been focused on responsibility accounting and management reports since they are useful in measuring how well assigned responsibilities are being carried out.

With the continuing trend toward decentralization, transfer pricing has become more significant in cost accounting.

Decentralized Operations

13.2 CONCEPTS OF ORGANIZATION

In the past, the major emphasis in organizational planning was on optimizing economic resources to achieve company objectives. However, in recent years the value of human resources has been recognized and become an important consideration in planning. Organizational planning may thus be defined as "the process of logically grouping activities, delegating authority and responsibility, and establishing working relationships that will enable both the company and the employee to realize their mutual objectives."*

The principal approaches to arranging company activities are by (1) function, (2) product, and (3) geographic location.

13.3 FUNCTIONAL APPROACH

In the functional approach, company activities and responsibilities are organized according to major functions, such as marketing, manufacturing, and finance. Generally, control for each function resides at the vice-president level. For example, the marketing employees report upward from the

---

* *Corporate Organization Structures: Financial Enterprises*, Report No. 631, 1974. The Conference Board Inc., New York.

lowest operating level to the vice-president of the Marketing Division. An important disadvantage is that key decisions are made at the top and passed downward, which is often a time-consuming process.

EXAMPLE 1

Fig. 13-1 illustrates the functional organization of three divisions, Marketing, Manufacturing, and Finance, each headed by a divisional vice-president. To keep the chart uncluttered, further details are shown only for the Manufacturing Division, which is composed of three plants. Each plant manufactures industrial, consumer, or government products and is headed by a plant manager. The details for the Consumer Products Plant illustrate how further division by function might be accomplished. Each of the departments in the Consumer Products Plant is involved in one of three types of operation (forming, assembly, or finishing) and is headed by a department supervisor.

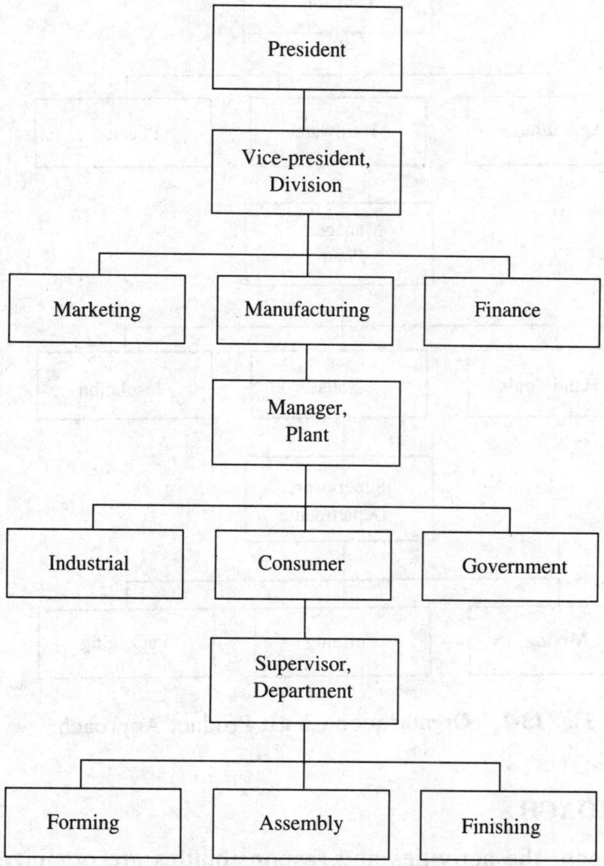

Fig. 13-1. Organization Chart: Functional Approach.

13.4 PRODUCT APPROACH

In the product approach, the activities and responsibilities of a company are organized according to the type of product or group of products manufactured. For example, instead of the one general marketing division for the company, as in Fig. 13-1, there would be three separate marketing departments. An important advantage in this approach is that it offers the possibility of more effective coordination of the activities and functions relating to a particular product.

EXAMPLE 2

Fig. 13-2 shows a product chart with three general product divisions: Agricultural, Hardware, and Plastics. Each product division would have its own Marketing, Manufacturing, and Finance Department (not shown). Further details for the Hardware Division show that it is composed of three plants (manufacturing hand tools, nails, or insulation), each having a plant manager. Further details are also given for the Nails Plant, which has three departments (Mixing, Forming, and Packaging), each with a department supervisor.

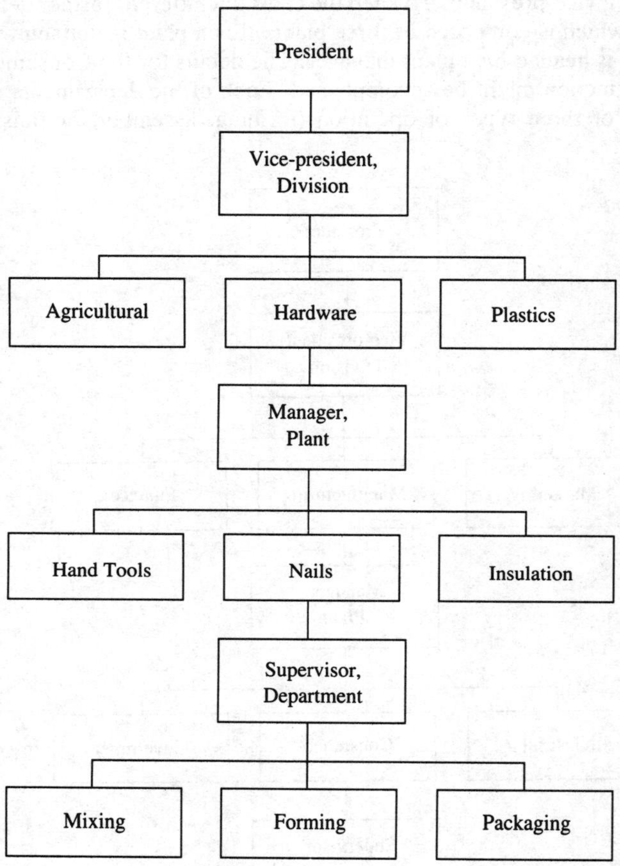

Fig. 13-2. Organization Chart: Product Approach.

13.5 GEOGRAPHIC APPROACH

In the geographic approach, the activities and responsibilities are organized according to geographical area. The managerial responsibility encompasses all functions and all products in a particular territory. This type of approach is often used when the product is bulky or heavy and substantial transportation charges are involved. Such charges are minimized when shipments are made from the plant or warehouse closest to the customer.

EXAMPLE 3

Fig. 13-3 shows an organization chart with three general divisions: North, South, and West. Further details for the South Division show that there are plants in Florida, Georgia, and South Carolina, each with a plant manager. The representative details for the Georgia plant show three departments, each with a departmental supervisor and producing plasterboard, glass, or roofing products.

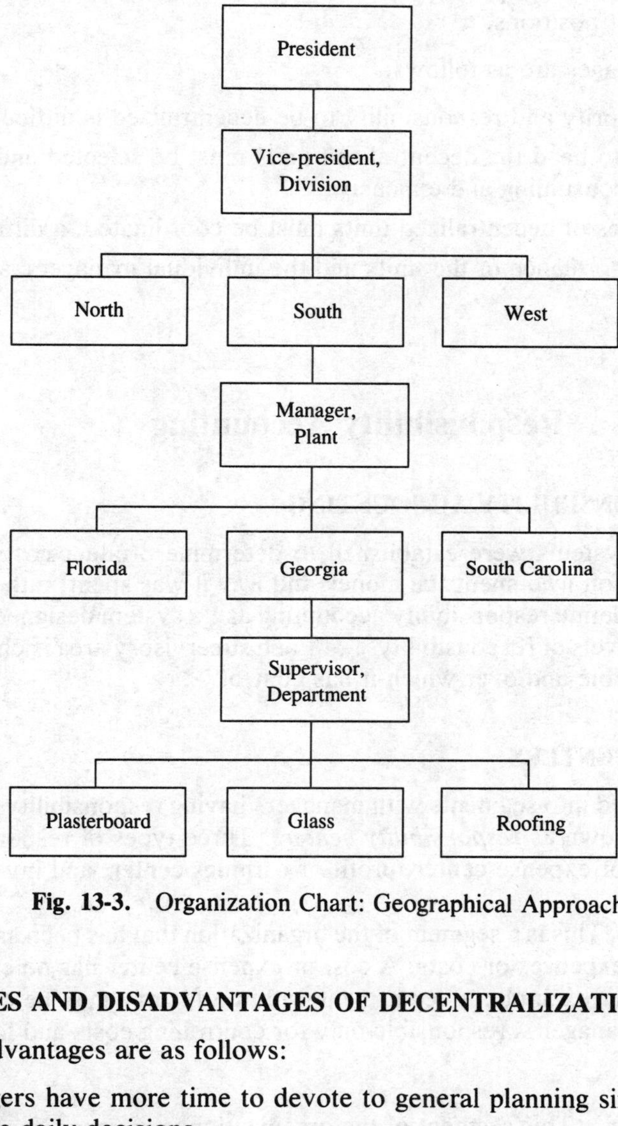

Fig. 13-3. Organization Chart: Geographical Approach.

13.6 ADVANTAGES AND DISADVANTAGES OF DECENTRALIZATION

The principal advantages are as follows:

(1) Top managers have more time to devote to general planning since they are not burdened with routine daily decisions.

(2) The decision-making task is distributed among more personnel so that each person has enough time to give matters sufficient attention.

(3) Better control can be achieved, as the manager can move quickly to make needed corrections.

(4) Managers are better motivated, as they have more control over those matters on which their performance is measured.
(5) Managers are more likely to exercise initiative in such matters as "comparison shopping" in order to reduce costs of outside materials. Comparison of internal and external costs tends to keep internal costs, such as transfer pricing of intracompany goods or services, in line.
(6) As managers become more proficient in decision making, they become more qualified for higher management positions.

The principal disadvantages are as follows:

(1) The extent of authority and responsibility to be decentralized is difficult to determine.
(2) Managers needed to head the decentralized units must be selected and trained, a process that is often time-consuming and expensive.
(3) The varied activities of decentralized units must be coordinated, a difficult task.
(4) Evaluating the performance of the units and the individual managers is often problematic.

Responsibility Accounting

13.7 NATURE OF RESPONSIBILITY ACCOUNTING

Originally, most cost systems were established to determine product costs. The emphasis in responsibility accounting is on *who* spent the money and *why* it was spent, rather than on *what* the expense was. Thus we can define responsibility accounting as "a system designed to accumulate and report costs by individual levels of responsibility. . . . Each supervisory area is charged only with the cost for which it is responsible and over which it has control".*

13.8 RESPONSIBILITY CENTERS

When an entity is divided into segments with managers having responsibility over specific areas, the segmented areas are known as *responsibility centers*. Three types of responsibility centers are commonly identified: cost or expense center, profit or earnings center, and investment center.

Cost or Expense Center. This is a segment of the organization that has been assigned control over only the incurrence of expenses or costs. A cost or expense center has no control over sales or marketing activities. For example, a department within a factory may be considered a cost or expense center if the manager is responsible only for controlling costs and has no responsibility over revenues.

Profit or Earnings Center. This segment of the organization is assigned control over both costs and revenues. Net income and contribution margins can therefore be computed for a profit center. For example, an entity that makes wood furniture may cut lumber in one department and assemble the furniture in another department. The first department can be considered a profit center if the cut lumber is "sold" to the second department. The selling price of this internal sale is called the *transfer price* (see Section 13.12 for further analysis of transfer pricing) and may be used as revenue for the first department.

* John A. Higgins, "Responsibility Accounting," *The Arthur Andersen Chronicle*, vol. C.

Investment Center. This center differs from a profit center in that it has control not only over revenues and costs but also over invested funds. If the manager of the lumber-cutting department also had control over how much was invested in the department, this segment would then be considered an investment center. In addition to net income and contribution margin, the return on investment can be computed for investment centers.

13.9 ESSENTIALS OF CONTROL

No matter how well-designed a system is, it will not be successful unless it has the support of the people who operate the system. The system must be based on *people responsibility*, as it is people who incur costs and should be held accountable for each expenditure. The principal controls for incurring of costs are as follows:

(1) An organization plan that establishes the objectives and goals to be achieved.

(2) Delegating the authority to incur costs and designating responsibility for such costs through a system of policies and procedures.

(3) Motivating individuals by developing standards of performance and offering incentives.

(4) Timely reporting and analysis of deviations in performance from stated goals or budgets by means of a system of records and reports.

(5) A system of appraisal or internal auditing to ensure that unfavorable variances are highlighted and that corrective measures are applied.

13.10 RESPONSIBILITY ACCOUNTING REPORTS

Responsibility accounting reports are prepared according to the levels of responsibility designated on the organization chart. At each level the direct costs incurred by the unit manager are listed, followed by the costs incurred by each of the subordinate managers. In some companies the indirect costs are also shown, so that top management and the unit manager can be aware of the total cost related to each unit.

On the responsibility reports a detailed breakdown of costs is shown for the lower levels. Reports prepared for vice-presidents usually show only plant totals. Vice-presidents who need more information can get it from the plant managers. At each level budgeted costs are compared with actual amounts. The resulting variances can then be analyzed at the appropriate levels.

Some companies prefer to designate the president's office as level 1 (or A) and the departments, or lower levels, as 2, 3, etc. Others prefer to use the reverse designation, with the lowest level as level 1 or A. In the following description, the highest level is designated as 1, but the reverse order is used in example 4.

Level 1: President. In the president's report the cost of that office is shown first, then the totals for the division for which each vice-president is responsible.

Level 2: Vice-President. On the report for the vice-presidents' level, the cost of that office is shown first and then the total for one of the three functions (Sales, Marketing, or Finance). Details of this report are illustrated for the Sales Division only. The total of the details on a vice-president's report equals one of the divisional totals on the president's report.

Level 3: Manager. In example 4 the Sales Division is divided into three territories, each with a plant manager. Each manager's report would show first the cost of that office, then the total cost for the territory. Expenses for territory 1 serve to illustrate the details of this report. The total of the details on each sales manager's report is also shown on the report for the next higher level, the vice-president of sales.

EXAMPLE 4

An organization chart (Fig. 13-4) and responsibility accounting reports for the Lynbob Company are presented below. The company has three levels of control: president, vice-president, and manager. This report emphasizes the sales function of the company by presenting the costs for sales managers and the vice-president of sales in detail.

Level 1: Sales Manager, Territory 1. These costs are directly controllable by the sales manager and are composed of office expenses and the expenses incurred by salespeople. The total controllable cost at this level becomes part of the cost of the vice-president of sales, and as such, is entered on the report for level 2.

Level 2: Vice-President, Sales. At this level, costs of the vice-president's office are shown, followed by the costs incurred by each of the three sales managers. The costs of the three sales territories were compiled from the reports prepared by the sales managers. The total controllable cost of this level becomes part of the cost of level 3, the president.

Level 3: President. In addition to the costs incurred by the president's office, included at this level are the costs of the vice-presidents of the three divisions of the company. The costs are compiled from the reports submitted by the vice-presidents.

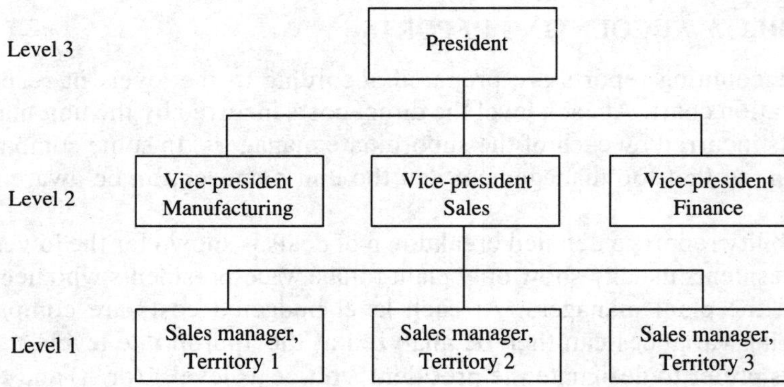

Fig. 13-4. Organization Chart: Levels Reversed.

Responsibility Reports
Controllable Costs
Month of April, 19XX

	Current Month Budget	Current Month Actual	(Favorable) Unfavorable Variance
Level 3: President			
President's office	$212,000	$208,600	$(3,400)
VP Sales	124,500	123,600	(900)
VP Finance	107,000	109,800	2,800
VP Manufacturing	125,800	131,000	5,200
Total controllable cost	$569,300	$573,000	$ 3,700
Level 2: VP Sales			
VP Sales office	$ 25,000	$ 22,300	$(2,700)
Territory 1	31,500	34,800	3,300
Territory 2	33,000	30,500	(2,500)
Territory 3	35,000	36,000	1,000
Total controllable cost	$124,500	$123,600	$ (900)
Level 1: Sales Manager, Territory 1			
Sales commissions	$ 14,500	$ 15,000	$ 500
Travel	13,000	17,000	4,000
Advertising	4,000	2,800	(1,200)
Total controllable cost	$ 31,500	$ 34,800	$ 3,300

13.11 ESSENTIALS OF GOOD PERFORMANCE REPORTS

Timely action reports are essential in responsibility accounting. Reports vary, of course, with needs and wishes of different managements, but the following basic considerations should govern the design and distribution of responsibility reports:

(1) ***Fit the report to the organization chart.*** Develop individual reports for each organizational level.

(2) ***Make reports timely.*** Determine whether the report should be submitted daily, weekly, monthly, etc.

(3) ***Use action reports.*** Present data in a manner that will motivate management to take corrective action.

(4) ***Issue reports sooner.*** Make flash reports when practical.

(5) ***Pinpoint responsibility.*** Make individual responsibility apparent in the reports.

(6) ***Simplify and clarify.*** Arrange data in logical sequence; interpret data; use short titles.

(7) ***Show comparisons, ratios, trends, etc.*** Show deviations as favorable or unfavorable.

(8) ***Make the system flexible.*** Revise reports as needed and change emphasis where required; issue special reports, if needed.

(9) ***Consider cost.*** Avoid duplication; obtain data from regular processing; investigate alternate methods of reproduction, presentation, etc., to reduce costs.

(10) ***Use visual aids.*** Use visual presentation; it saves management time, since relationships and trends are often clearer.

(11) ***Control distribution of reports.*** Make sure the individual responsible gets the report; fix responsibility for distribution and updating of list.

Transfer Pricing

13.12 SIGNIFICANCE OF TRANSFER PRICING

Transfer pricing refers to the basis for transferring goods or services from one affiliated unit to another within the company. With the continued trend toward decentralization, the problem of determining an equitable transfer price has become much more significant in cost accounting. The transfer price can have an important impact on the profit of each division and possibly on the performance evaluation of each division and division manager. The transfer price has an important effect on make-or-buy decisions, that is, whether to make, or continue to make an intermediate product for intracompany transfer or to buy the product outside the company.

13.13 OBJECTIVES OF TRANSFER PRICING

The most important overall objective of transfer prices is to ensure that the interests of any division do not conflict with the interests of the company as a whole. For example, a bonus plan may be based on sales volume rather than profit or return on investment, and a particular division may concentrate on selling products with high volume but low profit margins. The principal objectives of transfer pricing are to furnish data for:

(1) Pricing and capital-budget decisions
(2) Make-or-buy decisions
(3) Evaluation of divisional performance
(4) Evaluation of divisional managers' performance

13.14 TRANSFER PRICING METHODS

The particular pricing method chosen must be the one most suitable for company operations. The principal methods used to establish transfer prices are cost, cost plus, market price, negotiated price, dual prices, and incremental costs.

13.15 COST METHOD

Most companies use cost or cost plus for determining transfer prices. The cost may be based on actual, standard, variable, or any other reasonable estimate of cost. When either actual or full costs are used, there may not be enough incentive for the selling division to reduce inefficiencies or control its own costs. Generally, standard costs or budgeted costs are used since the selling division would try to keep its actual costs as close to the standard as possible.

When a decentralized company uses variable costs, difficulties may arise because of the wide differences between that price and the price to outsiders. Divisions with a large proportion of intracompany transfers are likely to show a low earnings ratio and low return on investment unless adjustments are made. One way to help solve this problem is by using dual prices, described in Section 13.19. Another way is to use cost plus a percentage of cost, which may bring the transfer price in line with the market price. This method is described next.

13.16 COST PLUS METHOD

Under this method a predetermined percentage is added to the cost. Thus if the cost is $0.60 per pound and the transfer price is *cost plus 30%*, the goods will be transferred at $0.78 per pound [$0.60 + $0.18, ($0.60 × 30%)]. Often, outlay costs or incremental costs are used as a base to which the percentage is added.

As described in Section 13.21, the percentage added on interdivisional profit has to be eliminated when the total company financial statements are prepared.

EXAMPLE 5

The J. Connell Company is an integrated manufacturing company with a number of autonomous divisions. Division A transfers all its output to Division B at a transfer price of $32 plus 25%, or $40. The manager of Division B complains that the transfer price is too high, since the same item can be bought outside the company for $37. The cost to Division A includes $28 of variable costs and $4 of fixed costs, at normal capacity. The division has some idle capacity at present. Should the item be purchased outside at the lower price?

	Division B Costs	Company Costs
Outside price	$37	$37
Transfer price	40	
Cost to company		32
Profit (loss)	$(3)	$ 5

Divisional results are a loss of $3 per unit when company products are used. However, for the company as a whole, results are a profit of $5 per unit. Therefore, it is preferable to continue transferring goods. However, to satisfy the manager of Division B, perhaps a shift to another transfer-pricing method should be considered.

13.17 MARKET PRICE METHOD

Use of the market-price method is generally satisfactory in the event that a competitive market price is obtainable. Often a transfer price lower than a competitive market price is justified since lower costs are involved due to the absence of advertising and other selling outlays. Advantages of this method include the fact that better control of purchases can be maintained and larger quantities can be produced and shipped at minimal cost. Furthermore, there is a guaranteed market, and there is assurance of good quality and dependable delivery.

The market-price method may have some disadvantages such as the unavailability of a market price for the exact product or for the intermediate product. In some cases the price obtained may not be reliable, or it may not be from a stable source. Sometimes a vendor will give a low bid for the first order and then increase the price for future orders. Generally, it is desirable to maintain contact with more than one seller or buyer so that reasonable and satisfactory market prices can be maintained.

EXAMPLE 6

The Panda Company has two manufacturing plants: Plant A, the processing unit, and Plant B, the finishing unit. Both plants are autonomous, so Plant A has the option of selling its finished product to Plant B or to outside customers. Plant B has the option of buying from Plant A or from outside suppliers. The sales price of Plant A's product is \$14 per unit, with variable costs of \$8 and fixed costs of \$4 per unit. The sale price of Plant B's product is \$22 per unit, with transfer costs of \$14 per unit and additional variable costs of \$4 per unit. Fig. 13-5 illustrates the transfer operation, and the profit is shown in the summary.

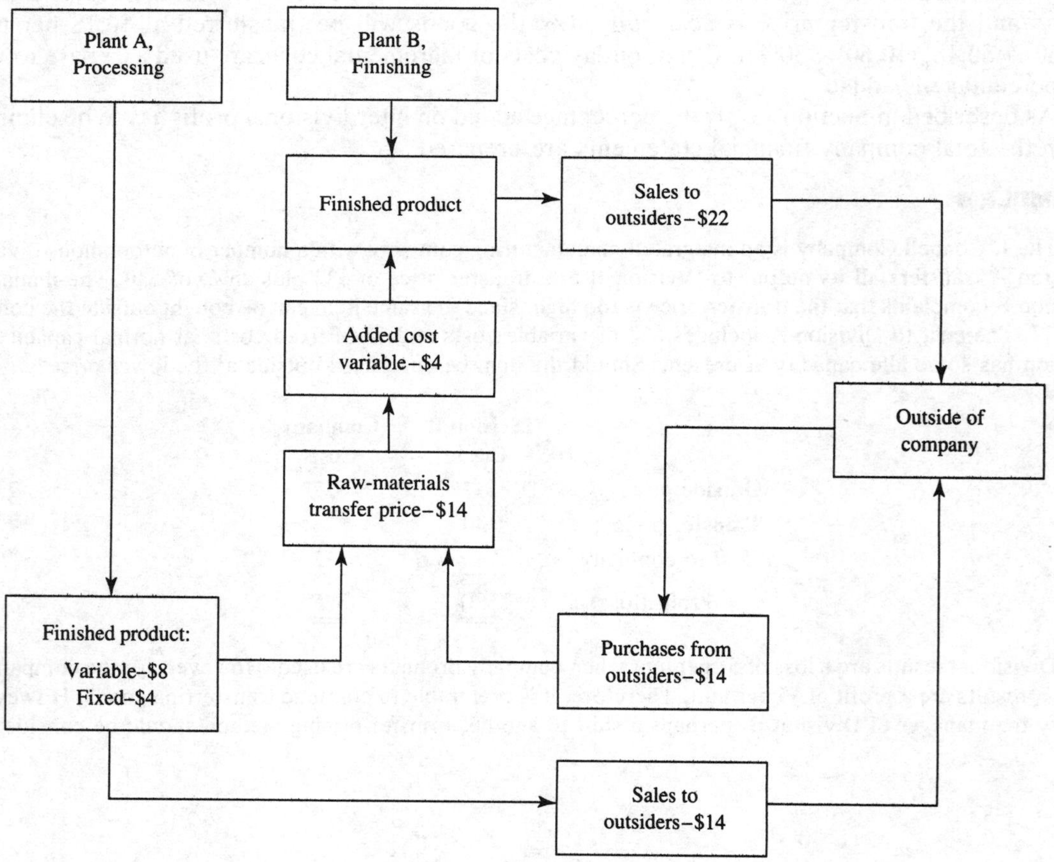

Fig. 13-5. The Panda Company, Transfer-Pricing Chart, 19XX.

Summary

	Plant A	Plant B	Company
Selling price	$14	$22	$22
Finishing			
Variable costs		$ 4	$ 4
Transfer price		14	
Processing			
Variable costs	$ 8		8
Fixed costs	4		4
Total costs	$12	$18	$16
Profit	$ 2	$ 4	$ 6

13.18 NEGOTIATED PRICE METHOD

Generally a negotiated price, which is arrived at through bargaining between the buying and selling divisions, gives division managers the greatest control over divisional profit. The serious difficulty with this method is that negotiations take time and require the development and analysis of much data. Also, there may be frequent requests for revisions. Possible overemphasis on divisional welfare rather than company welfare may result. Sometimes stalemates occur, and top management must intervene to resolve the issues. At times ill feelings may develop between the division managers involved that more than offset the benefits gained.

13.19 DUAL PRICES METHOD

In many cases a transfer price may cause much dissatisfaction for a divisional manager even though the company as a whole may earn a profit by transferring goods. For example, Division X transfers most of its output to Division Y at a price of $10. Everyone in company management is aware that the transfer price is significantly lower than the regular selling price ($14) and that the resulting profit of Division X will therefore be lower. Consequently, the manager of Division X is unhappy, since selling only to outsiders would greatly increase the profit of the division. The fact that divisional operating reports are widely distributed further aggravates the matter. As a result, the company is considering a switch to the dual pricing method, whereby Division Y would still be charged $10, the transfer price, but Division X would be given credit for a sale at the full market price of $14. In preparing the consolidated financial statements, this difference would have to be eliminated, as would any interdivisional profit.

13.20 INCREMENTAL COSTS METHOD

In certain situations, incremental costs may be the most appropriate transfer price. When a plant is operating with idle capacity and a special order is requested, incremental analysis should be employed to determine whether the special order should be accepted. In incremental analysis only the additional costs incurred in accepting an order are considered, and the allocation of existing fixed costs are ignored. Incremental analysis allows for no contribution margin and treats a division more as a cost center than as a profit center.

EXAMPLE 7

The typing pool is considered to be a service department of Ivy College. The pool charges its time at its total standard cost of $8 per hour; 80% of this amount is attributable to fixed charges. The English Department needs a special report typed. A typist is available with sufficient free time to do this job. The chairperson of the English

Department wants the report done at the lowest possible cost since the department is already overbudgeted for secretarial services. The report could also be typed at Redi-Type service company for $6 per hour. What should the chairperson do?

It would be in the best interest of Ivy College to have the report typed by its typing pool. The important cost to consider is not the $8 per hour total standard cost but the $1.60 per hour ($8 × 20% variable costs) additional costs incurred for paper, ribbons, etc., for this particular job. The chairperson should discuss incremental analysis with the manager of the typing pool and arrange for the English Department to be charged only $1.60 per hour for the special report. It would not be in the best interest of Ivy College for the English Department to pay $6 per hour externally for a service it can provide for $1.60 per hour.

13.21 ACCOUNTING ENTRIES

According to generally accepted accounting principles, profit can be made only on sales made outside the company. Therefore, it is necessary to eliminate entries of all intracompany profit when preparing company financial statements. Unless elimination entries are made, the sales, accounts receivable, cost of goods sold, and inventory accounts will be overstated by internal transfers.

In a large company, unearned profit may have to be eliminated at a number of different levels. For example, one plant may sell to another plant in the same division, thereby creating *interplant profit*; or to a plant in another division, creating *interdivisional profit*; or to an affiliated corporation, creating *intracompany profit*. Some companies may have more than one such profit account, but many use only one account and make adjustments to it at the end of each month. Generally, company statements are created at company headquarters, divisional statements at divisional headquarters, and plant statements (primarily cost details) at each plant. A monthly report containing the description, quantity, and cost of all goods received from affiliated units should be submitted by each plant to company headquarters. The markup on each item can then be determined and the total eliminated from intracompany profit.

EXAMPLE 8

The Brett Branning Company uses the cost plus transfer method at standard cost plus 25%. During June, Division A transferred materials with a standard cost of $6,000 to Division B at a transfer price of $7,500. At the end of the period, Division B had on hand $3,000 of transferred goods. The following shows the entries on the divisions' books and on the company headquarter's books when eliminations are made.

Divisions' Books
To record the transfers:

Division A

Accounts receivable, Division B	$ 7,500	
Interdivisional sales		$7,500
To record transfers by shipping division		
Interdivisional cost of goods sold	6,000	
Inventory		6,000
To record cost of transfers by shipping division		

Division B

Inventory	7,500	
Accounts payable, Division A		7,500
To record transfers by receiving division		

Headquarter's Books
Elimination entries needed:

Accounts payable, Division A	$ 7,500	
Accounts receivable, Division B		$7,500
To eliminate interdivisional payables and receivables		
Interdivisional sales	7,500	
Interdivisional cost of goods sold		6,000
Interdivisional gross profit		1,500
To close accounts and record gross profit		
Interdivisional gross profit	600*	
Inventory		600
To eliminate unrealized interdivisional gross profit		

* *Computation of interdivisional gross profit:*

$$\text{Gross profit included in inventory} = \frac{\$1{,}500 \text{ profit}}{\$7{,}500 \text{ purchases}} = 20\%$$

$$\text{Transferred inventory still on hand} \times \text{Gross profit included in inventory} = \$3{,}000 \times 20\% = \$600$$

Solved Problems

13.1 **Responsibility Report.** The Gifford Manufacturing Company produces cookie jars. All costs are accumulated from the responsibility centers as needed. The company's organization chart is shown in Fig. 13-6. Complete the following responsibility report.

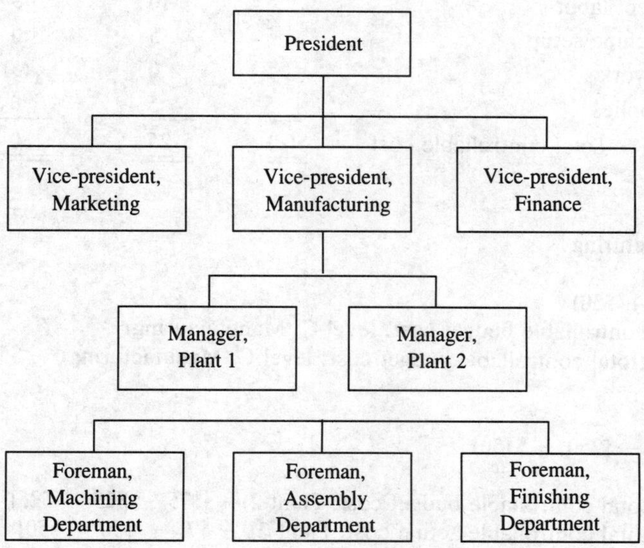

Fig. 13-6.

Responsibility Report
Month of September, 19XX

	Current Month		(Favorable)
	Budget	**Actual**	**Unfavorable Variance**
Level D: President			
President's office	$100	$ 90	$(10)
VP Marketing	400	(*c*)	50
(*a*)	(*d*)	(*e*)	(50)
(*b*)	200	220	20
Total controllable cost	$(*f*)	$(*g*)	$ 10
Level C: VP Manufacturing			
VP Manufacturing office	$250	$200	$(50)
Plant 1	(*h*)	50	(50)
Plant 2	150	200	50
Total controllable cost	$500	$(*i*)	$(50)
Level B: Manager, Plant 2			
Plant manager's office	$ 75	$ 75	$ 0
Machining Department	(*j*)	(*k*)	(*l*)
Assembly Department	25	50	25
Finishing Department	25	50	25
Total controllable cost	$(*m*)	$(*n*)	$(*o*)
Level A: Foreman, Machining Department			
Direct materials	$ 5	$ 5	$ 0
Direct labor	5	10	5
Machine setup	5	5	0
Rework	5	0	(5)
Supplies	5	5	0
Total controllable cost	$(*p*)	$ 25	0

SOLUTION

(*a*) VP Manufacturing
(*b*) VP Finance
(*c*) $450 ($400 + $50)
(*d*) $500 (total controllable budget cost, level C: Manufacturing)
(*e*) $450 [$500 (total controllable budget cost, level C: Manufacturing) − $50]
(*f*) $1,200
(*g*) $1,210
(*h*) $100 ($500 − $250 − $150)
(*i*) $450
(*j*) $25 [$150 (total controllable budget cost, Plant 2) − $75 − $25 − $25]
(*k*) $25 [$200 (total controllable actual cost, Plant 2) − $75 − $50 − $50]
(*l*) $0 ($25 − $25)
(*m*) $150 (*n*) $200 (*o*) $50 (*p*) $25

13.2 Transfer Pricing by Market Price Method. The Gates Corporation has two decentralized divisions. Division A manufactures its product at a variable cost of $5 per unit and a fixed cost of $2 per unit. The product, which has a competitive market price of $10 per unit, is transferred to Division B. The transfer price used by Gates is the competitive market price. Division B finishes the product, thereby incurring additional variable costs of $4 per unit. Division B sells the finished product outside the company for $16 per unit.

(*a*) Determine the profit for Divisions A and B and the Gates Corporation when 1,000 units are produced by Division A and transferred to Division B.

(*b*) In the above situation, are there any advantages in interdivisional transfers, or would purchases from, and sales to, the outside markets provide the same results?

SOLUTION

(*a*)

	Division A	Division B	Gates Corp.
Selling Price			
1,000 × $10	$10,000		
1,000 × $16		$16,000	$26,000
Manufacturing			
Variable costs (1,000 × $5)	(5,000)		
Fixed costs (1,000 × $2)	(2,000)		(7,000)
Finishing			
Variable costs (1,000 × $4)		(4,000)	
Transferred-in costs (1,000 × $10)		(10,000)	(14,000)
Profit	$ 3,000	$ 2,000	$ 5,000

(*b*) Assuming that a perfect market exists, the profit would be the same with either interdivisional transfers or outside market transactions. Differences would probably occur in such areas as administrative and marketing expenses, reliability of market and supplier, and ease of transactions. These factors would probably make interdivisional transfers preferable for both divisions and for the Gates Corporation.

13.3 Transfer Pricing at Cost, Cost Plus, and Market Price. The Playtime Manufacturing Co. produces toy dogs in three departments, Department X manufactures the parts, Department Y does the assembling, and Department Z does the finishing. No external market exists for the unassembled parts, and Department X uses its total cost as the transfer price when transmitting the parts to Department Y. Department Y assembles the parts and uses the current market price in its transfer of goods to Department Z. The current market price for unfinished, assembled toy dogs is $16 per unit. Department Z sells the finished toy dogs for $22 each.

The following information pertains to June, 19XX:

Department X

Sales to Department Y	15,000 units
Variable costs	$6 per unit
Fixed costs	$30,000

Department Y

Sales to Department Z	15,000 units
Variable costs (added in department)	$4 per unit
Fixed costs	$11,250

Department Z

Sales	15,000 units
Variable costs (added in department)	$3
Fixed costs	$15,000

(*a*) Compute the gross profit for the three divisions using Playtime Company's transfer price systems.

(*b*) Which department in (*a*) seems to be in an unusually good position? Why?

(*c*) Department X has repeatedly complained about its transfer price being based solely on total costs. The Playtime Co. is therefore changing Department X's transfer-price method from total cost to total cost plus 30%. Compute the new gross profit for X and show how it affects Departments Y and Z.

SOLUTION

(*a*)

Department X

Sales to Department Y (15,000 at $8)		$120,000
Less: Variable costs (15,000 at $6)	$ 90,000	
Fixed costs	30,000	120,000
Gross profit		-0-

Department Y

Sales to Department Z (15,000 at $16)		$240,000
Less: Transfer costs (15,000 at $8)	$120,000	
Variable costs (15,000 at $4)	60,000	
Fixed costs	11,250	191,250
Gross profit		$ 48,750

Department Z

Sales (15,000 at $22)		$330,000
Less: Transfer costs ($15,000 at $16)	$240,000	
Variable costs (15,000 at $3)	45,000	
Fixed costs	15,000	300,000
Gross profit		$ 30,000

(*b*) Department Y has the best of both worlds. It is transferring in goods at cost and transferring out goods at the current market price. This accounts for its high gross profit.

(*c*)

Department X

Sales to Department Y (15,000 at $10.40)		$156,000
$8 + ($8 × 30%) = $10.40		
Less: Variable costs (15,000 at $6)	$ 90,000	
Fixed costs	30,000	120,000
Gross profit		$ 36,000

Department Y

Sales to Department Z (15,000 at $16)		$240,000
Less: Transfer costs (15,000 at $10.40)	$156,000	
Variable costs (15,000 at $4)	60,000	
Fixed costs	11,250	227,250
Gross profit		$ 12,750

Department Z would be unaffected by the change in transfer-price method.

No doubt, Department Y will now argue that the transfer price charged by X is excessive. An equitable solution might be for management to readjust the transfer price to cost plus about 20%, which would give the two departments roughly the same profit.

13.4 Journal and Elimination Entries. Use the information from part (*c*) of the preceding problem (Department X sold to Department Y at cost plus 30%).

(*a*) Prepare the necessary journal entries to record the transactions. All interdepartmental transactions were recorded as accounts receivable, and no payments have been made. Department Z's sales were all cash transactions.

(*b*) Prepare all necessary elimination entries.

SOLUTION

(*a*) *Entries on Department X's books:*

Accounts Receivable, Department Y	$156,000	
Interdepartmental Sales		$156,000
Interdepartmental Cost of Goods Sold	120,000	
Inventory		120,000

Entries on Department Y's books:

Inventory	156,000	
Accounts Payable, Department X		156,000
Accounts Receivable, Department Z	240,000	
Interdepartmental Sales		240,000
Interdepartmental Cost of Goods Sold	227,250	
Inventory		227,250

Entries on Department Z's books:

Inventory	240,000	
Accounts Payable, Department Y		240,000
Cash	330,000	
Sales		330,000
Cost of Goods Sold	300,000	
Inventory		300,000

(*b*) *Elimination entries for worksheet:*

Accounts Payable, Department X	$156,000	
Accounts Receivable, Department Y		156,000
Accounts Payable, Department Y	240,000	
Accounts Receivable, Department Z		240,000
Eliminates interdepartmental receivables and payables		
Interdepartmental Sales, Department X	$156,000	
Interdepartmental Cost of Goods Sold		120,000
Interdepartmental Gross Profit		36,000
Interdepartmental Sales, Department Y	240,000	
Interdepartmental Cost of Goods Sold		227,250
Interdepartmental Gross Profit		12,750
To close accounts and show gross profit		

Since Department Z sold all its merchandise to outsiders, its departmental gross profit has been realized.

13.5 Five Methods of Transfer Pricing. Divisions J and T are two decentralized divisions of the Sweet Candy Company. Division J manufactures the candy, and Division T packages and distributes the candy at a sales price of $0.15 per unit. Division J transfers 60% of its output to Division T, the remainder being sold to outside markets. The following are the expected revenues and expenses for 19XX:

	Division J	**Division T**
Sales	4,000,000 units	All units received from Division J
Variable costs	$0.02 per unit	$0.04 per unit*
Fixed costs (annual)	$80,000	$40,000*

* Does not include costs from Division J.

Compute the gross profit for Divisions J and T for each of the following transfer price methods:

(*a*) Market transfer price when the market price for Division J's product is $0.07 per unit
(*b*) Cost transfer price (using full costs)
(*c*) Cost plus transfer price when the markup on total cost is 40%
(*d*) Negotiated transfer price when the negotiated price is $0.06 per unit
(*e*) Dual transfer price based on market price and total cost

SOLUTION

(*a*) **Market Transfer Price**

Division J

Sales to outside markets (1,600,000 at $0.07)	$112,000	
Sales to Division T (2,400,000 at $0.07)	168,000	$280,000
Less: Variable costs (4,000,000 at $0.02)	$ 80,000	
Fixed costs	80,000	160,000
Gross profit		$120,000

Division T

Sales (2,400,000 at $0.15)		$360,000
Less: Cost of units from Division J (2,400,000 at $0.07)	$168,000	
Other variable costs (2,400,000 at $0.04)	96,000	
Fixed costs	40,000	304,000
Gross profit		$ 56,000

(*b*) **Cost Transfer Price**

Division J

Sales to outside markets (1,600,000 at $0.07)	$112,000	
Sales to Division T (2,400,000 at $0.04)*	96,000	$208,000
Less: Variable costs (4,000,000 at $0.02)	$ 80,000	
Fixed Costs	80,000	160,000
Gross profit		$ 48,000

* *Calculation:* Variable costs ($0.02) + Fixed costs ($80,000 ÷ 4,000,000) = $0.04.

Division T

Sales (2,400,000 at $0.15)		$360,000
Less: Cost of units from Division J (2,400,000 at $0.04)	$ 96,000	
Other variable costs (2,400,000 at $0.04)	96,000	
Fixed costs	40,000	232,000
Gross profit		$128,000

(*c*) **Cost Plus Transfer Price**

Division J

Sales to outside markets (1,600,000 at $0.07)	$112,000	
Sales to Division T (2,400,000 at $0.056)*	134,400	$246,400
Less: Variable costs (4,000,000 at $0.02)	$ 80,000	
Fixed costs	80,000	160,000
Gross profit		$ 86,400

* *Calculation:* Total costs ($0.04) + Markup ($0.04 × 40% = $0.04 + $0.016 = $0.056).

Division T

Sales (2,400,000 at $0.15)		$360,000
Less: Cost of units from Division J (2,400,000 at $0.056)	$134,400	
Other variable costs (2,400,000 at $0.04)	96,000	
Fixed costs	40,000	270,400
Gross profit		$ 89,600

(*d*) **Negotiated Transfer Price**

Division J

Sales to outside markets (1,600,000 at $0.07)	$112,000	
Sales to Division T (2,400,000 at $0.06)	144,000	$256,000
Less: Variable costs (4,000,000 at $0.02)	$ 80,000	
Fixed costs	80,000	160,000
Gross profit		$ 96,000

Division T

Sales (2,400,000 at $0.15)		$360,000
Less: Cost of units from Division J (2,400,000 at $0.06)	$144,000	
Other variable costs (2,400,000 at $0.04)	96,000	
Fixed costs	40,000	280,000
Gross profit		$ 80,000

(*e*) **Dual Transfer Price**

For goods transferred, Division J receives credit at full market price, and Division T is charged the cost transfer price.

Division J

Sales to outside markets (1,600,000 at $0.07)	$112,000	
Sales to Division T (2,400,000 at $0.07)	168,000	$280,000
Less: Variable costs (4,000,000 at $0.02)	$ 80,000	
Fixed costs	80,000	160,000
Gross profit		$120,000

Division T

Sales (2,400,000 at $0.15)		$360,000
Less: Cost of units from Division J (2,400,000 at $0.04)	$ 96,000	
Other variable costs (2,400,000 at $0.04)	96,000	
Fixed costs	40,000	232,000
Gross profit		$128,000

13.6 **Effects of a Change in Transfer Price.** The ABC Dinghy Co. has several decentralized divisions, two of which are manufacturing and finishing. All divisions operate as profit centers and are free to buy from, and sell to, external markets. The finishing division had always purchased its intermediate goods from the manufacturing division at a price of $225 per unit. Now the manufacturing division says it must raise its price to $250 to cover its increased costs of $200 per unit variable costs and $50 per unit fixed costs. The finishing division will require 500 units.

How would the ABC Dinghy Co. be affected under the following independent circumstances?

(*a*) The finishing division purchases its goods from external markets for $235 per unit. No additional uses are found for the manufacturing division.

(*b*) The finishing division purchases its goods from external markets for $235 per unit. The manufacturing division incurs $20,000 in cash savings to other divisions.

(*c*) The finishing division purchases its goods from external markets for $235 per unit. The manufacturing division sells 300 units of its product to outside sources for $270 per unit.

SOLUTION

(*a*)

	Per Unit Costs		
	Finishing Division	Manufacturing Division	ABC Dinghy Company
Outside purchase	$235	$50*	$285*
Transfer purchase	250	0	250
Savings (loss)	$ 15	NA	$(35)

* Regardless of whether or not the manufacturing division is active, it will incur fixed costs for as long as it exists. Therefore, the cost to the company for the outside purchase is the purchase price plus the manufacturing division's fixed costs.

The finishing division saves $15 per unit (or $17,500 for the 500-unit order) by purchasing outside, but the company loses $35 per unit on the purchase. From the above it can be seen that the market price would have to be below $200 per unit ($250 total costs − $50 fixed costs) in order for the company to benefit from an external purchase in the situation outlined.

The above is generally presented in a different format as follows:

Purchase from outsiders (500 units at $235)	$117,500
Less: Variable cost savings (500 units at $200)	100,000
Cost to ABC Dinghy Co.	$ 17,500

(*b*)

Purchase from outsiders (500 units at $235)		$117,500
Less: Variable cost savings (500 units at $200)	$100,000	
Cash savings by other divisions	20,000	120,000
Savings to ABC Dinghy Co.		$ 2,500

(*c*)

Sales to outsiders (300 units at $270)	$ 81,000	
Less: Variable costs (300 units at $200)	60,000	
Contribution margin from outside sales		$ 21,000
Purchase from outsiders (500 units at $235)	$117,500	
Less: Variable costs (500 units at $200)	100,000	17,500
Profit to ABC Dinghy Co.		$ 3,500

Index